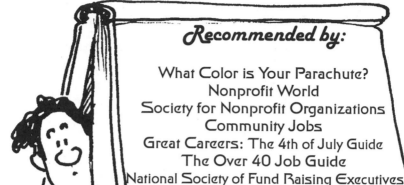

A perfect **10**

NON–PROFITS'
JOB FINDER

DANIEL LAUBER

THIRD EDITION
1994—1995

For quantity discounts and permissions, contact the publisher:
Planning/Communications
7215 Oak Avenue, River Forest, Illinois 60305; phone: 708/366-5200

Distribution to the trade by:
National Book Network
4720-A Boston Way, Lanham, MD 20706; phone: 301/459-8696

Front cover design by Salvatore Concialdi

Graphics used by permission from *Megatoons* by Phil Frank,
Presentation Task Force, and *PC/Graphics Deluxe*.

Disclaimer of All Warranties and Liabilities
The author and publisher make no warranties, either expressed or implied, with respect to the information contained herein. The information about job sources reported in this book is based on facts conveyed by their publishers and operators either in writing or by telephone interview. The author and publisher shall not be liable for any incidental or consequential damages in connection with, or arising out of, the use of materials in this book.

Library of Congress Cataloging—in—Publication Data
Lauber, Daniel.

    Non–Profits' Job Finder / Daniel Lauber. — 3rd edition
    p.   cm.
    Includes bibliographical references and index.
    ISBN: 1–884587–02–X (hard cover): $32.95 — 0–9622019–8–7 (paperback): $16.95

    1. Job hunting —United States—Information services —Handbooks, manuals, etc. 2. Nonprofit organizations —United States – Information services —hand-books, manuals, etc. 3. Occupations –United States – handbooks, manuals, etc. 4. Job hunting —United States — Bibliography. I. Title.

    HF5382.75.U6L328   1994

    331.12'8'0973—dc20   93–45781
                                                      CIP

Table of contents

Foreword

Good news! The non–profit world is no longer an ivory tower for idealists who don't mind living on pennies for a cause. In the 1990s, you need not be poor to do good. But you do need strong business skills (financial planning, marketing, management) or pragmatic operational abilities to earn higher salaries and to keep your NPO (non-profit organization) afloat. A good heart and wishing won't make it so.

My comments stem from personal experience. Before I became a careers columnist, I spent several years working for two NPOs — a United Way and a Girl Scout Council, both in St. Louis, Missouri. Those were some of the happiest days of my life. The interaction with people of good cheer was delightful.

NPOs typically attract volunteers and when people are interacting on a volunteer basis; they often are at their very best, making them a joy to be around. Further, it was clear that the job I was doing in providing staff support and guidance to a large team of volunteers mattered a great deal to the lives and well–being of legions of beneficiaries.

Three years ago I discovered Daniel Lauber's outstanding research accomplishment, now titled the ***Government Job Finder***. This remarkable book helps readers go beyond the usual guidance in finding government employment by leading them to more than 1,400 sources of information on openings in the public sector, sources ranging from specialty/trade periodicals to job hotlines to job–matching services. In my column, I called the book ***"the most comprehensive compendium*** of resources for government job hunters I've ever seen"* — and I meant it. I added, *"**If you have a fair idea of the type of government job you want, this is a dynamite job hunting tool."**

Now Lauber has done it again, spending untold hours in completing another magnificent research project. He has uncovered and identified more than 1,000 sources of job leads in the non-profit sector: ***Non–Profits' Job Finder***. Jobs that focus on bettering prospects for education, housing, food, health, justice, safety, and peace. Jobs that make a difference. Jobs that make the world a better place to live.

I've never met Daniel Lauber, but I have enormous respect for his uncommon willingness to turn over every rock and look in every crevice to find a source on the topic which he is researching. The man is obsessive about collecting data. I like that. I think you will too, after reading this book.

Are you a motivated, concerned person? Do you have a sense of mission for a higher purpose? Do you feel your job should be as important as the chief executive's?

If so, a non-profit organization may offer exactly the outlet for self-actualization you've been searching for. The ***Non–Profits' Job Finder*** will make your search much more efficient than it could have been until now, because this book provides instant access to a department store level of job leads.

You deserve an easier time finding work. After all, you're dedicating yourself to helping society cope with the multitude of serious unmet needs it faces. With the ***Non–Profits' Job Finder*** in hand, I wish you Job Speed.

Joyce Kennedy (signature)

Joyce Lain Kennedy
Nationally–syndicated careers columnist and author

Acknowledgments

Nobody could have produced this book and its two companion volumes, the *Government Job Finder* and *Professional's Private Sector Job Finder* (and *The Ultimate Job Finder* computer software), without a lot of help. In the year it took to research and write these volumes, my research associate and I contacted about 6,000 potential sources of job vacancies, internship opportunities, and grants before selecting the most effective ones for inclusion in these books. In addition, we took this task pretty seriously and **verified our job, internship, and grant sources** as thoroughly as possible by obtaining a copy of printed sources, calling job hotlines, or interviewing the publisher or operator.

This book could not have been prepared without the very kind cooperation of the people who publish and operate the job sources enumerated in these pages. I offer my deepest gratitude to them for providing the information needed to determine if the job–quest aides they produce and operate would really help people seeking work in the non–profit sector.

This third edition is substantially different from the two previous editions. Not only have more than 250 new job and grant sources been added, and new information furnished on most of the original job and grant sources, but we've expanded our coverage of online job sources and the sources for each individual state.

I would particularly like to thank my research associate Laura Southwick for a job well done. Little did she know when she took this job how much time she'd spend on the phone and in the library tracking down job and grant sources.

Thanks go also to Joyce Lain Kennedy for her support and the very kind *Foreword* she wrote for this book. All career writers appreciate her efforts to keep her readers informed of new, effective careers books from small publishers. I just hope I get to meet her one of these days.

And I thank our readers who continue to spread the word about our books. I'm glad that our books have helped ease the pain of the job search for so many people.

Most of all, I thank my wife, Diana, for not only putting up with my eccentricities while researching and writing this book (during which I did a very accurate impression of an obsessed workaholic), but for also offering valuable advice on the manuscript as well as moral support when the going got tough. I doubt if I could have written this book, much less three books at once, without her love and understanding.

"America's Job Finders for the 1990s" is an ongoing, interactive effort. Please share your discoveries of effective job sources with other job seekers by using the **Reader Feedback Form** on page 298 to report any new job sources you discover and let us know if a job source listed here has moved or changed its offerings. The changes you tell us about will appear in the free **Update Sheet** you can obtain after June 1, 1994 by following the instructions that begin on page 300. With this *Update Sheet,* you can keep track of any changes that have occurred in the sources described in this book.

Thanks for purchasing the *Non–Profits' Job Finder.* If you follow the suggestions in Chapter 1 on how to get the most out of this book, it will help you find the non–profit sector job you want, where you wish to live.

Daniel Lauber

Daniel Lauber
January 18, 1994

Chapter 1

How to get the most out of the Non–Profits' Job Finder

Read this chapter first

Despite the "recession that won't quit," you still care enough to want to be part of the ten percent of the populace that works in the non–profit sector. Until now, you had to rely almost solely on word–of–mouth to find jobs in the non–profit sector. Few of the good folks who are dedicated enough to teach or otherwise work in non–profits know about the wealth of job sources where they can find the jobs that don't get advertised in the local classifieds. And that's a good thing because career experts estimate that less than 20 percent of all job vacancies are advertised in the local classifieds. But if you know where to look for the job vacancies available

1

each month that aren't advertised in the local classifieds, your job quest can turn into a successful journey with the proverbial happy ending: the job you want, in the place you wish to live.

The *Non–Profits' Job Finder* provides everything you need to know to locate job vacancies, internships, and grant opportunities in the U.S. and abroad — it's literally a **one–stop shopping center for job vacancies in the non–profit sector**. In addition, the *Non–Profits' Job Finder* offers solid, no–nonsense advice on writing effective cover letters and resumes as well as preparing for job interviews.

Even if you're not one of those lucky people who knows exactly the type of work you want, the *Non–Profits' Job Finder* is the place to start your job search. Used in conjunction with books that help you decide what career to pursue — such as *What Color is Your Parachute?; Change Your Job, Change Your Life; and Zen and the Art of Making a Living* — the entries in the *Non–Profits' Job Finder* will give you a good idea of the current job outlook in each occupation. Each description of a job source tells you how many job openings are advertised or listed in that job source. You can get a real good idea if the professions that interest you are also likely to have job vacancies.

In addition, you can use the many directories of foundations and grant givers described in the *Non–Profits' Job Finder* to identify foundations and corporate givers for which you may wish to work, as well as to identify grants you might seek for yourself or your agency or school.

Whether you know the kind of job you want, or you are using this book to help determine what field you wish to enter, ***it is essential that you read this chapter before you go any further in this book. If you don't read this chapter first, you will not be able to find all the job sources that will help you.*** If you follow the suggestions this chapter presents for using the *Non–Profits' Job Finder*, job openings in all segments of the non–profit sector will soon be at your fingertips. If you're the impatient type and can't bring yourself to read this chapter first, at least read "The Quick & Easy Job Finder" page later in this chapter.

One of the most difficult parts of job hunting involves finding out what jobs are available in the geographic area in which you wish to apply your skills. Naturally, most job seekers turn to the local classifieds — where, at best, only 20 percent of job vacancies are advertised — to find a new position, or they use their contacts to network to identify vacancies even before they are advertised and find vacancies that don't get advertised.

But few people realize that the best jobs are *not* advertised in the local classifieds. You'll find them advertised in specialty periodicals, often published by professional or trade associations; on job hotlines, often accessible at no cost to the job seeker; in job–matching services, frequently free to the job seeker, or available at very low cost; and through computerized job databases and online services which are often free or very inexpensive to use. I'm not talking about just a few jobs here. Thousands upon thousands of jobs are advertised every month almost exclusively through these means.

The *Non–Profits' Job Finder* will lead you to the periodicals, job–matching services, job hotlines, online services, and computerized job databases that announce non–profit sector job openings in your specialty. It will also guide you to resume databases that many non–profits use to hire employees. And because it is often necessary to contact an agency directly to learn about job openings, this book identifies hundreds of directories of non–profits, schools, and associations to enable you to write to the correct person to inquire about job vacancies and/or to request that job announcements be sent to you.

In addition, this volume offers concise advice to help you prepare more effective cover letters and resumes. It also suggests techniques for preparing for a job interview so you can present the best possible portrait of yourself to the interviewer. The following chapters of this book also describe salary surveys that will enable you to be more effective when negotiating salary. Not only does this information clear up common misconceptions held by many entry–level job seekers, but it also serves as a refresher course for long–employed practitioners who have been out of the job market for years.

The *Non–Profits' Job Finder* provides all the information you need to find and be hired for the non–profit sector job you want, in the location you desire.

Job search strategies

There are at least two basic ways to find job openings in the non–profit sector. One is the direct approach, in which you find actual job openings. The second is more circumspect, where you use networking contacts to locate job opportunities or you write, often "blindly," to possible employers to learn if they have any job openings, or if they expect any in the near future. The *Non–Profits' Job Finder* furnishes vital information to use both techniques successfully.

Using the direct approach

Periodicals

Newspapers. Always start with your local newspaper's classified and display advertising. Even if only seven to 20 percent of job openings get advertised in the classifieds, there's no good reason to completely ignore them. In some locales, the Sunday edition of the local newspaper may be

FEIFFER®

the only accessible source for local job openings. In some states, a major newspaper is the best source for job ads for locations throughout the state, and in areas like New England, throughout the region. The *Non–Profits' Job Finder* identifies these newspapers in the chapter that presents job sources for individual states. If you wish to see classifieds from newspapers in other parts of the country, we identify a number of periodicals and online computer services that compile want ads from many papers throughout the country. These are noted near the beginning of Chapter 2.

A growing number of newspapers have placed their classified sections onto "online" computer databases or bulletin boards you can access with a computer modem. Since this technology is so new, and the life of some of these bulletin boards has been so fleeting, we've decided to leave them out of this edition of this book. We're afraid that many of them will be discontinued between the time this book is written and the time you read it. We will add them to a future edition once they become more stabilized.

But not only do the local classifieds rarely carry ads for jobs outside your local area, the best jobs are rarely even advertised in the local classifieds. That's why you need the other job sources described in the *Non–Profits' Job Finder*.

For some jobs, the local classifieds remain the best source of job vacancies. Most of these jobs are very locally–oriented professions, such as taxi drivers, which rarely have any reason to seek employees outside the local geographic area. The local classifieds are also the best job sources for so–called minimally skilled labor positions such as janitors and dish washers that do not require advanced skills. This book will not help you locate job vacancies in those specialties.

Even though most secretarial positions are advertised in the local classifieds, the *Non–Profits' Job Finder* does include several nationwide job sources for secretaries. These are noted in the Index.

Specialty periodicals. The specialty periodical that a professional association or private publisher produces is one of the best sources for non–profit sector job vacancies and business opportunities that aren't advertised in the local classifieds, as well as for job openings located outside your local area. These are described in the chapters that follow. Chapter 2 introduces you to the job sources that cover the whole spectrum of the non–profit sector. Beginning with Chapter 3, each chapter presents job sources for one or several related occupations. As explained later in this chapter, you should also consult the Index to locate job sources that are listed in places you would not intuitively expect them to be placed.

The vast majority of the specialty magazines are available to the general public, usually at higher subscription rates than for members. Some of these are available only to organization members. The *Non–Profits' Job Finder* presents full information on these periodicals so you can focus on the ones most likely to carry ads for jobs for which you are qualified and in which you are interested.

Job listing periodicals. The best source of jobs in a particular specialty is usually a periodical devoted primarily or entirely to job ads or announcements. The number of job ads in a typical issue ranges from about a dozen to several hundred.

As with specialty periodicals, a job listing periodical may be available only to members of the organization that publishes it. Most, however, are available to nonmembers as well, although members often receive the job magazine for free as part of their membership package or for a reduced fee.

Since so many professional organizations publish job ads in their periodicals, the *Non–Profits' Job Finder* also tells you about several directories of associations so you can track down any that might have escaped our attention. As you read this book, you'll find that some job listing periodicals are also published by private businesses rather than non–profit professional or trade associations.

State chapters of professional or trade associations. Many of the associations that publish periodicals with ads for non–profit sector positions have state or regional chapters that also announce job openings in their chapter newsletters. Unfortunately, few of these national federations can readily tell you which of their chapters publish job ads. You will have to contact an organization's national office to obtain the proper addresses and phone numbers to reach the chapter president or newsletter editor who can tell you if their newsletter features job openings. Throughout this book, the address and phone number given for a publication or job service issued by an association is almost always that for the association's headquarters.

You'd be very prudent to join the national professional association for your occupation. Not only will this give you access to the association's job services and periodicals which may be available only to association members, but simply belonging to the association demonstrates a tangible commitment to your profession that most employers like to see. In addition, most professional association include in their membership package publications at no extra cost that offer a great way to continue your professional education.

Positions wanted. In addition to listing jobs which are available, many of these periodicals let job seekers advertise themselves under a category like "Positions Wanted." Many of these are identified in the *Non–Profits' Job Finder*. Before seeking to place a "Positions Sought" ad, you'd be prudent to first examine the periodical. Try to get a sample copy or examine one in a library. After you've identified the periodicals in which you want

The Quick & Easy Job Finder

If you just can't read all of Chapter 1 first, follow these steps to find sources of jobs, internships, and grants in the U.S. and abroad. But if you're really smart, you'll read Chapter 1 first.

In the U.S.

Start with the "Table of Contents." Select and read the appropriate chapter(s) for your occupation.

Look up your occupation in the Index to find job sources not located where you would intuitively expect them to be.

Be sure to also examine the job sources described in Chapter 2 since these cover all occupations in the non–profit sector.

For sources of jobs, internships, and grants unique to each individual state, look up the states that interest you in Chapter 31.

Look in the Index under "Grants" to find nationwide sources of grants for different specialties.

Outside the U.S.

For jobs and internships, read Chapter 16, "International Jobs."

Look under "Foreign jobs" in the Index to find sources for foreign jobs not listed in Chapter 16.

For grants, read Chapter 13, "Grants and foundations," and look in the Index under "Grants."

All sources of job vacancies, internships, and grant opportunities described in the *Non–Profits' Job Finder* were verified in late 1993. Please use the *Reader Feedback Form* on page 298 to let us know of any changes you discover.

to advertise yourself, contact them directly to learn if they publish "Position Wanted" ads, if they have any restrictions that limit such self–advertising to members only, the rates charged, and whether you can publish a "blind" ad without your name in it. In a blind ad, a box number at the publication is given for responses. The periodical regularly mails the responses to you. This way you can remain anonymous and avoid tipping off your current employer that you are in the job market.

Inspect some periodicals first. The *Non–Profits' Job Finder's* descriptions of each periodical will give you a good idea whether it's worth subscribing to it. But in a few cases you can't really decide without seeing a sample copy. Many publishers will be happy to send you a complimentary sample copy to help you decide if you want to subscribe. Others charge a few dollars for a single issue.

In addition, you can inspect many of the periodicals listed in the *Non–Profits' Job Finder* at your local public library or a university library. The libraries of professional associations are also likely to carry relevant periodicals. But when you're actively looking for a new job, it is usually worth the cost to subscribe to a periodical rather than rely on library copies since subscribers invariably receive their periodicals at least a few days before they are available at any library.

Internships. Throughout the chapters that follow, you'll come upon some directories of internships and a few periodicals that carry internship announcements. These directories function more like the periodicals described above since they provide job descriptions for the internships they list. *Also be sure to consult the Index under "Internships" to find job sources that include internships.*

Job ads in print. The *Non–Profits' Job Finder* tells you everything you need to know about each periodical so you can make an informed decision whether to subscribe without having to call or write the publisher for more information. Periodicals are listed under the heading "Job ads in print." Included in each periodical's entry is the following information:

- *Periodical's title.*
- *Address for subscriptions.*
- *Publisher's phone number.* Toll–free "800" numbers are given when available.
- *Frequency of publication.* To clear up the confusion, "biweekly" means every two weeks; "bimonthly" means every two months. "Semi-monthly" is twice a month.
- *Subscription rates.* Both rates are given when a professional or trade association charges different rates for nonmembers and members. Contact the association for membership dues. Sometimes annual dues don't cost much more than the price of an annual subscription.

Prices given are for surface mail delivery to addresses in the United States and its possessions. Entries note when different rates are charged for Canada, Mexico, and/or other foreign countries. Most subscription rates are annual rates. Rates for shorter periods of time are noted. Contact a periodical if you wish to subscribe for more than 12 months since many offer discounts for two– or three–year subscriptions. Although prices are accurate as of the date on which we obtained them, they are certainly subject to change without notice at any time.

☞ *Special information about the periodical.* If a periodical is regional in scope, the states within its region are noted. Also provided is any additional pertinent information that will help you decide if the periodical is worth your attention.

☞ *Heading under which job openings appear.* For the periodicals that contain articles as well as job listings, the heading under which job ads appear is given.

☞ *Number of job openings in a typical issue.* "Few job ads" means no more than two or three appear in the average issue. Each entry (there are a handful of exceptions) will tell you how many jobs were advertised in a typical issue during 1993. If the economy remains static in 1994, you can assume that roughly the same number of jobs will be advertised in 1994. If the economy should miraculously boom, anticipate more job ads in each issue during 1994 and beyond.

Job–matching services and job banks

Many private companies, trade and professional organizations, and state governments operate services in which the resumes of job candidates are matched with positions for which they qualify. These services can be quite effective for professionals as well as individuals seeking support, technical, trades, or labor positions in the non–profit sector.

Some services supply a form for the job candidate to complete, while others allow you to submit your usual resume. Most input the information you submit into a computer database while others operate manually. Some charge job candidates for their services, while others do not (they will usually charge employers a fee to access the candidates' resume database). The job–matching services operated by state Job Service Offices are free. These are described in Chapter 31.

A growing number of universities and colleges now participate in special computerized job–matching services strictly for their graduates' use. Since you can simply ask your school's placement office for details on any such services in which it participates, we decided not to include them in the *Non–Profits' Job Finder*.

Attractive as these services sound, they can be agonizingly slow in getting you a job interview. Despite all the hype that surrounds them, most of these are relatively new services without proven track records. If you are the sort of person who is likely to quickly find a job by using other methods, you may also be matched to a job pretty quickly when using one of these services. But if you've been having trouble getting hired when using other job–search methods, you should probably not expect instant results using a job–matching service.

Job–matching services and job banks are listed under the heading "Job services." Entries that describe these services provide the following information:

☐ *Name of the service and operator of the service.*

☐ *Operator's address and phone number.* Please call only during normal weekday business hours unless noted otherwise.

☐ *Type of resume used.* Does the service require you to fill out the service's own resume data form or do you submit your own regular resume? If you submit your own resume, how many copies should you send in? Many job–matching services, especially the free ones, send your original resume to the potential employer. Those will require you to submit multiple copies of your resume.

☐ *How the service operates.* Is the service computer–based or manually operated?

☐ *Who contacts whom?* Does the job service tell the job candidate that an employer would like to contact her for an interview, or does the potential employer simply contact selected candidates directly? To protect your confidentiality (vital if your current employer uses the job service to hire new employees), can you be listed by a code number rather than by name?

☐ *Length of time resume is kept on file.*

☐ *Fees for applicants, if any.* Fees were accurate as of the end of 1993. These fees, though, are no exception to the adage "things change."

☐ *Other pertinent information.* A job service may be available only to members of the organization that operates it. A few privately–operated job services attempt to compensate for past (and, to be candid, current) discrimination against minorities or women and, therefore may serve only members of the discriminated–against group.

Online job databases

This decade has witnessed a proliferation of online job databases which anybody can access using a home computer and modem. This electronic job search revolution enables you, from your armchair, to see the growing number of job ads that appear on many of the nation's electronic bulletin boards. These online services enable you to read ads for the latest job openings and, if you wish, download them onto your own computer where you can print them out and even build your own job database.

Generally speaking, it is worth your while to contact the operator of any online job database you wish to use to learn the details of how to hook up and what the costs are. Many of these online job databases tend to be a bit ephemeral. Only a few of those operating in 1989 still exist. Charges are subject to frequent changes.

A good number of universities and colleges participate in special online job databases for use strictly by their graduates. Since you can simply ask your school's placement office for details on any such services in which it participates, we decided not to include them in the *Non–Profits' Job Finder*.

In this book, online job databases are listed under "Job services." The *Non–Profits' Job Finder* offers the following information on each of the online job databases it describes:

☞ *Name of online job database service.*

☞ *Name of the association or private business that operates the online job database service.*

☞ *Operator's address and regular telephone number.*

☞ *Online job database service phone number.* Each listing will give you the voice phone number of the company that operates the service. The entry will also give you the phone number to dial with your modem to access the service when there are no charges to use the service other than the cost of a phone call, frequently long distance, or the entry tells you what the charges are.

☞ *Costs.* If there are any costs required to use an online job database service, we'll tell you about them. These include a monthly subscription fee, connection charge, telecommunications charge for each minute you're connected, and/or a software starter kit which is usually inexpensive or free. If the entry gives the phone number for your modem to call, be sure to note if it begins with "900." There is a per minute charge in addition to normal phone line charges for numbers that begin with a 900 area code.

📁 ***Hours the online job database service operates.*** You can assume that you can access each of these any time you want unless operating hours are provided.

📁 ***When job listings are changed.*** So you don't waste time calling too often, most of the entries note when job listings are updated.

📁 ***Types of jobs included.*** When an online job database is for specific types of jobs that may not be readily apparent from its name, we'll tell you the types of jobs featured.

📁 ***Membership requirements, if any.*** The description of a online job database service notes when it is available only to subscribers or to a sponsoring association's members.

To find job sources that move...

If you write to a job source and it has moved without leaving a forwarding address (or its forwarding order has expired), first call it at the phone number given in the *Non–Profits' Job Finder*. If that number has been disconnected and no forwarding number is given, see if your local library has a phone directory for the city the publisher was last in, or call directory assistance in that city (area code + 555–1212).

If that doesn't work, see your library's directories of periodicals, online services, or associations which give addresses and phone numbers.

If you still can't find the new address or phone number, use the *Reader Feedback Form* on page 298 to let us know and we will send you the new address or phone number if we have it.

If you do find a new address or phone number, please use the *Reader Feedback Form* on page 298 to let us know so we can put the change in the *Update Sheet* (see page 300).

Job hotlines

Many professional and trade associations operate job hotlines which usually offer a prerecorded announcement of job openings. These hotlines have become much more sophisticated than just two years ago thanks to the wonders of the "automated attendant" device. You will almost certainly need a touch–tone phone to call them because the recorded voice at the other end will give you instructions that can be implemented only with a touch–tone phone. The most sophisticated job hotlines allow you to specify the geographic area(s) in which you are interested and the types of jobs about which you want to hear.

Some of the less high tech hotlines simply give you a recording that lists jobs. You have no control over what you hear. Often you will first hear a list of all the job titles available. If you want to hear a detailed description and how to apply for a particular position that was just listed, keep listening because that information is often conveyed next.

When you call a few of these hotlines, a live person will answer and read job openings to you. Other job hotlines can be accessed by computer (via a modem) to generate printed listings. Those that are accessible by computer modem are noted. Some of these job hotlines offer thousands of job openings.

Pay attention to the area code of the job hotline you are about to call. If the area code is "900," the call not only isn't free, but you will be charged an additional fee directly on your phone bill. When a "900" number is listed here, the charges are generally identified.

All of the job hotlines presented in this book either cover the entire non–profit sector or a specific occupation. A good number of universities, colleges, and institutions, like the University of South Carolina (803/777–2100 for administrative jobs, 803/777–6900 for secretarial/clerical positions, 803/777–7728 for technical jobs), operate their own job hotlines that announce job openings only at their school or institution. Listing all of these could fill another book.

In fact, they did fill another book: ***Job Hotlines USA: The National Telephone Directory of Employer Joblines*** (Career Communications, Inc., $24.95, 128 pages, published each May; since you can't find it in bookstores, it's available in the catalog at the end of this book). You'll find several hundred job hotlines operated by universities, colleges, and institutions across the country that announce jobs available only for their institution. Job hotlines are listed two ways: alphabetically by name, and geographically by state and city.

In the *Non–Profits' Job Finder,* job hotlines appear under the heading "Job services." If a job hotline operated by a government entity is free, the

Non–Profits' Job Finder simply gives you the phone number to call. But for job hotlines operated by associations or a business where there may be a charge to use it, the following information is presented:

☐ **Name of the job hotline.**

☐ **Name of the entity that operates the hotline.**

☐ **Operator's address and regular voice telephone number.**

☐ **Hotline's phone number.** A small, but growing number of hotline operators offer a "Telephone Device for the Deaf" number as well. These are identified in bold face type as **TDD** phone numbers.

☐ **Hours the hotline operates.** Most of these recordings can be called 24–hours a day, eight days a week. Operating hours are listed if they are limited.

☐ **When job listings are changed.** So you don't waste time calling too often, most of the listings note when recordings are updated.

☐ **Types of jobs included.** Some job hotlines are for specific types of jobs that may not be readily apparent from the name of the hotline.

☐ **Membership requirements, if any.** The description of a hotline notes when a hotline is available only to subscribers or only to the sponsoring association's members.

Using the indirect approach

Unfortunately, many employers are less than aggressive when announcing job openings. Some non–profits and colleges will, upon request, place job candidates on a mailing list to receive announcements of certain types of job openings. Others will tell you about jobs available at the time you contact them. And in some instances, you just get lucky by contacting the right person at the right time. The directories in the *Non–Profits' Job Finder* help you find that right person.

Using directories and computer databases

National directories. The *Non–Profits' Job Finder* includes descriptions of hundreds of directories of non–profit entities to steer job seekers to the right person concerning possible job openings in a wide variety of non–profit specialties. Speaking directly to the right person can give you a genuine competitive edge. It tells the hiring person that you've done your homework. Also, you can learn a lot more about the nature of vacant jobs and the character of the hiring agency by talking to someone who is "in the know" than just by reading job ads. As noted in the chapter on interviewing, you would be most prudent to know something about the company for which you are applying for a job when you enter the job interview.

Many of the directories enumerated in this book include the name of a agency's director of personnel or human resources. Most do not. You can, however, use these to contact a company and ask to whom to send a job inquiry or application.

Directories are also useful for networking purposes. They give you an opportunity to identify people who already work for the company to which you want to apply. By knowing who they are when you meet them at professional gatherings, you can "network" with them and place yourself in a position to hear about vacancies even before they officially occur. For details on the networking game, see books like *The New Network Your Way to Job and Career Success* by Ron and Caryl Krannich (available from Planning/Communications' catalog at the end of this book).

State Directories. While we do not generally include state directories of non–profit entities, we do include state directories of foundations and other grant sources. These are described in Chapter 31. In addition, a number of directories for some specialties are available in a nationwide format or for individual states.

Libraries. Some of the directories listed in the *Non–Profits' Job Finder* are rather lengthy tomes that cost the proverbial arm and a leg. No rational individual would spend the hundreds of dollars many of these cost. Fortunately, most of them are available at well–stocked public libraries and can also be found through interlibrary loan systems. Reference libraries and libraries at colleges and universities are even more likely to carry the directories described in this book. Libraries of professional associations are also likely to carry relevant directories.

Directories are listed throughout this book under the heading "Directories." The following details are furnished for each of the directories described in the *Non–Profits' Job Finder:*

🗀 *Title.*

🗀 *Publisher.*

🗀 *Publisher's address and phone number.* Please call only during normal weekday business hours.

🗀 *Price.* Members of an association that publishes a directory can usually purchase it at a lower price than nonmembers, or receive it free as part of their membership package. The price of the most recent edition is given. Subsequent editions may cost more. When a directory is available only to association members, this restriction is noted. Some directories are available free to qualified "professionals." To obtain a free copy, you almost always must complete an application form which you can obtain from the publisher.

🗀 *Frequency of publication.* Most of these directories are published annually or less frequently. The handful that are updated and repub-

lished several times a year are sold by subscription. The date of the most recent edition is usually given as well as how often the directory is published. If possible we give you the month in which a directory is published so you can decide if you want to obtain it now or wait for the next edition.

📂 ***Description of contents.*** Information on the subjects a directory covers is provided when the directory's title doesn't adequately describe its contents. When it's helpful, indexing information is presented. The number of entries and pages is usually provided, especially for the really large and expensive directories.

The number of computer databases that are essentially directories of non–profit agencies, schools, or foundations continues to grow. Their big advantage is that you can often set specific search criteria to find the employers that interest you. Some of these databases are available through the types of online services described earlier in this chapter. Others are available on computer disks. Still others come on CD–ROMs (compact disk, read–only memory) which require you to have a CD–ROM player attached to your personal computer.

As with the directories discussed immediately above, you can use computer databases to construct a list of non–profits for which you may wish to work. You can also use them to learn more about non–profit entities with which you have an interview coming up.

All three types of these databases are listed under "Directories" in the *Non–Profits' Job Finder*. The same sort of information that is furnished about directories is provided for these databases. However, for online database services, we'll also give you details on how to access the database by computer modem.

Salary surveys

As the last chapter of the *Non–Profits' Job Finder* explains, the more a job applicant knows about the wage scales in the locale or region for a particular position, the better he can negotiate salary and meet the employer's expectations in the job interview. In addition, knowing differences in salary between states and regions can help you decide where to look for a job.

Consequently, the following chapters include books, monographs, and articles that report the results of salary surveys. Many trade and professional associations collect salary data but do not widely publicize their findings. To obtain salary information on the professions for which salary survey information is not listed, contact the appropriate professional or trade association directly. To find associations not mentioned in this book, see the directories of associations cited in Chapter 2.

Salary surveys appear under the heading "Salary surveys." The descriptions of these salary survey books include:

📁 *Title.*

📁 *Publisher.*

📁 *Publisher's address and phone number.* Please call only during normal weekday business hours.

📁 *Price.*

📁 *Most recent publication date or frequency of publication.*

📁 *Survey coverage.* Entries often include details of how data is presented (by size of city, type of city, region, etc.).

How to use this book most effectively

Nationwide job–hunting helpers. The periodicals, job hotlines, job–matching services, and directories described in the *Non–Profits' Job Finder* can be divided into two classes based on the subject area they cover. The periodicals and other job–hunting aides that feature job openings for a broad spectrum of non–profit sector specialties, are listed in Chapter 2. The chapters that follow Chapter 2 focus on an individual specialty, or on related fields. When one or more specialties are closely related, a cross reference is provided to alert you to examine the job sources for the related specialties as well.

Local sources of non–profit sector vacancies. The other set of job–search aides presents information on jobs available within each state. Nearly all these job sources include the broad range of non–profit sector job specialties. Chapter 31 which covers "state–by–state job sources" identifies these periodicals, job hotlines, job–matching services, directories, and salary surveys.

Area codes change

Ma Bell is rapidly adding new area codes. So if you get a recording that your call cannot be completed, it is very possible that only the area code has changed. Call your local Bell System telephone operator for the new area code. If he can't help you, call the operator for your long distance service.

Executive search and recruiting. The *Non–Profits' Job Finder* does not offer information on individual executive search or recruiting firms. Describing them would fill a whole book. Some of the executive search firms described in the companion book, the *Professional's Private Sector Job Finder* (available from Planning/Communications' catalog at the end of this book) cover positions in the non–profit as well as private sector.

Cover letters, resumes, and interviews. Chapter 32 presents succinct guidelines for writing cover letters and for preparing and designing resumes. Two sample cover letters and resumes are presented. Chapter 33 explains how to prepare for job interviews, what to wear, and how to perform at the interview. It addresses some of the many myths regarding job interviews.

How to find
professional and support positions

Start with the nationwide job–quest aides identified in Chapter 2. These job helpers are quite broad in coverage. Each issue of these periodicals is almost certain to include ads for professional positions in most, if not all, of the classifications into which occupations are divided in the chapters that follow.

Next, turn to chapters whose titles tell you they are likely to include your specialty. These chapters are cross–referenced so periodicals, job–matching services, job hotlines, computerized job databases, online services, directories, and salary surveys that serve more than one discipline can be easily found. Virtually all of the job–search aides identified here are nationwide in scope. Any regional and state job sources for a particular field are generally listed here with the nationwide job sources, rather than in the state–by–state chapter.

You'll find that the number of items presented in each chapter varies significantly. There are simply more job sources available for some specialties than for others. For those specialties with few job sources, you will have to rely more heavily on the job sources in Chapter 2 and in Chapter 31, the state–by–state chapter.

Be sure to also look in the *Index* where you will find references to job sources for specialties that are not listed where you would intuitively expect them to be. When you find your specialty in the Index, be sure to read the whole section in which that specialty is listed because there are often several entries for that specialty in addition to the one on the page of the index entry.

Many chapters of this book start with a set of job sources that cover a broad subject area. Following the initial section on "general" job sources that cover all facets of that field are sections that focus on more specialized areas. For example, the "Education" chapter starts with "Education in general" and then continues with narrower disciplines labeled "Administrators," "Elementary and secondary education," "Higher education," "International education," and "Trades and vocational education." Don't look just in the section on your specialty. Also see the initial section on general sources at the beginning of the chapter because many of those job sources will include your specialty. And be sure to also look in the Index for different specialties in education that appear elsewhere in this book.

Finally, turn to Chapter 31, "State–by–state job and grant sources" for job–search aides that cover individual states. Be sure to read the material at the beginning of the chapter. Job sources for a state include local newspapers that cover the whole state or a multi–state region; state–operated job–matching services; books on finding a job in a major city; and how to locate state Job Service offices. This chapter also explains how to identify the local and state chapters of professional associations that may publish a newsletter with job ads or operate a job service.

How to find jobs and internships abroad

Chapter 16 reports on sources of job vacancies and internships located outside the U.S. After reading Chapter 16, be sure to also look up "Foreign jobs" in the Index to find those job sources located elsewhere in the *Non–Profits' Job Finder*. For grants, be sure to read Chapter 13, "Foundations and grants," and to look under "Grants" in the Index.

How to find grant opportunities

The chapter "Foundations and grants" provides information on sources of grants that are national in scope. For information on grants available within individual states, see Chapter 31, "State–by–state job and grant sources," which includes many directories of foundations and other grant sources for most states.

In addition, be sure to see the Index entries under "Grants." A good many sources of grants for different specialties are described in other chapters of this book and can be found by using the Index entries.

If you wish to work for a foundation, the foundation directories described in Chapter 13, "Foundations and grants" and in Chapter 31, "State–by–state job and grants sources" serve as excellent sources of information on these foundations. Unfortunately, they rarely include the name of the personnel director, but you can always call the foundation if you want that bit of information.

If you follow these suggestions, you will find all the job sources cited in the *Non–Profits' Job Finder* for the non–profit sector specialty or specialties in which you want a new job or internship. Armed with this information, you will be able to find the most desirable jobs, internships, or grant opportunities where you want to live.

Chapter 2

General job sources

Sources of job vacancies in the non–profit sector are either for a specialty or for the full spectrum of occupations within the non–profit arena. This chapter presents the most effective job sources that cover everything within the non–profit sector. Each of the chapters that follows covers a specific area such as the arts, association management, education, housing, museums, organizing, religion, or social services. To find all the job sources that will help you land a new job, you should consider the ones in this chapter as well as those in the chapter or chapters that cover your specific occupation. Also, be sure to consult the Index for additional references to the specialties that interest you.

For some fields, the best job sources that include non–profit sector positions are those that actually focus more on government jobs or private sector positions. In those instances, you will be referred to one or both of the companion books to this volume, the *Government Job Finder* or the *Professional's Private Sector Job Finder*. For your convenience, the catalog at the end of this book describes these books in detail and tells you how to obtain them. Many of the job sources in those two books include a moderate number of non–profit sector positions in addition to government or private sector positions. We had to divide the job sources into three separate books. Otherwise we'd have wound up with one hard–to–handle 1,200 page tome that would have cost over $50. Since most people only need one book, this seemed the best approach to take.

General job sources

How to proceed. The periodicals, job services, directories, and salary surveys described in this chapter are broad in scope: each covers a wide variety of non–profit sector disciplines. As noted in Chapter 1, you should examine these first to see which of them will be most helpful to your job search.

After examining the job sources in this chapter, you should see the more narrowly–focused sources in the chapters that follow. Also be sure to look in the Index at the end of this book to find job sources in an occupation that are not listed where you would intuitively expect to find them.

Job ads in print

Community Jobs (ACCESS: Networking in the Public Interest, 50 Beacon St., Boston, MA 02108; phone: 617/720–5627) monthly, individuals: $29/three–month subscription, $39/six–month subscription; also available at bookstores. Each issue lists about 200 to 350 job vacancies and internships in the non–profit world. Regional biweekly editions for New York and New Jersey,

Job sources are presented under these labels:

Job ads in print, Job services, Directories, Salary surveys

Within each classification, job sources are listed in this order: Those with the broadest coverage and the most job openings come first, followed by those with a more narrow focus and/or fewer job openings. Job sources that cover the same specialties are generally listed consecutively.

Chicago, and the District of Columbia are available free upon request with subscriptions to *Community Jobs*; see the entries for the appropriate states in Chapter 31.

The Chronicle of Philanthropy (P.O. Box 1989, Marion, OH 43305; phones; 800/347–6969, 202/466–1032) 24 issues/year, $67.50/annual subscription, $36/six–month subscription. The "Professional Opportunities" section advertises 60 to 90 job openings in all aspects of the non–profit world, from grant writers to CEOs.

The NonProfit Times (Davis Information Group, 190 Tamarack Cr., Skillman, NJ 08558; phone: 609/921–1251) monthly, $49/annual subscription, free/qualified full–time non–profit executives, write for qualification form. "The National NonProfit Employment Marketplace" carries 20 to 30 ads for all sorts of positions with non–profits, particularly administrative.

The Employment Review (Recourse Communications, P.O. Box 1040, Warwick, RI 02887–1040; phone: 401/732–9850) ten issues/year, $9.95/six–issue subscription, $19.95/annual subscription, $2.50/single issue. Hundreds of jobs are advertised under the categories: professional, health care, general, and engineering. The most ads are in engineering and health care. A moderate number of these positions are in the non–profit sector.

National Business Employment Weekly (P.O. Box 435, Chicopee, MA, 01021–0435; phone: 800/562–4868) weekly, $35/eight–week subscription, $199/annual subscription, $3.95/single issue; also available at newspaper stands and bookstores. Forty or so ads for middle to senior level positions in the non–profit sector appear in a special section in the first and third issue each month. Hundreds more positions for professionals and managers in the private sector also appear in each issue.

The Black Collegian (Black Collegiate Services, 1240 S. Broad Ave., New Orleans, LA 70125; phone: 504/821–5694) quarterly, $10/annual subscription (U.S.), $15/foreign. The annual jobs issue published in March or April includes advertisements for 50 to 150 professional positions under "JASS" and in display ads throughout the magazine.

Careers and the disABLED (Equal Opportunity Publications, 150 Motor Parkway, Suite 420, Hauppauge, NY 11788–5145; phone: 516/273–8743) quarterly, $8/annual prepaid subscription. Over 40 display ads throughout this magazine feature positions for college graduates from employers who certify they are equal opportunity employers who will hire people who have disabilities. Readers can submit their resume to the magazine which then forwards them to advertising employers the job seeker names–for free.

Equal Opportunity (Equal Opportunity Publications, 150 Motor Parkway, Suite 420, Hauppauge, NY 11788–5145; phone: 516/273–0066) three issues/year, $13/annual subscription, free to minority college graduates and professionals. Over 25 display ads throughout this magazine feature positions in all areas.

Career/#1 Woman (Equal Opportunity Publications, 150 Motor Parkway, Suite 420, Hauppauge, NY 11788–5145; phone: 516/273–8743) three issues/year, $13/annual subscription, free to female college graduates and female students within two years of graduation (request application form). A handful of the dozen or so job ads that appear throughout the magazine are for positions in the non–profit sector. A reader can submit her resume to the magazine which then forwards it to advertising employers she specifies–for free.

Working Options (Association of Part–Time Professionals, 7700 Leesburg Pike, Suite 216, Falls Church, VA 22043; phone: 703/734–7975) 10 issues/year, $45/available only to members. The typical issue includes about five positions under "Part–Time Job Leads Non–Profit Organizations."

Successful Nonprofits (Development and Technical Assistance Center, 70 Audubon St., New Haven, CT 06510; phone: 203/772–1345) quarterly, $18/annual subscription. "Classified Advertisements–Employment Opportunities" includes just one or two ads for jobs with non–profits.

The Nation (P.O. Box 10791, Des Moines, IA 50347–0791; phone: 212/242–8400) weekly, $48/annual subscription, $66/elsewhere. Ads for jobs with non–profits dominate the dozen or so job ads in the "Classifieds" section.

Roll Call (Levitt Communications, 900 Second St., NE, Washington, DC 20002; phone: 202/289–4900) twice weekly, $195/annual subscription. Among the 15 or more job ads under "Roll Call Classifieds–Employment," are positions with non–profit organizations that require a knowledge of politics and Capitol Hill: lobbyists, government affairs/relations directors, legislative assistants, press directors, etc.

The National Directory of Internships (National Society for Experiential Education, Suite 207, 3509 Haworth Dr., Raliegh, NC 27609–7229; phone: 919/787–3263) published in November of odd–numbered years, $29.50/non-member (U.S.), $25.50/member (U.S.), add $4.85/shipping to Canada, add $8.15/shipping to Mexico, contact for shipping to other countries. Lists 28,000 internship opportunities in 75 different fields with chapters on the arts, business, clearinghouses, communications, consumer affairs, education, environment, health, human services, international affairs, museums and history, public interest, sciences, women's issues, and resources for international internships.

The New Careers Directory: Internships in Technology and Social Change (Student Pugwash USA, 1638 R St., NW, Suite 32, Washington, DC 20009; phone: 202/328–6555) $18, $10/students (add $3 shipping), last published in 1993. Offers full details on where and how to apply for internships and entry–level jobs with non–profits and government agencies in the environment and energy, development, communications, peace/security, health, law, and general science.

Summer Jobs '94 (Peterson's Guides; available from Planning/Communications' catalog at the end of this book) $15.95, 344 pages, annual. Describes over 20,000 summer job openings in the United States and Canada with environmental programs, resorts, camps, amusement parks, expeditions, theaters, national parks, and government. Each detailed em-

---

To see classifieds from around the country...

The National Ad Search (P.O. Box 2083, Milwaukee, WI 53201; phones: 800/992–2832, 414/351–1398) 50 issues/year, $40/six–week subscription, $75/three–month subscription, $145/six–month subscription, $235/annual subscription. Call for a free sample. Over 2,000 classified ads are reprinted from 75 newspapers around the country. Although most are for private sector positions, a good number of the job ads are for non–profit vacancies in education, health care, and science.

Classifacts (North American Classifacts, Suite 305, 2821 S. Parker Rd., Aurora, CO 80014; phone: 303/745–1011) $29.95/four–week subscription plus $4.95/shipping, $4.95/each additional week (includes shipping), extra charges to receive material via fax, modem, or overnight mail. When this service started in September 1993, 54 newspapers were participating. By the end of 1994, it expects to have over 100 newspapers take part. Participating newspapers place all their classified job ads in *Classifacts'* job database. You can have *Classifacts* search this database for up to three different job titles, either nationally, by state, or by city. The results of the search are then sent to you by mail, or if you choose to pay an additional charge, by fax, modem, or overnight mail. Call 303/745–1011 in Denver to get the toll–free number for your region of the country. Then call that "800" number to subscribe to this service. The live operator will help you decide which job titles to search for. Currently operators are on hand every day except Saturday, from 8 a.m. to 10 p.m. Eastern Standard Time. As business builds, the operators expect *Classifacts* to become a 24–hour service.

---

ployer description includes salary and benefits, employer background, profile of employees, and whom to contact to apply. Includes category, employer, and job title indexes.

Job services

Non–Profit Organization Search (ACCESS: Networking in the Public Interest, 50 Beacon St., Boston, MA 02108; phone: 617/720–5627) $25. You specify up to four regions, states, or cities you prefer and which of 23 job categories interest you. ACCESS searches its extensive database of non–profit organizations to find up to 100 that meet your criteria. The report you get gives the name, address and phone number for each organization along with a description of it. While this service doesn't direct you to organizations that necessarily have current job openings, it does enable you to identify organizations for which you may wish to work so you can set up informational interviews and contact them to learn about future openings.

Here's everything you need to know to use this service. Send ACCESS your check and the following information: your name, address, and phone number; and the geographic areas you want searched: up to four cities, regions, and/or states. Then specify which of the following organizational focus categories you want included in your search (give them the code letter for each one): A–Arts, culture, humanities; B–Education/instruction and related; C–Environmental; D–Animal related; E–Health (general and rehabilitative); F–Health (mental health, crisis); G–Health (diseases, disorders, medical discipline and support organizations); H–Health (diseases, disorders, medical disciplines–research); I–Crime and delinquency prevention; J–Employment/jobs; K–Food, nutrition, agriculture; L–Housing/shelter; M–Public Safety, emergency relief; N–Recreation; O–Youth development; P–Human services; Q–International/Foreign; R–Civil rights, social action, advocacy; S–Community improvements and building; T–Philanthropy and voluntarism; U–Research, science, planning, technology; V–Social sciences; W–Public policy, government agencies, consumer protection; X–Religion and spiritual development; Y–Mutual/membership benefit organizations.

ACCESS Resumé Bank for Staff/Board Diversity (ACCESS: Networking in the Public Interest, 50 Beacon St., Boston, MA 02108; phone: 617/720–5627), $5. The purpose of this resume database is to give employers who wish to conduct a more inclusive job search that includes people of all races and levels of physical abilities, access to the resumes of individuals of color or who have physical disabilities. It is also used to identify people interested in serving on an organization's board of directors. Call or write to obtain the resume application form. Submit it and your resume, both of which will be placed in this computerized job bank. When a non–profit employer sends in a "candidate request form," the computer spews out the resumes of job candidates who match the job's requirements. A hard copy of these resumes is sent to the employer who is then responsible for contacting the job candidate for an interview.

APTP Job Referral Service (Association of Part–Time Professionals, 7700 Leesburg Pike, Suite 216, Falls Church, VA 22043; phone: 703/734–7975) $5/members only. Jobseeker fills out services resume form and the job service sends the seeker job descriptions and they are responsible for contacting the employer.

Public Allies Program (Public Allies, 815 15th St., NW, Suite 610, Washington, DC 20005; phone: 202/638–3300) free. The idea behind this service is to make it financially feasible for young adults, particularly from non–wealthy households, to pursue a career in the non–profit sector. Beginning in autumn 1992, the Public Allies Program will place 60 young adults in jobs with non–profits in Chicago, the District of Columbia, and the northern Rockies (Montana, Wyoming, and Idaho). While employed in these jobs, the PAP will help them defer the cost of their student loans and provide an "additional stipend" to supplement their salaries. PAP expects to expand nationwide as time goes by.

E–Span Jobsearch (E–Span Employment Advertising Network, 8440 Woodfield Crossing, Suite 170, Indianapolis, IN 46240; phones: 800/682–2901, 317/469–4535) requires computer modem: free/via Prodigy®, $4/month plus $4 per hour via America OnLine®. Also available through CompuServe, BIX, Internet, and GEnie. You can get a free trial introduction to the system via your modem by dialing: 317/469–4522 (2,400 baud, 7 bits, even parity, 1 stop bit; at the log in prompt, type in lower case: jobs). Formerly called ADNET ONLINE, this job vacancy database covers the whole gamut of the employment world. The job candidate gets a menu that lists 14 job categories (the number of job ads in a recent week are in parentheses) that they claim include positions with non–profits: executive, CEO, plant management, and division management (111); engineering, construction, maintenance, and facilities (324); data processing, computer operations, and telecommunications (189); sales, marketing, advertising, and communications media (234); accounting, finance, and general administration (145); human resources, labor relations, training, and safety (89); purchasing, transportation, and traffic (76); manufacturing, production, quality, and materials (167); management–hotel, restaurant, food, retail, and property (92); natural and physical sciences (134); social sciences (52); education (113); legal occupations (32); and health professions (64).

Once you select one of the 14 categories, you get a more specific menu of classifications with the number of job ads in each. Then you get another menu with narrower classifications, and the number of job ads in each, from which you select your specialty. Then you can browse the ads for each job and take down the information needed to apply.

Career Placement Registry (Career Placement Registry, Inc., 302 Swann Ave., Alexandria, VA 22301; phones: 800/368–3093, 703/683–1085) registration fees: $15/students, others by salary sought: $25/through $20,000 salary, $35/$20,001–$40,000 salary, $45/$40,001+. Complete detailed data entry form. Resume information kept in database for six months. Database updated weekly. Maintains resume database that employers access through DIALOG Information Services computer network. Employers contact registrant directly. Over 11,000 governments and non–profit organizations–all potential employers–have access to CPR's database.

4-Sights Network (16625 Grand River, Detroit, MI 48227; phone: 313/272–3900) free. This is part of a national computer system for people who are blind or visually–impaired. It requires the use of a computer modem. Set your communications program with the following parameters: full duplex, VT–100 or TTY emulation, up to 9,600 baud; choose either 8–bit word, 1 stop bit, no parity. Then dial 313/272–7111. When you have reached 4–Sights, type the single word *newuser* in lower case letters at the login: prompt. Answer the questions about yourself and type in a personal code name of three to seven characters in lower case letters. Then select a password of three to seven lower case characters. This information will be recorded by the 4–Sights system administrator on the next business day so that the next time you call 4–Sights you can simply use your login and password to enter the system. You would be prudent to contact 4–Sights for instructions on how to dial 4–Sights and get around the program.

4–Sights maintains a *Job Placement Exchange* on this computer database. Contact 4–Sights for instructions on how to add your resume to the database. The database contains both a roster of jobs and resumes of persons looking for employment. The idea is to connect people who are blind or visually–impaired with job opportunities and specialized training.

Also on this database is 4–Sights' *Occupational Information Library for the Blind*. This database directory describes over 500 jobs successfully performed by people who are blind or visually–impaired. It itemizes the educational requirements, technical devices needed to accomplish each job listed, and the sort of organizations or businesses most likely to hire people for each job. Jobs listed range from simple tasks in agriculture or manufacturing to positions that require advanced degrees. This directory is a great resource of career ideas for individuals who have a visual impairment or who are blind.

To access the OILB, follow the instructions given above for entering the 4–Sights Network. Once on 4–Sights, type *oilb* at the first "Ok: prompt." Then choose to run the OILB program and follow the instructions to search through the ten "job families" or create a personal profile that identifies job titles that match your interests. You may download onto your computer those job descriptions that interest you.

Saluki Hotline (Southern Illinois University, Career Services, Woody Hall, Carbondale, IL 62901) members only, $36/per year, $26/students. Call 618/453–4571, 618/453–4572, –4573, and –4574 to receive a member hotline number for a 24–hour recording of job openings. It will ask you to select up to three career codes which give you access to more than 300 jobs in all areas. Updated two or three times per week.

Directories

Good Works: A Guide to Careers in Social Change (Barricade Books, for your convenience, this book is available from Planning/Communications; see the catalog at the end of this book) $18, 1991, new edition in April 1994. Describes over 800 non–profits that facilitate social change. Each entry tells you to whom to apply for a job, the phone number and address, the staff size and composition, how many job openings are typical each year, salary range, internships, and where it advertises job openings. There's also a directory of "networks:" clearinghouses, action–research projects, and training schools. If you are looking for an employer that offers jobs that will let you help make the world a better place to live, this book is an essential resource.

National Directory of Nonprofit Organizations (Taft Group, 12300 Twinbrook Pkwy., Suite 520, Rockville, MD 20852–9830; phones: 800/877–8238, 301/816–0210) $399, two volumes, published each summer. Details are presented on over 256,000 private, non–profit organizations. Each entry includes the name and address, annual income, and activities. Volume one ($296) lists 167,000 organizations with over $100,000 annual income. The second volume ($182) lists 106,000 non–profits with $25,000 to $99,999 annual revenues.

Nonprofit Employer Directory (ACCESS: Networking in the Public Interest, 50 Beacon St., Boston, MA 02108; phone: 617/720–5627) $42.90, published each April. Lists organizations alphabetically. Each entry includes address, phone, staff size, mission, year funded, executive director, and coded fields.

The National Service Guide: How You Can Find Opportunities That Make a Difference (ACCESS: Networking in the Public Interest, 50 Beacon St., Boston, MA 02108; phone: 617/720–5627) contact for price (it will be under $10), 40 pages, 1994. This directory includes all Voluntary Action Centers and National Service Corps as well as information on other potential employers in the non–profit sector and other resources for finding job openings in the non–profit sector.

Finding a Job in the Nonprofit Sector (Fund Raising Institute, Taft Group, 12300 Twinbrook Pkwy., Suite 520, Rockville, MD 20852–9830; phones: 800/877–8238, 301/816–0210) $95/paperback (subtract ten percent for prepaid order) plus $3/shipping, 696 pages, 1991. This huge book includes profiles on over 1,000 of the largest non–profit organizations in the U.S. Another 4,000 non–profit organizations, all with annual incomes over $10 million, receive briefer listings in this directory. Each listing identifies the entity's non–profit activity, annual income, and address (and usually phone number). The more extensive entries also include whom to contact for a job, the number of employees, typical types of jobs, preferred college majors or other special requirements, and benefits/special attractions. If you are conducting a broad search for jobs in the non–profit sector, this book is well worth its price tag.

Doing Well by Doing Good: The Complete Guide to Careers in the Nonprofit Sector (Fund Raising Institute, The Taft Group, 12300 Twinbrook Pkwy., Suite 520, Rockville, MD 20852–9830; phones: 800/877–8238, 301/816–0210) $27.95/hard cover plus $3/shipping, 220 pages. In addition to presenting job–search strategies, this book includes a sample list of large non–profit organizations and information on training opportunities.

1994 Internships (Peterson's Guides; available from Planning/Communication's catalog at the end of this book) $29.95, published every October. This 422–page book provides detailed descriptions and application instructions for paid and unpaid internships with over 1,700 organizations and companies, including a good number of non–profits. It includes geographic and alphabetical indexes, and details on regional and national internship clearinghouses.

Volunteerism: Organizations, Training, Programs, and Publications (R.R. Bowker; available through Reed Reference Publishing, P.O. Box 31, New Providence, NJ 07974; phone: 800/521–8110) $119 plus 7 percent shipping, 1,164 pages, 1991. Provides details on over 5,300 volunteer organizations in over 80 areas, including substance abuse, AIDS, teenage pregnancy, homelessness, environment, literacy, people with disabilities, senior citizens, and physical and mental health. Although this directory's title suggests volunteerism, the organizations it describes generally do have some paid staff to coordinate all the volunteers.

Pros & Cons of the Peace Corps (Overseas Development Network, 333 Valencia St., Suite 330, San Francisco, CA 94105; phones: 415/331–4204, 415/731–4205) $10, annual, 1993. Listing of association members and nonprofit organizations by phone number and background of organization.

Job Hunter's Sourcebook: Where to Find Employment Leads and Other Job Search Resources (Gale Research, Inc., 835 Penobscot Bldg., Detroit, MI 48226–4094; phone: 800/877–4253) $57, 1,106 pages, 1993. This tome lists specialty periodicals that often include help wanted ads; placement and job referral services; employer directories and networking lists; handbooks and manuals about each profession; employment agencies and search firms; and other leads, primarily associations that don't offer any job services but can provide general information about a profession.

This is a great source for identifying job recruiters and executive search firms for the 150 careers into which the book is divided. It also identifies extremely useful books and manuals that will help you learn about a specific field. Unfortunately, when it lists periodicals, it doesn't tell you anything about them except the address and phone number. A large number of the periodicals mentioned in the book do not, and have never, carried job ads.

Washington Information Directory (Congressional Quarterly, Inc., 1414 22nd St., NW, Washington, DC 20037; phones: 800/673–2730, 202/887–8500) $89.95, 1,100 pages, June 1993. Divides the federal government into 18 broad subject categories and furnishes detailed information on each federal department and agency. Also provides details on regional federal information sources, non–governmental organizations in the Washington area, and Congressional committees and subcommittees.

Career Opportunities in International Development in Washington D.C. (Overseas Development Network, 333 Valencia St., Suite 330, San Francisco, CA 94103; phones: 415/451–4202, 415/431–9205) $10, annual. Lists association members and nonprofit organizations by phone number and organizational background.

Associations Yellow Book (Monitor Publishing Co., 104 Fifth Ave., 2nd Floor, New York, NY 10011; phone: 212/627–4140) semiannual, $165/annual subscription, 900 pages. Being published twice a year makes this volume perhaps the most accurate directory of professional associations for government employees.

Encyclopedia of Associations (Gale Research, Inc., 835 Penobscot Bldg., Detroit, MI 48226; phone: 800/877–4253) Volume 1: *National Organizations of the U.S.* $340/set of three parts, published each July, includes entries on over 22,000 associations including hundreds for government professionals. Usually available at public libraries. Volume 2: *Geographic and Executive Indexes*, $275, published each July, enables you to locate organizations in a particular city and state to identify association executives. Volume 3: *Supplement,* $295, published every November provides full entries on associations not listed in Volume 1.

The *Encyclopedia of Associations* is available on the DIALOG online computer service (File number 114) on which records can be accessed by name, key word, description, publications, and other fields. For information on online subscriptions, contact DIALOG Information Services (3460 Hillview Ave., Palo Alto, CA 94304; phone: 800/334–2564).

Asian–Americans Information Directory 1992–93 (Gale Research, Inc., 835 Penobscot Bldg., Detroit, MI 48226–4094; phone: 800/877–4253) $75, 461 pages, 1991. Describes over 5,200 national, regional, state, and local organizations, agencies, institutions, programs, and publications concerned with the life and culture of Americans with an Asian heritage. Each entry includes contact person, address, phone, fax, and, usually, a description. This is a good, almost affordable source for identifying non–profit organizations with this specialty for which you may wish to work.

Black Americans Information Directory (Gale Research, Inc., 835 Penobscot Bldg., Detroit, MI 48226–4094; phone: 800/877–4253) $75, 500 pages, 1993. Describes over 4,800 national, regional, state, and local organizations, agencies, institutions, programs, and publications concerned with black or African–American life and culture. Each entry includes contact person, address, phone, fax, and, usually, a description. This is a good, almost affordable source for identifying non–profit organizations with this specialty for which you may wish to work.

Hispanic Americans Information Directory (Gale Research, Inc., 835 Penobscot Bldg., Detroit, MI 48226–4094; phone: 800/877–4253) $89.50, 750 pages, 1993. Describes over 4,800 national, regional, state, and local organizations, agencies, institutions, programs, and publications concerned with the life and culture of Americans with an Hispanic heritage. Each entry includes contact person, address, phone, fax, and, usually, a description. This is a good, almost affordable source for identifying non–profit organizations with this specialty for which you may wish to work.

Native Americans Information Directory (Gale Research, Inc., 835 Penobscot Bldg., Detroit, MI 48226–4094; phone: 800/877–4253) $75, 371 pages, 1993. Describes nearly 4,500 national, regional, state, and local organizations, agencies, institutions, programs, and publications concerned with Native American life and culture. Each entry includes contact person, address, phone, fax, and, usually, a description. This is a good, almost affordable source for identifying non–profit organizations with this specialty for which you may wish to work.

Women's Information Directory (Gale Research, Inc., 835 Penobscot Bldg., Detroit, MI 48226–4094; phone: 800/877–4253) $75, 763 pages, 1993. Describes nearly 6,000 national, regional, state, and local organizations, agencies, institutions, programs, and publications concerned with women in the United States. Each entry includes contact person, address, phone, fax, and, usually, a description. This is a good, almost affordable source for identifying non–profit organizations with this specialty for which you may wish to work.

Directories in Print (Gale Research, Inc., 835 Penobscot Bldg., Detroit, MI 48226–4094; phone: 800/877–4253) $270, published in even–numbered years, 2,155 pages in two volumes; *Supplement,* $165, 200 pages, published in odd–numbered years. Details on 14,000 directories in the U.S. and worldwide. In addition to traditional print directories, this includes directories published on CD–ROMs, as online databases, diskettes, microfiche, and mailing labels.

National Trade and Professional Associations of the United States (Columbia Books, 1212 New York Ave., NW, Suite 300, Washington, DC 20005; phone: 202/898–0662) $65. With information on over 7,250 trade and professional associations, this annual volume enables you to identify any professional associations beyond those included in this volume.

Salary surveys

Compensation in Nonprofit Organizations (Abbott, Langer & Associates, 548 First St., Crete, IL 60417; phone: 708/672–4200) Part 1: Professional Societies and Trade Associations, $135; Part 2: Excluding Professional Societies and Trade Associations: $150; both combined: $225, 843 pages, annual. Based on information from 2,128 non–profits for over 40,000 positions in 87 different job categories.

Nonprofit World Salary Survey (The Society of Nonprofit Organizations, Suite 1, 6314 Odana Road, Madison, WI 53711; phone: 800/424–7367) appears in *Nonprofit World* magazine, usually the May/June issue, $12/single copy. This is a four–page summary of the Abbott, Langer & Associates survey described immediately above.

Comp Key Effective Compensation: A Key to Nonprofit Success (Applied Research & Development Institute, 1805 S. Bellaire St., Suite 219, Denver, CO 80222; phone: 303/691–6076) $29.95 plus $3.50 shipping, 1990. Compares salaries and benefits based on data from over 900 non–profits.

The American Almanac of Jobs and Salaries 1994–1995 (Avon Books, 105 Madison Ave., New York, NY 10016; phone: 800/762–0779) $17, 638 pages, 1993. This is a good general source on salaries. It covers a broad spectrum of careers. However, it is not nearly as job specific as the salary studies conducted by trade and professional organizations.

American Salaries and Wages Survey (Gale Research, Inc., available from Planning/Communications as a special order, phone: 800/829–5220) $95, 1,125 pages, 1993. Covers more than 4,500 occupational classifications with salary ranges, entry level, highest paid. Figures are derived from more than 300 publications issued by federal, state, and local governments, and professional organizations.

Available Pay Survey Reports: An Annotated Bibliography (Abbott, Langer & Associates, 548 First St., Crete, IL 60417; phone: 708/672–4200) Part 1: U.S. surveys, $350; Part 2: Non–U.S. surveys, $125. Covers over 1,100 individual pay survey reports. Heavily indexed to help you find the specialities that interest you.

Chapter 3

Agriculture

Agriculture

*Also see entries in the "Environment" and "Forestry and horticulture" chapters. For many more job sources for private sector and government positions, see the **Professional's Private Sector Job Finder** and **Government Job Finder** respectively.*

Job ads in print

Agronomy News (American Society of Agronomy, 677 S. Segoe Rd., Madison, WI 53711; phone: 608/273–8080) monthly, $7/annual subscription, included in membership package. About 30 openings for agronomists and crop and soil scientists are described under "Personnel."

Phytopathological News (American Phytopathological Society, 3340 Pilot Knob Rd., St. Paul, MN 55121; phone: 612/454–7250) monthly, free to members only. About ten positions in plant pathology, genetics, or pesticides with the Department of Agriculture and extension services appear under "Classified."

Alternative Agriculture News (Henry A. Wallace Institute for Alternative Agriculture, Suite 117, 9200 Edmonton Rd., Greenbelt, MD 20770; phone: 301/441–8777) monthly, free/members only, $16/annual dues. Few ads in the typical issue.

American Journal of Alternative Agriculture (Henry A. Wallace Institute for Alternative Agriculture, Suite 117, 9200 Edmonton Rd., Greenbelt, MD 20770; phone: 301/441–8777) quarterly, $24/annual subscription (U.S.), $26/Canada and Mexico, $28/elsewhere. Two or three jobs ads appear in alternative agriculture.

Job service

Career Development and Placement Service (American Society of Agronomy, 677 S. Segoe Rd., Madison, WI 53711; phone: 608/273–8080) $15/annual fee, free to members, resume on file 12 months, $7.50 fee to update resume during that year. The job seeker submits a copy of her resume. When a match is made, the resume is forwarded to the interested employer who is responsible for contacting the job seeker for an interview.

Chapter 4

Animals

Job ads in print

The Animals' Agenda (Animal Rights Network, P.O. Box 6809, Syracuse, NY 13217; phone: 800/825–0061) six issues/year, $22/annual subscription, $28/Canada and Mexico, $35/elsewhere. Fewer than five jobs and internships with animal shelters appear under "Classified–Employment."

Animal Keepers Forum (American Association of Zoo Keepers, 635 S.W. Gage Blvd., Topeka, KS 60606–2066; phones: 800/242–4519, 913/272–5821) free/members only; annual dues: $30/full–time zoo keeper, $25/affiliates and associates, $20/libraries. Six to eight vacancies for animal keepers, veterinary technicians, and education specialists appear under "Opportunity Knocks."

Shoptalk (American Humane Association, 63 Inverness Dr. East, Englewood, CO 80112; phone: 303/792–9900) bimonthly, $10/year annual subscription (U.S.), $25/elsewhere. As many as six jobs for animal care and control professionals (including administrative) appear in a typical issue under "Employment."

Communique Magazine (American Association of Zoological Parks and Aquariums, Oglebay Park, Route 88, Wheeling, WV 26003; phone: 304/242–2160) monthly, free/members only; annual dues range from $35 to $110; write for dues schedule. Jobs are listed under "Position Directory."

Journal of the American Veterinary Medical Association (American Veterinary Medical Association, 1931 N. Meacham Rd., Suite 100, Schaumburg, IL 60173; phone: 708/925–8070) biweekly, $100/annual nonmember subscription (U.S.), $120/foreign, included in dues. Among the 300 to 450 "Classifieds" are many positions for veterinarians and veterinary technicians.

Veterinary and Human Toxicology (c/o Comparative Toxicology Laboratories, Kansas State University, Manhattan, KS 66506–5606; phone: 913/532–4 Blvd., Suite 100, Trenton, NJ 08618; phone: 609/882–5600) eleven issues/year, bimonthly, $50/annual subscription (U.S.), $60/Canada, $70/elsewhere. Forty to 50 openings, including positions for veterinarians, toxicologists, biologists, and health professionals appear under "Job Opportunities." A membership directory of related organizations is published once a year in this journal.

Journal of Animal Science (American Society of Animal Science, 309 W. Clark St., Champaign, IL 61820; phone: 217/356–3182) monthly, $160/annual nonmember subscription, free/members. The typical issue includes ads under "Placement" for about five professor positions in animal science, agronomy, agriculture, and veterinary science.

Job service

AVMA Job Placement Service (American Veterinary Medical Association, 1931 N. Meacham Rd., Suite 100, Schaumburg, IL 60173; phone: 708/925–8070) free/members only. Complete an application form and this service will match you with vacancies in government, clinical practice, private industry or college universities.

Directories

Directory of Animal Care and Control Agencies (American Humane Association, 63 Inverness Dr. East, Englewood, CO 80112; phone:303/792–9900) $50 (or $2 per state listing) for non–profit agencies, $500 (or $10 per state listing) for individuals and profit–making organizations, 200 pages. Covering over 3,600 animal care and control agencies in the U.S. and

Canada, this directory is maintained on computer and is published in a binder. Agencies are listed alphabetically by state and city. This directory is also available as cheshire or pressure sensitive labels.

Zoological Parks and Aquariums in the Americas (American Association of Zoological Parks and Aquariums, Oglebay Park, Route 88, Wheeling, WV 26003; phone: 304/242–2160) $63/nonmembers, $33/members, published in the summer of even–numbered years.

ACVS Directory of Diplomates (American College of Veterinary Surgeons, 4330 East West Highway, Suite 1117, Bethesda, MD 20814; phone: 301/718–6504) $15, printed in late autumn of odd–numbered years.

Grants for Environmental Protection & Animal Welfare (The Foundation Center, 79 Fifth Ave., New York, NY 10003–3076; phones: 800/424–9836, within New York State call 212/620–4230) $65 plus $4.50/shipping, October 1993. Describes recent foundation grants of at least $10,000 given for animal protection and welfare, wildlife preservation, zoos, botanical gardens, and aquariums. This directory is useful for identifying foundations and grant recipients for which you may wish to work.

California Museum Directory: A Guide to Museums, Zoos, Botanic Gardens, and Historic Buildings Open to the Public (California Institute of Public Affairs, P.O. Box 189040, Sacramento, CA 95818; phone: 916/442–2472) $25, 1992, 192 pages. Each entry includes name, location, mailing address, telephone, hours open, tours available, whether admission is charged, publications issued, and descriptions of collections of 1,200 institutions. Listings are by location, with indexes of names, subjects, and counties.

Chapter 5

Arts and entertainment

*The job sources here include positions in the non–profit sector. You'll find a much greater number of job sources for the art and entertainment world in the **Professional's Private Sector Job Finder.***

Arts and entertainment in general

Job ads in print

WESTAF's Artjob (Western Arts Federation, 236 Montezume Ave., Santa Fe, NM 87501; phone: 505/988–1166) biweekly, $36/annual subscription, $24/six–month subscription, each issue contains over 100 vacancies in theater, dance, and music: arts administration, performance, production, technical, and academia as well as information on grants, residencies, internships, and competitions.

National Arts Placement Affirmative Action Arts Newsletter (National Art Education Association, 1916 Association Dr., Reston, VA 22091–1590; phone: 703/860–8000) nine issues/year, $45/annual nonmember subscription (U.S.), $50/foreign, $20/members. Each issue overflows with 75 to 100 positions in dance, art, music, and theatre.

CAA Careers (College Art Association, 275 Seventh Ave., New York, NY 10001; phone: 212/691–1051) bimonthly, $27/annual nonmember subscription (U.S.), $34/foreign, free/members. Close to 200 positions for all aspects of art are in a typical issue (the largest issue is January). Jobs include studio artists, graphic artists, printmakers, painters, photographers, sculptors, art and drawing instructors, art historians, internships, art education, conservators, administrative positions with museums and galleries, and many more.

National Arts Placement (National Art Education Association, 1916 Association Drive, Reston, VA 22091–1590; phone: 703/860–8000) nine issues/year, $45/annual subscription (U.S.), $55/foreign; prepaid. As many as 150 job openings with two–year and four–year institutions and other entities can fill these pages: administration, art teaching, art therapy, museum curators, art history, art studios, graphic designers, arts councils, internships, fellowships, grants, assistantships, and competitions.

Entertainment Employment Journal (Suite 815, 7095 Hollywood Blvd., Hollywood, CA 90028; phone: 213/969–8500) semiweekly, $95/annual subscription (U.S.), $101/annual subscription (Canada), $60/six–month subscription (U.S.), $35/three–month subscription (U.S.). From 25 to 50 jobs in all aspects of the entertainment industry fill these pages.

NAEA News (National Art Education Association, 1916 Association Drive, Reston, VA 22091–1590; phone: 703/860–8000) bimonthly, free/members only, $50/active member annual dues, $40/associate members, $20/student dues. "Placement" lists five to 30 teaching and administrative positions in art education in the U.S. and elsewhere.

New Art Examiner (Chicago New Art Association, 1255 S. Wabash, Chicago, IL 60605; phone: 312/786–0220) 10 issues/year, $35/annual subscription. About four "Employment Opportunities" for administrators of art centers and galleries are advertised in the usual issue as are around 20 "Exhibition Opportunities."

Guild News (Graphic Artists Guild of New York, 11 W. 20th St., New York, NY 10011; phone: 212/463–7730) quarterly, available only to members. Three or four positions for graphic artists appear under "Job Opportunities."

Jobline News (Graphic Artists Guild of New York, 11 W. 20th St., New York, NY 10011; phone: 212/463–7730) semiweekly (said soon to be weekly in September 1993), $60/six month member subscription. 10 to 15 job ads for graphic designers, illustrators , surface and textile designers , and computer artists.

Bulletin (National Association of Artists' Organizations, 918 F St., NW, Washington, DC 20004; phone: 202/347–6350) bimonthly, available only to members. About two positions in art administration appear under "Help Wanted."

Audition News (Chicago Entertainment Company, 6272 W. North Ave., Chicago, IL 60639; phone: 312/637–4695) monthly, $24.95/annual subscription, $14.95/six–month subscription. Dozens of job openings appear throughout. Positions are mostly in acting, singing, and dancing, as well as in production. Covers the midwest.

Daily Variety (5700 Wilshire Blvd., Suite 120, Los Angeles, CA 90036; phone: 213/857–6600) daily, $145/annual subscription. As many as 50 openings in all aspects of entertainment appear under "Job Opportunities."

Performing Arts Forum (International Association of Performing Arts Administrators, 4920 Plainfield NE, Suite 3, Grand Rapids, MI 49505; phone: 616/364–3000) eight issues/year, $25/annual nonmember subscription, free/members. One or two positions for arts administrators (CEO of performing arts center, senior arts positions, director of marketing) are under "Position Openings." Two internships a year are offered to post–graduates and students currently enrolled in graduate arts management, public administration, law, or business programs. Application deadline early April.

Employment Opportunities (National Guild of Community Schools of the Arts, P.O. Box 8018, Englewood, NJ 07631; phone: 201/871–3337) monthly, free/members only. About four job vacancies for administrators in art schools (music, dance, and visual arts education) are announced in the typical issue.

Community Arts News (c/o Springfield Arts Council, P.O. Box 745, Springfield, OH 45501; phone: 513/324–2712) quarterly, free. At the end of this newsletter, you'll find two or three announcement of job vacancies in community and multi–media arts, performing arts, classes, exhibitions, and administration.

The Washington International Arts Letter (Allied Business Consultants, P.O. Box 12010, Des Moines, IA 50312; phone: 515/255–5577) ten issues/year, contact for current subscription rates. "Deadlines" features details on 30 to 50 grants, awards, and residency programs in administration, architecture, design, film/TV/radio, music, performing arts, photography, research and training, visual arts, and writing.

Arts & Cultural Funding Report (Education Funding Research Council, 4301 N. Fairfax Drive, Suite 875, Arlington, VA 22203; phone: 703/528–1000) monthly, $138/annual subscription. Reports on available federal and foundation grants. The "Grants Alert" section announced specific grant deadlines.

Maquette (International Sculpture Center, 1050 17th St., NW, Suite 250, Washington, DC 20036; phone: 202/785–1144) bimonthly, $40/annual subscription (U.S. and Canada), $55/elsewhere. "Opportunities" lists five to 15 jobs for sculptors and artists as well as dozens of competitions, grants and fellowships, residencies, calls for artists, and studio exchanges. Also lists "Wanted/Apprenticeships."

Sculpture (International Sculpture Center, 1050 Potomac St., NW, Washington, DC 20007; phone: 202/965–6066) bimonthly, $40/annual subscription (U.S. and Canada), $55/elsewhere. "Opportunities" lists five to 15 jobs for sculptors and artists as well as dozens of competitions, grants and fellowships, residencies, calls for artists, and studio exchanges. Also lists "Wanted/Apprenticeships."

Job service

Sculpture Source (International Sculpture Center, 1050 17th St., NW, Suite 250, Washington, DC 20036; phone: 202/785–1144) $40/annual nonmember registration fee, free/members. Registrants complete this service's forms and also submit slides of their work. The computerized database is used to match sculptors with potential art sponsors. Over 1,200 referrals were made in 1990.

Directories

American Art Directory, 1991–1992 (R. R. Bowker; available through Reed Reference Publishing, P.O. Box 31, New Providence, NJ 07974; phone: 800/521–8110) $186 plus 7 percent shipping and handling, published in February of odd–numbered years, 820 pages. Offers details on more than 7,000 art organizations, museums, libraries, schools, and galleries throughout the U.S. and Canada.

Who's Who in American Art (R.R. Bowker; available through Reed Reference Publishing, P.O. Box 31, New Providence, NJ 07974; phone: 800/521–8110) $176 plus 7 percent shipping and handling, published in February of odd–numbered years, 1,473 pages. Lists over 11,800 artists, critics, curators, administrators, librarians, historians, collectors, and dealers in the U.S., Mexico, and Canada.

Who's Who in Entertainment 1992–1993 (Marquis Who's Who; available from Reed Reference Publishing, P.O. Box 31, New Providence, NJ 07974; phone: 800/521–8110) $235 plus 7 percent shipping and handling, 702 pages, annual. Provides complete and accurate biographical information on more than 18,000 individuals in the entertainment business from actors, directors, and technicians to educators, agents, and executives.

International Directory of Arts 1993/94 (K.G. Saur; available from Reed Reference Publishing, P.O. Box 31, New Providence, NJ 07974; phone: 800/521–8110) $225 plus 7 percent shipping and handling, published annually each February, 1,900 pages, two–volume set. Lists over 150,000 names and addresses in 137 countries of art restorers, publishers, libraries, art dealers, galleries, museums, associations, and more.

National Association of Artists' Organizations Directory (National Association of Artists' Organizations, 918 F St., NW, Washington, DC 20004; phone: 202/347–6350) $25/nonmembers, free/members, published in spring of even–numbered years.

Art & Auction International Directory (P.O. Box 11344, Des Moines, IA 50340; phones: 800/777–8718, 212/582–5633) 11 issues/year, $42/annual subscription (U.S.), $54/Canada, $90/Europe; single issue available for $12 in book stores. Essentially a directory of over 7,000 antique dealers and shows, auction houses, art galleries, art services, and art fairs.

Sunshine Artists (Sun Country Enterprises, 1736 North Highway 427, Longwood, FL 32750–1700; phone: 407/332–4944) monthly, $24.50/annual subscription (U.S.), $48.50/Canada and Mexico. Features a calendar directory of art fairs and craft shows in the U.S. and Canada.

Where It's At: A Guide to Arts and Crafts Shows (7204 Buckmell Dr., Austin, TX 78723; phone: 512/926–7954) ten issues/year, $23.95/annual subscription, $11.95/three–month subscription, $5/single issue. This is essentially a monthly directory of arts and crafts shows in these "southwestern" states: Alabama, Arizona, Arkansas, Colorado, Georgia, Kansas, Louisiana, Mississippi, Missouri, New Mexico, Oklahoma, Tennessee, and Texas. This directory lists up to 5,000 shows per year and each issue is updated monthly with 350 to 400 shows.

Art in America (Brant Art Publications, 575 Broadway, New York, NY 10012; phones: 800/925–0859, 212/941–2800) monthly, single issue: $4.75 plus $3/shipping (U.S.), $5/shipping (foreign), August issue costs $12 plus $3/shipping (U.S.), $5/shipping (foreign); $39.95/annual subscription (U.S.), $59.95/Canada, $69.95/elsewhere. This directory contains an alphabetical list by city and state of museums, galleries, non–profit exhibition spaces, corporate consultants, private dealers, and print dealers. It provides basic information plus a short description of the type of art shown and artists presented. The August issue is an enlarged annual guide edition. This is often available at bookstores or newsstands.

National Directory of Grants & Aid to Individuals in the Arts, 8th Edition (Allied Publishing, P.O. Box 12010, Des Moines, IA 50312; phone: 515/255–5577) biannual, last published April 1993. $30/nonmembers, $22/members. Grant information on the arts, education, and scholarships.

National Guide to Funding in Arts and Culture (The Foundation Center, 79 Fifth Ave., New York, NY 10003–3076; phones: 800/424–9836, 212/620–4230) $125, May 1992. Describes over 4,200 foundations and corporate direct giving programs including 9,500 of the grants they've made to theaters, museums, archaeology projects, orchestras, dance groups, and others.

Grants for Arts, Culture & the Humanities (The Foundation Center, 79 Fifth Ave., New York, NY 10003–3076; phones: 800/424–9836, within New York State call 212/620–4230) $65 plus $4.50/shipping, October 1993. Describes recent foundation grants of at least $10,000 given to arts and cultural organizations, historical societies and historic preservation, media, visual arts, performing arts, music, and museums. This directory is useful for identifying foundations and grant recipients for which you may wish to work.

Handel's National Directory for the Performing Arts (R.R. Bowker; available from Reed Reference Publishing, P.O. Box 31, New Providence, NJ 07974; phone: 800/521–8110) $250 plus 7 percent shipping and handling, two–volume set, 2,289 pages, 1992. This directory provides virtually every professional dance, music, and theatre organization in the U.S. as well as educational institutions that offer training and degrees in the performing arts. *Volume One: Performing Arts Organizations and Facilities* alphabetically lists organizations and facilities by state, city within state, and arts area. Listings contain the names of artistic and administrative management, board, paid staff, budget and attendance statistics, type of facility and stage, building costs, architect, resident group, facility rental information, and more. *Volume Two: Performing Arts Educational Institutions* lists alphabetically universities, colleges, schools, and institutions offering degrees and courses in dance, music, and theatre. These two volumes must be purchased together.

International Association of Performing Arts Administrators Membership Directory (IAPAA, 4920 Plainfield, NE, Suite 3, Grand Rapids, MI 49505–1010; phone: 616/364–3000) free/members only, annual.

Music and dance

Job ads in print

Music Faculty Vacancy List (CMS Publications, PO Box 8208, Missoula, MT 59807; phones: 800/729–0235, 406/728–2002) monthly; $30/annual subscription. Lists all types of positions in college music teaching. As of this writing, this newsletter has expanded its scope to include performing positions in orchestras. The average issue lists 40 to 80 positions. Mailing label service available. $75/1,000 address labels of institutions, faculty members, and departments.

Job Bulletin (New England Conservatory of Music, 290 Huntington Ave,. Boston, MA 02115) monthly, $28/annual subscription. Lists jobs in university and public school music education, performance, and arts administration.

New York Opera Newsletter (P.O. Box 278, Maplewood, NJ 07040; phone: 201/378–9549) 11 issues/year, $40/annual subscription. From 30 to 50 positions (primarily for singers, some musicians) with opera companies and choruses with symphony orchestras appear under "Auditions." Despite the periodical's title, these jobs come from across the country.

Newsline (Opera America, 777 14th St., NW, Suite 520, Washington, DC 20005; phone: 202/347–9262) monthly, available only to members, salary–based dues system starts with $25/students. Three to ten positions in opera management are listed under "Positions Available."

Conducting Service Announcements (American Symphony Orchestra League, 777 14th St., NW, Suite 500, Washington, DC 20005; phone: 202/628–0099) monthly, free/members only, $75/annual dues. About five to ten job openings for conductors are in the typical issue.

Musician Service Announcements (American Symphony Orchestra League, 777 14th St., NW, Suite 500, Washington, DC 20005; phone: 202/628–0099) monthly, free/members only, $75/annual dues. About five to ten work opportunities for classical musicians are in the typical issue.

Update (American Alliance for Health, Physical Education, Recreation and Dance, 1900 Association Dr., Reston, VA 22091; phone: 703/476–3400) eight issues/year, $45/annual nonmember subscription, free/members; $85/annual dues. "Job Exchange" features 30 or more jobs with largely universities as well as numerous graduate assistantships and grants.

Journal PERD (American Alliance for Health, Physical Education, Recreation and Dance, 1900 Association Dr., Reston, VA 22091; phone: 703/476–3400) monthly, $65/annual nonmember subscription. The "Classifieds" feature about five positions with camps and universities.

Dance/USA Journal (Dance/USA 777 14th St., NW, Washington, DC 20005; phone: 202/628–0144) quarterly, $30/annual nonmember subscription (U.S. and Canada), $60/elsewhere, free/members. Around ten positions for dancers, administrators, trainers, etc. appear under "Positions Available."

Musical American: International Directory of Performing Arts (Musical American Publishing, 825 Seventh Ave., New York, NY 10019; phone: 212/265–8360) $75 includes shipping. Published each December. Lists performers, managers, festivals, concert sites, and schools–only for classical music.

The Village Voice (P.O. Box 4088, Syracuse, NY 13217; phone: 800/825–0061) weekly, $28.95/six–month subscription, $47.95/annual subscription (U.S.), $79.20/foreign. The classifieds section has about 50 job openings under "Music Notes–Public Notice–Musicians," and 15 under "Stage & Screen Notes–Jobs & Auditions." Includes both performing and behind the scenes positions.

Job services

Resume Clearinghouse (American Symphony Orchestra League, 777 14th St., NW, Suite 500, Washington, DC 20005; phone: 202/628–0099) free/members only. You complete their registration form and submit it with your resume. When matched to a job opening, your resume is sent to the employer who is responsible for contacting you directly. Fields covered include: classical musicians, conductors, and arts administration (primarily orchestras, but also some theater) in management, development, marketing, operations, education, and public relations.

Job Express Registry (American Dance Guild, 31 W. 21st St., Third Floor, New York, NY 10010; phone: 212/627–3790) monthly, $33/three–month nonmember subscription, $18/members. Fifteen to 20 job ads for positions in dance administration and education fill this newsletter.

Directory

Stern's Performing Arts Directory (33 W. 60th Street, 10th Floor, New York, NY 10023; phones: 212/248–8937, 800/458–2845) $65, issued each September. Lists ballet companies, modern dance and tap, choreographers nationwide, college and summer study programs, singers, duos, chamber music, and opera companies.

Theater

Job ads in print

THEatre JOBLIST: The National Employment Service Billboard for Theatre Arts (THEater Service, P.O. Box 15282, Evansville, IN 47716–0282) phone: 812/474–0549) 11 issues/year, $45/annual nonmember subscrip-

tion, $30/members of Association for Theatre in Higher Education; $36/members of Alliance for Theater and Education or United States Institute for Theatre Technology. From 15 to 90 positions appear throughout for technicians, designers, and mostly for college teaching positions.

Casting Call (Mel Pogue Enterprises, 3365 Cahuenga, Hollywood, CA 90068; phone: 213/874–4012) biweekly, $36/annual subscription, $1/single issue. About 40 positions for just about any aspect of show biz appear under "Auditions."

Callboard (Theatre Bay Area, 657 Mission, Suite 402, San Francisco, CA 94105; phone: 415/957–1557) monthly, $32/annual subscription (includes membership in TBA), single copy available at Bay Area bookstores. Over 20 technical, production, acting, and administrative positions appear under "Job Bank." "Auditions" features about 35 opportunities. These openings are located almost entirely in the San Francisco Bay Area.

Newsletter (Box Office Management International, 333 E. 46th St., New York, NY 10017; phone: 212/949–7350) eight issues/year, free/members only. About four positions in box office management appear under "BOMI/Search."

Job Contact Bulletin (Southeastern Theatre Conference, P.O. Box 9868, Greensboro, NC 27429–0868; phone: 919/272–3645) monthly, available only to members: $40/annual member subscription, $15/member students. From 20 to 50 ads for everything in theater except actors appear in the typical issue.

Teaching Theatre (International Thespian Society, 3368 Central Parkway, Cincinnati, OH 45225; phone: 513/559–1996) quarterly, available only to members. Features three or four positions for directors and drama teachers under "Positions Available."

ArtSEARCH (355 Lexington Ave., New York, NY 10017; phone: 212/697–5230) 23 issues/year, $48/annual subscription. Features from 200 to 400 positions in theater for administrators, actors, dancers, musicians, designers, technicians, production, marketing, interns, and faculty.

Short Subjects (Greater Philadelphia Cultural Alliance, 320 Walnut St., Suite 500, Philadelphia, PA 19106; phone: 215/440–8100) 11 issues/year, $20/annual subscription, $2.50/per issue. Under "Job Bank" you'll find around 20 ads in the Philadelphia area for administrative positions, entry level to executive directors, and occasionally volunteer/intern/fellowship opportunities.

Job service

Job Bank (Greater Philadelphia Cultural Alliance, 320 Walnut St., Suite 500, Philadelphia, PA 19106; phone: 215/440–8100) free. You may send your resume, which is kept on file for one to two years. Employers may look through these resumes for employees in administration, marketing, production, development, teaching and other support positions in the cultural arts field. The service will give a copy of your resume to the potential employer who is then responsible for contacting you.

Directories

Directory (Southeastern Theatre Conference, P.O. Box 9868, Greensboro, NC 27429–0868; phone: 919/272–3645) available only to members. The major value of this directory is its list of theater companies that belong to the SETC.

American Association of Community Theatre Membership Directory and Handbook (AACT, 6915 Cass, Omaha, NE 68132; phone: 402/553–4890) free/members only, published each October.

Regional Theatre Directory (American Theatre Works, Inc., P.O. Box 519, Dorset, VT 05251; phone: 802/867–2223) $14.95, published each spring. Lists regional theaters and programs for the U.S.

Summer Theatre Directory (American Theatre Works, Inc., P.O. Box 519, Dorset, VT 05251; phone: 802/867–2223) $14.95, published each winter. Covers the May to September theater season in the U.S., Canada, and Great Britain.

Theatre Directory of the Bay Area (Theatre Bay Area, 657 Mission, Suite 402, San Francisco, CA 94105; phone: 415/957–1557) $24/nonmembers, $18/members. Published in March of odd–numbered years. Provides details on the theater companies in the nine–county San Francisco area.

Theatre Directory 1993–1994 (Theatrical Communications Group, 355 Lexington Ave., New York, NY 10036; phone: 212/697–5230) $5.95, issued each September. Lists names, addresses, phones, and faxes of theatres and artistic directors.

GPCA Membership Directory and Resource Guide (Greater Philadelphia Cultural Alliance, 320 Walnut St., Suite 500, Philadelphia, PA 19106; phone: 215/440–8100) $23, issued annually. Lists GPCA members, non-profit art and cultural organizations in the Philadelphia area, government guide to officials in the area, media sources and non–profit resource organizations, and consultants from the Philadelphia area.

Visual arts and film

Job ads in print

Afterimage (Visual Studies Workshop, 31 Prince St., Rochester, NY 14602; phone: 716/442–8676) 10 issues/year, $30/annual subscription (U.S.), $35/foreign. Under "Notices–Etc." there are listed about 15 to 20 jobs in media arts and photography, curators, administrative, and visual arts museums. In addition, there are about ten grants, five internships and residencies, plus 30 notices to submit to exhibitions.

Documentary Editing (Association for Documentary Editing, c/o Department of History, University of South Carolina, Columbia, SC 29208; phone: 803/777–6526) quarterly, free/members only. Four or five jobs for documentary editors appear under "Positions Available."

The Independent (Foundation for Independent Video and Film, 625 Broadway, New York, NY 10012; phone: 212/473–3400) 10 issues/year, individual issues available at newsstands for $3.50, free/members. The "Notices–Opportunities–Gigs" section lists five positions for in video/television direction, marketing, curators, media artists–anything to do with film and video.

Chapter **6**

Association management

Be sure to also see the job sources described in Chapter 2.

Job ads in print

CEO Job Opportunities Update (Suite 1190, 1575 I St., NW, Washington, DC 20005; phone: 202/408–7900) biweekly, $90/seven–issue subscription, $160/13–issue subscription, $300/annual. Each issue features about 50 to 75 vacancy announcements for chief operating officers or executive directors for all sorts of non–profit associations as well as around 50 to 75 vacancies for senior staff.

ASAE Career Opps (Suite 1190, 1575 I St., NW, Washington, DC 20005; phone: 202/408–7900) biweekly, nonmembers: $47/five–issue subscription, $97/12 issues, $177/24 issues; members of the American Society of Association Executives: $47/six–issue subscription, $97/14 issues, $177/28 issues. Each issue contains ads for about 170 jobs with non–profit associations that have annual salaries ranging from $30,000 to $50,000. About half the jobs are located in the Washington, D.C. area and the rest are scattered throughout the country.

Association Trends (Martineau Corporation, 7910 Woodmont Ave., Suite 1150, Bethesda, MD 20814; phone: 301/652–8666) weekly, $72/annual subscription (U.S.), $108/foreign. Ads for 15 or more job vacancies for secretaries to executive directors are in these "Classifieds." The magazine also publishes job seeker ads under "Free Resumes." For a $52 fee, your 30–word resume appears in three consecutive issues of *Association Trends*. As part of this service, you also submit ten copies of your resume. When an interested employer contacts the newspaper, they send out your resume. You also receive a copy of each issue of the newspaper in which your ad appears.

NSFRE Executive Search Service Newsletter (National Society of Fund Raising Executives, Suite 700, 1101 King St., Alexandria, VA 22314; phone: 703/684–0410) monthly, $25/nonmember annual subscription, free/members. About 25 vacancies for development professionals, fund raisers, and other association personnel appear under "ESS Employment Opportunities."

The NonProfit Times (190 Tamarack Cr., Skillman, NJ 08558; phone: 609/921–1251) monthly, free to qualified non–profit organization executives, $49/annual subscription for others. Jobs listed under "National Employment Non–Profit Marketplace." Among the 30 jobs per issue are management positions with non–profit associations.

Association Management (American Society of Association Executives, 1575 I St., NW, Washington, DC 20005; phone: 202/626–2723) monthly, $30/annual nonmember subscription (U.S.), $35/Canada, $40/elsewhere, $24/members. The "Executive Search" section includes about three or four executive director positions with trade or professional associations. Includes "Positions Wanted."

NEA Now (National Education Association, 1201 16th St., NW, Washington, DC 20036; phone: 202/833–4000) weekly, free/members only. Each issue includes ads for ten to 20 jobs at the National Education Association's headquarters in Washington and with its many state affiliates throughout the country.

NEA Vacancy List (National Education Association, Employment Office, 1201 16th St., NW, Washington, DC 20036; phone: 202/833–4000) weekly, free. An individual can request a copy of this list just *once* by calling 202/822–7613. Organizations can request a free subscription. This list gives full details on all jobs that are on the *NEA Vacancy Telephone* described below under "Job services," as well as details on job openings with the NEA's state affiliates.

Not sure where to find your occupation?

Then read Chapter 1 which tells you how to find all the job sources for your specialty. Even though it doesn't have much of a plot, it's well worth your valuable time.

Job services

Jobseeker Service (Martineau Corp., 7910 Woodmont Ave., Suite 1150, Bethesda, MD 20814; phone: 301/652–8666) $52. Send ten copies of your resume (up to three pages long) and a 30–word classified ad. Your ad, with a box number, will run in three consecutive issues of *Association Trends*, described above under "Job ads in print." Unless otherwise requested, your resume will be sent to all employers who ask for it. The employer is responsible for contacting you for an interview. A typical issue sports about a dozen of these ads under "Free Resumes."

ASAE Referral Service (American Society of Association Executives, 1575 I St., NW, Washington, DC 20005; phone: 202/626–2723) $80/nonmembers, $40/members. Submit fee with seven copies of your resume and a completed application form. Your resume will be kept on file for nine months. When the service matches you with an appropriate vacancy with an association, it sends your resume to the association which is then responsible for contacting you.

ASAE Executive Search (American Society of Association Executives, 1575 I St., NW, Washington, DC 20005; phone: 202/626–2723) free. This is a genuine executive search service for higher level positions with associations.

NEA Vacancy Telephone (National Education Association, Employment Office, 1201 16th St., NW, Washington, DC 20036; phone: 202/822–7641) free. Call 202/822–7642 24–hours a day to hear a recording that describes job vacancies at NEA's headquarters in the nation's capitol. Usually five to ten positions are available, although in recessionary times there are sometimes none.

Directory

Directory of Association Meeting Planners & Conference/Convention Directors (The Salesman's Guide; available from Reed Reference Publishing, P.O. Box 31, New Providence, NJ 07974; phone: 800/521–8110) $217 plus 7 percent shipping and handling, 1,000 pages, 1993 edition. Includes more than 8,600 national associations that hold more than 22,000 conventions, seminars, and meetings with 12,500 meeting planners by city and state.

Salary surveys

NSFRE Membership Profile and Salary Survey (National Society of Fund Raising Executives, 1101 King St., Suite 700, Alexandria, VA 22314; phone: 703/684–0410) $20/nonmembers, free/members, printed every three years, last published December 1992. A list of association members cross–referenced by salary, education level, type of organization, and geographic location.

Cordom's Salary Survey of Nonprofit Organizations (Association Trends, 7910 Woodmont Ave., Suite 1150, Bethesda, MD 20814–3015; phone: 301/652–8666) $90 plus $5.25/shipping, published each autumn. Covers over 110 Washington, D.C. area non–profit organizations.

Salary Survey (Association Trends, 7910 Woodmont Ave., Suite 1150, Bethesda, MD 20814; phone: 301/652–8666) $135.25 plus $5.25/shipping, published annually. Prepared by the Greater Washington Society of Association Executives' Association, this covers District of Columbia area non–profit groups.

Compensation and Benefits Survey (Association Trends, 7910 Woodmont Ave., Suite 1150, Bethesda, MD 20814; phone: 301/652–8666) $159 plus $5.25/shipping, published in even–numbered years. Prepared by the Chicago Society of Association Executives, this survey reports on salaries and benefits at Chicago area non–profits.

Chapter 7

Computers

Computers

Clearly few job sources focus on jobs with computers specifically in the non–profit sector. See the **Professional's Private Sector Job Finder** for a much more extensive set of job sources in computers, data processing, and electronics, albeit they will be largely for positions in the private sector.

Job ads in print

Computer (IEEE Computer Society, 10662 Los Vaqueros Cr., Los Alamitos, CA 90720–1264; phone: 714/821–8380) available only to members. Two to 15 pages of "Career Opportunities" are listed.

Directory

Directory of Computer and High Technology Grants (Research Grant Guides, P.O. Box 1214, Loxahatchee, FL 33470; phone: 407/795–6129) $44.50 plus $4 shipping, prepaid, published in April of odd–numbered years. Describes over 4,400 funding opportunities from 640 funding sources.

Chapter 8

Education

Be sure to also look up specific specialties in the Index of this book.

Job ads in print

NESC Newsletter (National Education Service Center, P.O. Box 1279, Dept. NP, Riverton, WY 82501; phone: 307/856–0170) weekly, September through February: $37/one–month subscription, $125/five–month subscription, $10/trial issue. March through August: contact NESC for an order form because you can choose the months for which you wish to receive the newsletter as well as indicate the subject areas in which you are interested. In the course of a year, over 72,000 job ads for teachers and administrators in public and private elementary and secondary schools appear under "Help Wanted," and "Professional Services Offered." Also includes post–secondary positions.

Education Bulletin (Career Development Coop Education Placement Services, Emporia State University, 1200 Commercial, Box 4014, Emporia, KS 66801–5087; phone: 316/343–5407) weekly March through August, monthly the rest of the year, $31.43/six–month subscription, $56.57/annual subscription. Hundreds of teaching positions appear in each issue. In the course of a year, over 9,000 positions are advertised.

The Job Search Handbook for Educators (Association for School, College and University Staffing, Inc., 1600 Dodge Ave., S–300, Evanston, IL 60201–3451; phone: 708/864–1999) $8 (prepaid no credit cards), 50 pages, annual. This fabulous resource includes about 40 display ads for teaching positions at all levels. In addition it offers a great list of over 100 universities that publish their teacher vacancy lists (price and frequency of publication is provided; you'll have to use directories of universities to find the address and phone number of those that interest you. See the directories section of this chapter under "Higher Education." Also included is a list of U.S. state teacher certification officers as well as over a dozen articles on the hiring process in the U.S. and overseas, and summary of supply/demand report in the U.S.

The National Ad Search (P.O. Box 2083, Milwaukee, WI 53201; phones: 800/992–2832, 414/351–1398) 50 issues/year, $40/six–week subscription, $75/three–month subscription, $235/annual subscription, $15/one–week trial subscription. Call toll–free number for a free sample copy. Each issue over-flows with 2,000 classified ads reprinted from 75 newspapers around the country. Job ads are divided into 54 disciplines including education. This is a good source for finding classified ads for teachers and administrators from other cities.

Career Focus (New Mexico State University, Placement and Career Serv-ices, P.O. Box 30001, Dept. 3509, Las Cruces, NM 88003–0001; phone: 505/646–1631) biweekly, $12.60/six–month subscription. Features brief descriptions of at least 200 jobs openings, largely west of the Mississippi, in education, liberal arts, and other fields. Issues have ranged from 32 to 56 pages.

Job Bulletin #1 (Center Career Services, University of Washington, 301 Loew Hall, Mailstop FH–30. Seattle, WA 98104; phone: 206/543–9104) weekly, $40/three–month subscription. Includes ads for teachers and ad-ministrators at all levels of education. Over 30 ads are in the typical issue. While advertised jobs can be anywhere in the country, most jobs advertised here are located in Oregon and Washington State.

TEACHING Exceptional Children (Council for Exceptional Children, 1920 Association Drive, Reston, VA 22091; phone 703/620–3660) quarterly, $30/annual non–member subscription (U.S.), $35/foreign (surface), $55/for-eign (airmail), free/members. From six to 30 ads for special education teachers and administrators are listed under "Classified." Includes all levels of education.

Exceptional Children (Council for Exceptional Children, 1920 Association Drive, Reston, VA 22091; phone 703/620–3660) bimonthly, $45/annual subscription (U.S.), $51/foreign. "Professional Opportunities" carries about 15 ads for positions in all aspects of special education: teaching, administration, university staff.

LDA Newsbriefs (Learning Disabilities Association, 4156 Library Rd., Pittsburgh, PA 15234; phone: 412/341–1515) $13.50/annual nonmember subscription (U.S.), $30/foreign, free/members. "Classified Ads" runs ads for three to ten openings for teachers of students who have learning disabilities.

Reading Today (International Reading Association, 800 Barkdale Rd., Newark, DE 19714; phones: 800/628–8508, ext. 49, 302/731–1600 ext. 245) contact for details, free/members. Includes two to five ads for reading teachers.

Journal of Reading (International Reading Association, 800 Barkdale Rd., Newark, DE 19714; phones: 800/628–8508, ext. 49, 302/731–1600 ext. 245) eight issues/year, $38/annual subscription. Includes occasional ads for reading teachers.

The Reading Teacher (International Reading Association, 800 Barkdale Rd., Newark, DE 19714; phones: 800/628–8508, ext. 49, 302/731–1600 ext. 245) nine issues/year, $38/annual nonmember subscription, free/members. Includes occasional ads for reading teachers.

Update (National Association for Sport and Physical Education, 1900 Association Drive, Reston, VA 22091; phone: 703/476–4310) eight issues/year, $45/annual nonmember subscription (U.S. and Canada), $53/elsewhere, free/members. Fifteen to 20 jobs are listed on last page for coaches, athletic directors, and health and physical education teachers.

The Science Teacher (National Science Teachers Association, 1742 Connecticut Ave., NW, Washington, DC 20002; phone: 202/328–5800) nine issues/year, $52. Three to six ads for science teachers and administrators appear under "Classified."

Science Education News (Directorate for Education and Human Resources, American Association for the Advancement of Science, 1333 H St., NW, Washington, DC 20005; phone: 202/326–6620) eight issues/year, free. Under "Opportunities," this newsletter frequently reports about non–profits that need teachers and researchers.

Minority Funding Report (Government Information Services, 1611 N. Kent St., Suite 508, Arlington, VA 22209; phone: 703/528–1000) monthly, $128/annual subscription. The "Education Grants Week" section reports on two to four education grants. Another two to ten more grants in housing, health care, and other fields are also reported.

Initiatives (National Association for Women in Education, 1325 18th St., NW, Suite 210, Washington, DC 20036; phone: 202/659–9330) quarterly, $40. Ten to 30 jobs appear under "JOB LINE."

Job services

National Resume Bank (Suite 330, 3637 4th St., North, St. Petersburg, FL 33704; phone: 813/896–3694) $25/three–month resume listing, $40/six months; to update your resume listing, send five copies of your resume with the $5 update fee. To get on this resume database, you must send in your check along with five copies of your resume. Unless you request your name, address, and phone number to be hidden from prospective employers' view, you will be contacted directly by employers interested in you. Includes jobs in education.

National Association of Teachers Agencies (Education Job Search, P.O. Box 223, Georgetown, MA 01833; phone: 508/352–8473) price: five percent of your first year salary. Contact EJS for full details on how this service operates. You complete the application form used by this job–matching service. When matched with a teaching or administrative vacancy, your form is sent to the hiring agency which is responsible for contacting you.

Employment Information Services (Professional Development Resource Center, School for International Training, P.O. Box 676, Kipling Rd., Brattleboro, VT 05302; phone: 802/258–3397, ext. 258, free/available only to alumni of World Learning, Inc. and School for International Training. Alumni may request regular mailings of employment opportunities in their specialty. Contact for details. Alumni may also call in evenings between 6:30 p.m. and 10 p.m. (eastern standard time) to hear a list of job vacancies.

CU Career Connection (University of Colorado, Campus Box 133, Boulder, CO 80309–0133; phone: 303/492–4127) $30/two–month fee entitles you to a "passcode" which unlocks this job hotline. You need a touch–tone phone to call and request the field in which you are interested in hearing job openings. The hotline is turned off Monday through Friday, 2 to 4 p.m. for daily updating.

Faculty Exchange Center (952 Virginia Ave., Lancaster, PA 17603; phone: 717/393–1130). Contact for information about domestic teacher exchange programs.

kiNexus (Information Kinetics, Inc., Suite 560, 640 N. LaSalle St., Chicago, IL 60610; phones: 800/828–0422, 312/642–7560) $30/annual fee, $50/confidential listing (so your present employer can't learn that you are looking for a job), free if you are a student at one of the 1,500+ universities that subscribe to this service–check with your school's placement office. This is an online resume database service for college students and graduates with

up to five years work experience. You complete their resume form and kiNexus puts your information into the computer. If you request the higher–cost "confidential" option, you'll be assigned a number. When a prospective employer wishes to interview you, you will be asked by kiNexus if you wish to be interviewed. Only after you agree to be interviewed will your name, address, and phone be given to the employer. The universities that subscribe to kiNexus can ask kiNexus staff to conduct searches to identify candidates for specific teaching or administrative positions, or can conduct their own searches since the database is online. The potential employer is responsible for contacting job candidates for an interview.

DORS (Defense Outplacement Referral System) (Operation Transition, DMDC, Suite 155–A, 99 Pacific St., Monterey, CA 93940; phone: 800/727–3677) free, available only to military service personnel and their spouses. Your resume is kept on file for up to 90 days after separation from the military. Obtain DORS' "mini–resume" form from a local military installation transition office. You can update your resume for free at a transition office. Around 4,000 employers, including school districts and universities, access this resume database and can conduct their own searches for job candidates.

Directories

ASCUS National Directory for Employment in Education (Association for School, College and University Staffing, Inc., 1600 Dodge Ave., S–300, Evanston, IL 60201–3451; phone: 708/864–1999) $20, annual. Lists ASCUS member teachers by institution with cross–references by subject areas taught and an alphabetical listing of members.

National Directory of Job and Career Fairs for Educators (Association for School, College and University Staffing, Inc., 1600 Dodge Ave., S–300, Evanston, IL 60201–3451; phone: 708/864–1999) $10, 40 pages, annual. Each entry includes the data and name of the job or career fair, location, sponsoring institution, who may attend, fees, number of employers and candidates expected to attend, fee and deadlines for employers wishing to exhibit, and contact person.

Private Independent Schools (Bunting and Lyon, 238 N. Main St., Walling-
ford, CT 06492; phone: 203/269–3333) $95, published each April. Lists
information about private independent schools throughout the world.

**Directories of State Public School Systems and State Certification Offices
in the U.S.** (Careers/Consultants in Education, 615 Main Street, Suite 455,
Stroudsburg, PA 18360; phone: 305/974–3511) $5 to $10, depending on
state. Each directory provides the addresses and phone numbers for every
public school district and state teacher certification office in one state.

National Association for Women in Education Membership Handbook
(NAWE, 1325 18th St., NW, Suite 210, Washington, DC 20036; phone:
202/659–9330) free/members only, released each September. Lists member teachers and administrators.

National Black Child Development Institute Membership Directory (NBCDI,
1463 Rhode Island Ave., NW, Washington, DC 20005; phone: 202/387–
1281) $60/nonmembers, $30/members, published every January and July.
Members are engaged in health education and child welfare.

Job Banks (National Clearinghouse for Professions in Special Education, The
Council for Exceptional Children, 1920 Association Dr., Reston, VA 22091;
phone: 703/264–9477) free. This four–page list includes state and private
agencies that have information on job vacancies in 26 states.

Grants for Literacy, Reading & Adult/Continuing Education (The Foundation Center, 79 Fifth Ave., New York, NY 10003–3076; phones: 800/424–
9836, within New York State call 212/620–4230) $65 plus $4.50/shipping,
October 1993. Describes recent foundation grants of at least $10,000 given
to organizations that support literacy, reading, and adult basic education
and continuing education programs. This directory is useful for identifying
foundations and grant recipients for which you may wish to work.

Salary survey

ALISE Library and Information Science Education Statistical Report (Association for Library and Information Science Education, 4101 Lake Boone
Trail, Suite 201, Raleigh, NC 27607; phone: 919/787–5181) $34/nonmem-
ber (U.S.), $34/foreign, $24/members, published each May. Includes a
salary survey of teachers in member schools.

Administrators

Job ads in print

National Job Register for School Administrators (Empire State Building, Suite 3308, New York, NY 10118) biweekly, $50/annual subscription, $40/six–month subscription. About 300 vacancies for superintendents, central office personnel, and school positions (principals, department heads, etc.) fill the typical issue.

Leadership News (American Association of School Administrators, 1801 N. Moore St., Arlington, VA 22209; phone: 703/528–0700) 19 issues/year, free/members only. "Job Bulletin" includes 50 ads for school district super-intendents, deputy administrators, and university administrators.

Education Week (Editorial Projects in Education, 4301 Connecticut, NW, Suite 250, Washington, DC 20008; phone: 202/364–4114) 40 issues/year, $59.94/annual subscription (U.S.), $82.94/annual (Canada), $92.94/else-where (surface mail), $124.94/elsewhere (air mail). About 50 to 100 ads primarily for school superintendents, principals, and administrators (only a few teaching positions) are in "The Marketplace."

AACRAO Employment Referral Bulletin (American Association of Colle-giate Registrars and Admissions Officers, 1 Dupont Cr., NW, Suite 330, Washington, DC 20036–1171; phone: 202/293–9161) monthly, $25/six–month subscription, $50/annual subscription. Each issue is crammed to the gills with ads for positions in admissions and records.

Data Dispenser (American Association of Collegiate Registrars and Admis-sions Officers, 1 Dupont Circle, NW, Suite 330, Washington, DC 20036–1171; phone: 202/293–9161) ten issues/year, included in dues, $30/annual nonmember subscription, free/members. Four to eight ads for university level registrars, admission officers, and administrators appear under "Pro-fessional Positions Classifieds."

Employment Opportunities (National Guild of Community School of the Arts, P.O. Box 8018, Englewood, NJ 07631; phone: 201/871–3337) monthly, free/members only. About four job vacancies for administrators in art schools (music, dance, and visual arts education) are announced in the typical issue.

NACAC Bulletin (National Association of College Admission Counselors, 1631 Prince Street, Alexandria, VA 22314–2818; phone: 703/836–2222) monthly, $25/annual nonmember subscription, free/members. Three to five job ads are listed under "Career Corner."

Outlook (American Association of University Women, 1111 16th St., NW, Washington, DC 20036; phone: 202/785–7745) four issues/year, free/mem-bers only. The "Classifieds" include ads for three to five administrative openings in higher education.

CUPA News (College and University Personnel Association, 1233 20th St., NW, Washington, DC 20036; phone: 202/429–0311, ext. 23) semimonthly, $75/nonmember annual subscription, $50/members. Two to six jobs for human resource professionals are listed under "Classified."

Spotlight (College Placement Council, 62 Highland Ave., Bethlehem, PA 18042; phones: 800/544–5272, 215/868–1421) 21 issues/year, $72/annual nonmember subscription, included in membership package. Under "Job-wire" there are usually five to ten openings for personnel directors, recruiters, and career counselors.

NASFAA Newsletter (National Association of Student Financial Aid Administrators, 1920 L St., NW, Suite 200, Washington, DC 20036–5020; phone: 202/785–0453) biweekly, free/members only. "Job Classified" carries about six ads for financial aid administrators.

APPA Newsletter (APPA: The Association of Higher Education Facilities Officers, 1446 Duke St., Alexandria, VA 22314; phone: 703/684–1446) eight issues/year, $40/nonmember annual subscription to both this magazine and *Facilities Manager* described immediately below, free/members. "Job Corner" runs ads for ten to 15 positions: controls engineers; directors of physical plant; director of architecture, engineering, and construction; plant engineers; custodial services; project, civil, and operating engineers.

Facilities Manager (APPA: The Association of Higher Education Facilities Officers, 1446 Duke St., Alexandria, VA 22314; phone: 703/684–1446) quarterly, $40/nonmember annual subscription to both this magazine and *APPA Newsletter* described immediately above, free/members. "Job Corner" carries ads for about six positions: controls engineers; directors of physical plant; director of architecture, engineering, and construction; plant engineers; custodial services; project, civil, and operating engineers.

NCURA Newsletter (National Council of University Research Administrators, 1 Dupont Circle, NW, Suite 420, Washington, DC 20036; phone: 202/466–3894) bimonthly, free/members only. About one to four ads for research administrators appear throughout the newsletter.

ASBO Accents (Association of School Business Officials, International, Membership Department, 11401 N. Shore Dr., Reston, VA 22090–4232; phone 703/478–0405) monthly, $68/annual subscription. About ten ads for school administrators appear under "Jobs Bank."

Business Officer (National Association of College and University Business Officers, 1 Dupont Cr., Suite 500, Washington, DC 20036; phone: 202/861–2500) monthly, $50/members only. Five to seven ads for college and university business officers (fiscal officers, controller, vice chancellors for business affairs, budget and planning) materialize under "Classifieds."

Position Registry (National Association of College and University Attorneys, 1 Dupont Cr., NW, Suite 620, Washington, DC 20036; phone: 202/833–8390) semimonthly, $50/annual nonmember subscription, $25/members. Three or four attorney positions with universities or colleges are in each issue.

Job services

Placement Service (Harold Webb Associates, Ltd., 545 Lincoln Ave., Suite 6, Winnetka, IL 60093; phone: 708/446–8637) free. Contact this service for an application form. It places school district superintendents, principals, executive directors, and persons of administrative positions. Contact for further information.

P.E.N. (National Association of Student Financial Aid Administrators, 1920 L St., NW, Suite 200, Washington, DC 20036–5020; phone: 202/785–0453) $22/member subscription to Post–Secondary Education Network, $42/nonmembers, plus $8/per month usage fee. Accessible by computer modem, this computer job database enables you to locate openings for financial aid administrators. Contact NASFAA for details.

National Academic Advising Association Placement Service (NAAA, c/o Dr. G. Robert Standing, Advising and Orientation, California State University at Chico, Chico, CA 95929–0725; phone: 916/898–5712) free/members only; $40/annual dues, $15/students. You submit four copies of your resume and a completed application form. When a match is made, a copy of the job announcement is sent to you and you are free to contact the employer. Positions are for academic advisors at the college and university level. This is a relatively new service that is beginning to grow.

Directories

AACRAO Member Guide (American Association of Collegiate Registrars and Admissions Officers, 1 Dupont Circle, NW, Suite 330, Washington, DC 20036–1171; phone: 202/293–9161) $60/nonmembers, free/members, published every December.

NACAC Membership Directory (National Association of College Admission Counselors, 1631 Prince Street, Alexandria, VA 22314–2818: phone: 703/836–2222) $40/nonmembers, free/members, issued each September.

National Association of Student Personnel Administration Membership Handbook (NASPA, 1875 Connecticut Ave, NW, Suite 418, Washington, DC 20009; phone: 202/265–7500) $25/nonmembers, first copy free/members, published every September.

NASFAA National Membership Directory (National Association of Student Financial Aid Administrators, 1920 L St., NW, Suite 200, Washington, DC 20036–5020; phone: 202/785–0453) $50/nonmembers, free/members, issued each January.

CUPA Membership Directory (College and University Personnel Association, 1233 20th St., NW, Washington, DC 20036; phone: 202/429–0311) $150/nonmembers, $25/members, issued annually. Lists human resource administrators at universities and colleges.

NCURA Membership Directory (National Council of University Research Administrators, 1 Dupont Circle, NW, Suite 420, Washington, DC 20036; phone: 202/466–3894) free/members only, published every April.

APPA Membership Directory (APPA: The Association of Higher Education Facilities Officers, 1446 Duke St., Alexandria, VA 22314; phone: 703/684–1446) free/members only, published each January.

IACLEA Membership Directory (International Association of Campus Law Enforcement Administrators, c/o Peter Berry, 638 Prospect Ave., Hartford, CT 06105; phone: 203/233–4531) $50/nonmembers, free/members, annual.

Buyers Guide and Membership Directory (Association of School Business Officials, International, Membership Department, 11401 N. Shore Dr., Reston, VA 22090–4232; phone 703/478–0405) free/members only, issued each March. Lists businesses that serve schools as well as school administrators by title.

NACUBO Membership Directory (National Association of College and University Business Officers, 1 Dupont Cr., Suite 500, Washington, DC 20036; phone: 202/861–2500) $110/nonmembers, $41/members, printed every January.

NACUA Membership Directory (National Association of College and University Attorneys, 1 Dupont Cr., NW, Suite 620, Washington, DC 20036; phone: 202/833–8390) free/members only, issued each October.

Salary surveys

National Study of Salaries and Wages in Public Schools (Educational Research Service, 2000 Clarendon Blvd., Arlington, VA 22201; phone: 703/243–2100) contact for price, published each February. This is the authoritative source of salary data for 33 categories of school personnel. Published in three volumes: salaries scheduled for professional personnel; salaries paid professional personnel; and salaries and wages paid to support personnel.

Administrative Compensation Survey (College and University Personnel Association, 1233 20th St., NW, Washington, DC 20036; phone: 202/429–0311, ext. 23) $175/nonmembers, $75/members, issued annually in January. Salaries of 160 positions in higher education from CEOs to deans to top management.

Salary Budget Survey Report (American Compensation Association, 14040 N. Northsight Blvd., Scottsdale, AZ 85260; phone: 602/951–9191) $80/nonmembers, $55/members, published each September. This survey is broken down into 45 industry groups nationally in four regions.

Elementary and secondary education

Also see the "Administrators" and "Education in general" sections earlier in this chapter.

Teaching Opportunities (Educator Information Services, 637 Georges Rd., North Brunswick, NJ 08902–3331; phone: 908/246–7046) nine issues/year, $94.50/annual subscription (individuals), $150/annual subscription (institutions), $15.50/single issue. Each issue includes information on over 800 vacancies in elementary and secondary education, primarily teaching positions, but also administrative, professional support staff, therapists, guidance, and vocational. Information provided includes the position, school district, administrator (name, address, phone), salary scale, closing date for applications, and starting date. This periodical is supplemented by the *Job Opportunity Express Service* described below under "Job services."

Teacher Magazine (P.O. Box 2091, Marion, OH 43305-2091; phone: 202/364–4114) nine issues/year, $18/annual subscription (U.S.), $33/Canada, $43/elsewhere (surface mail), $58/elsewhere (air mail). Over 20 positions for elementary and secondary teachers, including summer positions, appear under "Classified Advertising."

NASSP NewsLeader (National Association of Secondary School Principals, 1904 Association Drive, Reston, VA 22091; phone: 703/860–0200) monthly during school year, free/members. About five to ten job ads appear throughout the newsletter.

Education Grants Alert (Capitol Publications, 1101 King Street, Suite 444, Alexandria, VA 22314; phones: 800/327–7203, 703/683–4100) weekly, $299/annual subscription. Provides details on private and federal grants for kindergarten through twelfth grade programs.

Job services

National Teachers Clearinghouse (P.O. Box 1257, Boston, MA 02118–1257; phone: 617/267–3204) $25/one–month registration fee, $45/three–month fee, $65/six–month fee. To receive specific school openings submit the NTC's "Resume Form" which enables you to specify the type of position(s) and geographic location you prefer. Each additional position category is $15. Teaching positions are for kindergarten through community college. Positions are classified into: arts, elementary, counselor, English, foreign languages, mathematics, music, physical and health education, principals, science, social sciences, and special education.

You will receive a report twice a month (February through June, once a month from July through January) of open positions that match your interests and experience. You must contact the school to apply for the position.

Mailing lists for public school districts and private schools are available for purchase. $12/public schools, $12/private schools, $20/both (except California, Illinois, New York, Ohio, Pennsylvania, and Texas). $18/public schools, $18/private schools, $30/both (California, Illinois, New York, Ohio, Pennsylvania, and Texas only). Lists are printed on self–adhesive labels. A list of all state certification offices is available for $7.

Job Opportunity Express Service (Educator Information Services, 637 Georges Rd., North Brunswick, NJ 08902; phones: 800/969–4001, 908/246–7046) $65/basic regular package, $30/five additional notifications. Some job vacancies come in after the periodical *Teaching Opportunities* goes to press. Under the "basic regular package," you'll be notified by phone of up to five late-breaking vacancies that fit your certification(s), grade level preference, and zip code preference. These jobs are not published in *Teaching Opportunities*. Vacancies include elementary and secondary education, primarily teaching positions, but also administrative, professional support staff, therapists, guidance, and vocational. This periodical supplements the periodical *Teaching Opportunities* described above under "Job ads in print."

Directories

Directory of Public School Systems in the U.S. (Association for School, College and University Staffing, Inc., 1600 Dodge Ave., S–300, Evanston, IL 60201–3451; phone: 708/864–1999) $65, annual. Includes nearly 15,000 public school systems. Individual state directories can also be ordered for prices that range from $1 per state (minimum order $5) to $11 per state. Each entry includes the school district name, address, telephone number, hiring official, and grade levels and size of each district.

Handbook of Private Schools (Porter Sargent Publishers, Inc., 11 Beacon St., Suite 1400, Boston, MA 02108; phone: 617/523–1670) $77.41, 1,440 pages, annual. Includes over 1,700 elementary and secondary boarding and day schools: administrators, enrollment breakdown, faculty breakdown, curriculum, financial data, and school history.

Directory for Exceptional Children (Porter Sargent Publishers, Inc., 11 Beacon St., Suite 1400, Boston, MA 02108; phone: 617/523–1670) $52.84, 1,362 pages, last edition 1990–91. Reports on over 3,000 schools, facilities, and organizations that serve children and young adults who have developmental, organic, or emotional disabilities.

Schools Abroad of Interest to Americans (Porter Sargent Publishers, Inc., 11 Beacon St., Suite 1400, Boston, MA 02108; phone: 617/523–1670) $36.98, 592 pages, last edition was for 1991–92. Describes over 800 elementary and secondary schools in 130 countries.

Guide to Summer Camps and Summer Schools (Porter Sargent Publishers, Inc., 11 Beacon St., Suite 1400, Boston, MA 02108; phone: 617/523–1670) $22.55/paperback, $27.98/cloth edition, 492 pages, last edition 1990–91. Reports on over 1,100 camps and summer schools as well as specialized programs for children with learning, physical, or mental disabilities.

Directory of Day Schools in the United States and Canada (Torah Umesorah–National Society for Hebrew Day Schools, 5723 18th Ave., Brooklyn, NY 11204; phone: 718/259–1223) $13, last published in 1993.

National Guide to Funding for Elementary and Secondary Education (The Foundation Center, 79 Fifth Ave., New York, NY 10003–3076; phones: 800/424–9836, 212/620–4230) $135 plus $4.50/shipping, June 1993. Describes the programs of over 1,600 foundations and corporate direct giving programs that fund elementary and secondary school programs: nursery schools, bilingual education, dropout prevention, educational testing programs, and more. Includes a list of over 4,500 grants that have been funded.

Grants for Elementary & Secondary Education (The Foundation Center, 79 Fifth Ave., New York, NY 10003–3076; phones: 800/424–9836, within New York State call 212/620–4230) $65 plus $4.50/shipping, October 1993. Describes recent foundation grants of at least $10,000 given to elementary and secondary schools for academic programs, counseling, educational testing, drop–out prevention, teacher training and education, salary support, and school libraries. This directory is useful for identifying foundations and grant recipients for which you may wish to work.

Salary surveys

Teacher Supply and Demand in the United States (Association for School, College and University Staffing, Inc., 1600 Dodge Ave., S–300, Evanston, IL 60201–3451; phone: 708/864–1999) $10, annual. Includes average salaries by region and by teacher's degree for elementary/secondary teachers and special education teachers.

An Introduction to the K–8 Principalship (National Association of Elementary School Principals, 1615 Duke St., Alexandria, VA 22714; phone: 703/684–3345) free; you must send a self–addressed stamped (one ounce) number ten business envelope. This brochure includes a few paragraphs about earnings.

Higher education

Also see the section labeled "Administrators" earlier in this chapter and the section called "Trades and vocational education" where you'll find additional job sources for junior colleges.

Job ads in print

The Chronicle of Higher Education (P.O. Box 1955, Marion, OH 43306–2055; phone: 800/347–6969) 48 issues/year, $40.50/six–month subscription, $75/annual subscription. The "Bulletin Board" section contains hundreds of ads for teaching, research, and administrative positions. Also includes "positions wanted" ads as well as "faculty exchange" and "housing exchange."

Black Issues in Higher Education (Cox, Matthews, & Associates, Inc., 10520 Warwick Ave., Suite B–8, Fairfax, VA 22030–3136; phone: 703/385–2981) biweekly, $26/annual subscription first year, $40/first two years, $60/first three years. After 3 years rates go up. At least 250 ads for faculty positions are listed under "Position Announcements."

The Black Scholar (Black World Foundation, P.O. Box 2869, Oakland CA 94609: phone: 510/547–6633) four issues/year, $30/annual subscription (U.S.), $40/foreign, $50/institutions, $65/foreign institutions. Fifteen to 30 ads for university faculty and research positions are listed under "Classified Ads."

Affirmative Action Register (Warren H. Green, Inc., 8356 Olive Blvd., St. Louis, MO 63132; phones: 800/537–0655, 314/991–1335) monthly, individuals: $15/annual subscription, $8/six–month subscription; free to institutional and organizational minority, female, or disabled candidate sources. Dozens of university and college positions appear throughout this periodical.

Educational Researcher (American Educational Research Association, 1230 17th St., NW, Washington, DC 20036–3078; phone: 202/223–9485) nine issues/year, $37/annual nonmember subscription, free/members. Under "Classifieds," you'll generally find ten ads for faculty and research positions with schools of education and research and development organizations. But the fall issues carry over 20 job ads.

About Women on Campus (National Association for Women in Education, Suite 210, 1325 18th St., NW, Washington, DC 20036; phone: 202/659–9330) quarterly, $20/nonmembers, free/members. About 20 jobs ads are listed under "JOB LINE" for deans, counselors, and administrators in higher education.

Journal of Cultural Diversity (Association of Black Nursing Faculty in Higher Education, 5832 Queens Cove, Lisle, IL 60532; phone: 708/969–3809) quarterly, $25/annual subscription, $15/student. Twelve to 22 job ads are listed under "Classified" for university jobs, teaching, and administration. Jobs are primarily in sociology, ethnic studies, anthropology, and social work.

Careers and the disABLED (Equal Opportunity Publications, 44 Broadway, Greenlawn, NY 11740; phone: 516/261–9080) three issues/year, $8/annual prepaid subscription. About five display ads under "Equal Opportunity & Higher Education Careers" feature positions in higher education for college graduates from employers who certify they are equal opportunity employers who will hire people who have disabilities. Readers can submit their resume to the magazine which then forwards them to advertising employers the job seeker names — for free.

NUCEA News (National University Continuing Education Association, 1 Dupont Cr., Suite 615, Washington, DC 20036; phone: 202/659–3130) monthly, $45/annual nonmember subscription, free/members. Four job ads for continuing education faculty, conference planners, deans, directors, and administrators appear under "Recruiter Advertisements."

AECT Job Referral Newsletter (Association for Educational Communications and Technology) 1025 Vermont Ave., NW, Washington, DC 20005; phone: 202/347–7834) monthly, free/members only. Each issue contains at least 12 announcements of vacancies in higher education: media specialists, librarians, educational technology professors.

MLA Job Information List (Modern Language Association, 10 Astor Place, New York, NY 10003; phone: 212/614–6321) five issues/year, $35/annual subscription (U.S. and Canada), $47/elsewhere. Each issue contains 200 to 600 university and college job openings for teachers of English composition and literature in the U.S. and Canada, and another 200 to 600 for teachers of foreign languages.

College Language Association Journal (College Language Association, c/o Dr. Cason L. Hill, Morehouse College, Atlanta, GA 30314; phone: 404/681–2800) quarterly, $35/members only (U.S.), $36.50/Canada, $40.50/elsewhere. "CLA Placement Service" includes ads for two to 30 English and modern foreign language teaching positions at private and public two–year and four–year institutions.

Music Faculty Vacancy List (CMS Publications, P.O. Box 8208, Missoula, MT 59807; phones: 800/729–0235, 406/728–2002) monthly, $30/annual subscription. Lists all types of positions in college music teaching, administration, and research. As of this writing, this newsletter has expanded its scope to include performing positions in orchestras. The average issue lists 40 to 80 positions. You can purchase mailing labels for $75 per 1,000 address labels of institutions, faculty members, and departments.

NAFSA Job Registry (Association of International Educators, 1875 Connecticut Ave., Suite 1000, NW, Washington, DC 20009; phone: 202/462–4811) monthly, $18/members only, contact for membership details. About 20 job vacancies in international education are touted in the typical issue: foreign student advisors, study abroad advisors, ESL, foreign student admissions, and directors of international offices.

The NCAA News (National Collegiate Athletic Association, P.O. Box 7347, Overland Park, KS 66207–0347; phone: 913/339–1900) 46 issues/year, $24/annual nonmember subscription, $15/junior college and high school faculty and students, $12/faculty and students at NCAA member institutions. Around 20 to 60 job openings are advertised in "The Market" — athletics directors, trainers, athletic promotions, public relations, sports information, coaches, physical education instructors, and graduate assistants.

Journal of Physical Education, Recreation, and Sport (National Association for Sport and Physical Education, 1900 Association Dr., Reston, VA 22091; phone: 703/476–3410) nine issues/year, $65/annual subscription (institutions only, individuals cannot subscribe), free/members. The "Classified" section carries about ten ads for coaches, health, physical education instructors, and athletic directors.

AIN Notes (American Institute of Nutrition, 9650 Rockville Pike, #L–4500, Bethesda, MD 20814; phone: 301/530–7050) quarterly, $30/annual subscription. Four to 12 ads for college level personnel are listed under "Positions Available."

Anthropology Newsletter (American Anthropological Association, 4350 N. Fairfax Dr., Suite 640, Arlington, VA 22203; phone: 703/528–1902) nine issues/year, $55/annual nonmember subscription, free/members. "Placement" runs around 50 ads for faculty and research positions.

Positions for Classicists and Archaeologists (American Philological Association, Department of Classics, Box 117–A, Holy Cross College, Worcester, MA 01610; phone: 508/793–2203) monthly, $25/annual members only subscription (U.S.), $39/foreign; also available for $30/U.S., $44/foreign, as part of the APA's Placement Service's "Comprehensive Service" which is available only to members of APA or the Archaeological Institute of America (675 Commonwealth Ave., Boston, MA 02215). Each issue includes five to 20 ads for classicist and archaeologist faculty and research positions.

Perspectives (American Historical Association, 400 A St., SE, Washington, DC 20003; phone: 202/544–2422) nine issues/year, contact for subscription rates. "Employment Information" can carry as many as 100 job ads for history professors, librarians, and public historians.

History News Dispatch (American Association for State and Local History, 530 Church St., Suite 600, Nashville, TN 37219–2325; phone: 615/255–2971) monthly, $30/members only. About 20 to 35 ads for historians, archivists, and educators appear under "The Marketplace."

IMS Bulletin (Institute of Mathematical Statistics, 3401 Investment Blvd., Suite 7, Hayward, CA 94545; phone: 510/783–8141) bimonthly, $50/annual nonmember subscription, free/members; $50/annual dues. Ads for 15 to 30 faculty positions fill the "Employment Opportunities" section.

Geotimes (American Geological Institute, 4220 King St., Alexandria, VA 22302; phone: 703/379–2480) monthly, $24.95/annual subscription (U.S.), $38.95/foreign. Twenty to 30 ads for geologists, geographers, and scientists, generally in academics, are listed under "Classified Advertising."

ACSA NEWS (Association of Collegiate Schools of Architecture, 1735 New York Ave., NW Washington, DC 20006; phones: 800/232–2724, 202/786–2324) nine issues/year, $40/annual member subscription. About 15 to 20 ads for architecture faculty are listed under "Positions Available."

Higher Education Report (Association of Jesuit Colleges and Universities, 1 Dupont Circle, Suite 405, Washington, DC 20036; phone: 202/862–9893) ten issues/year, $17.50/annual subscription (U.S. and Canada). Five to 10 ads for faculty are listed under "Classifieds."

ACJS Employment Bulletin (Academy of Criminal Justice Sciences, Northern Kentucky University, 402 Nunn Hall, Highland Heights, KY 41099–5998; phone: 606/572–5634) eight issues/year, $30/annual nonmember subscription, free/members. About 20 job ads from academic institutions appear under "Job Opportunities."

The Criminologist (American Society of Criminology, 1314 Kinnear Rd., Suite 212, Columbus, OH, 43212; phone: 614/292–9207) bimonthly, $7.50/annual nonmember subscription (U.S.), $10/foreign, free/members. Ten to 12 jobs for probation officers, police, and faculty are listed under "Positions Announcements."

Journal of Social Work Education (Council on Social Work Education, 1600 Duke St., Alexandria, VA 22314; phone: 703/683–8080) three issues/year, free/members only, $80/annual dues. About four vacancies for university teaching positions in social work are in the typical issue.

Social Work Education Reporter (Council on Social Work Education, 1600 Duke St., Alexandria, VA 22314; phone: 703/683–8080) three issues/year, free/members only, $80/annual dues. About four vacancies for university teaching positions in social work are in the typical issue.

AHEA Action (American Home Economics Association, 1555 King St., Alexandria, VA 22314; phones: 800/424–8080, 703/706–4600) five issues/year, $7.50/annual nonmember subscription, free/members. About 30 vacancies for faculty and administrators in home economics appear in "Position Announcements."

Facilities Manager/APPA Newsletter (Association of Higher Education Facilities Officers, 1446 Duke St., Alexandria, VA 22314; phone: 703/684–1446) monthly, $40/annual nonmember subscription (U.S.), $50/elsewhere, free/members included in dues. Six to 15 jobs appear under "Job Corner" for facilities managers, energy managers, HVAC technicians, and other positions related to educational facilities management.

Financial Management (Financial Management Association, College of Business Administration, University of South Florida, Tampa, FL 33620; phone: 813/974–2084) quarterly, $50/annual subscription (U.S.), $50 plus postage/foreign. "Placement Clearinghouse" run ads for four to ten business school professor positions. Also includes "Positions Desired" listings.

Academy of International Business Newsletter (School of Business Administration, c/o Dr. Attila Yaprak, Wayne State University, Detroit, MI 48202; phone: 313/577–4487) quarterly, members only. "Job Mart" features five to ten ads for faculty and administrators in business schools.

The Women's Review of Books (Center for Research on Women, 106 Central St. Wellesley, MA 02181; phone: 617/283–2087) monthly, $17/annual subscription (U.S.), $22/Canada. A few university teaching, research, and administrative positions appear throughout the magazine and under "Job Opportunities."

The Technology Teacher (International Technology Education Association, 1914 Association Dr., Reston, VA 22091; phone: 703/860–2100) eight issues/year, $55/annual nonmember subscription, free/members. Just one or two display ads appear for university faculty.

American Association of Colleges for Teacher Education Briefs (AACTE, 1 Dupont Cr., NW, Suite 610, Washington, DC 20036; phone: 202/293–2450) biweekly, $25/annual nonmember subscription (U.S.), $35/foreign, free/members. Just one or two ads for deans and faculty are in an issue.

Mechanics (American Academy of Mechanics, 4205 EBUI, AMES 0411, University of California, 9500 Gilman Dr., La Jolla, CA 92093–0411; phone: 619/534–2036) ten issues/year, $64/annual nonmember subscription, $40/members, $78/(air mail), $40/members, $8/single issue. You must live in the America's to subscribe (this includes South and Central America). One to five ads for university faculty are in the typical issue.

NCRE Newsletter (National Council on Rehabilitation Education, c/o Dr. Julie Smart, Department of Special Education, Utah State University, Logan, UT 84322–2870; phone: 801/750–3269) quarterly, free/members only. "Positions" generally lists openings for two rehabilitation education or psychology positions.

Forest Products Journal (Forest Product Society, 2801 Marshall Ct., Madison, WI 53705; 608/231–1361) ten issues/year, $115/annual nonmember subscription, included in dues. "Positions Available" runs job ads for about four faculty and administrators at universities in fields that involve forest products.

Job services

Teachers Registry and Information Service (Council on Social Work Education, 1600 Duke St., Alexandria, VA 22314; phone: 703/683–8080) $125/nonmember seven–month registration fee, $70/nonmember full–time students, $70/members, $40/full–time student members. Fill out the registration form and submit the original plus ten copies. Registration is good for the October through April academic year. Your registration form is put on display at the annual program meeting and sent to schools of social work education actively looking for faculty and administrators. The university contacts you for an interview. In addition, you'll receive announcements of university openings in October, January, and March.

Academic Position Network (Suite 815, 245 E. Sixth St., St. Paul, MN 55101; phone: 612/225–1433) contact for details. This online academic position announcement service can be accessed by computer modem through Internet/Gopher.

National Faculty Exchange (c/o Betty Worley, Executive Director, 4656 W. Jefferson, Suite 140, Fort Wayne, IN 46804; phone: 219/436–2634). Contact for information about domestic exchange programs for college or university level teachers.

CLA Placement Service (College Language Association, c/o Dr. Earle D. Clowney, Director, Box 116, Clark Atlanta University, Atlanta, GA 30314; phone: 404/880–8546) free/members only. Submit your resume. When a match is made for an English and modern foreign language teaching position at a private or public two–year or four–year institution, you are sent information about the position and you are responsible for contacting the institution.

NCAA Ethnic Minority and Women's Vita Bank (National Collegiate Athletic Association, 6201 College Blvd., Overland Park, KS 66211; phone: 913/339–1906) free; open only to women or members of racial or ethnic minorities. If you are looking for a job in coaching, officiating, athletics administration, teaching and support services (athletics trainer, business manager, ticket manager, facility manager, sports information director, academic counselor, and more) submit a completed registration form, current resume, and names, addresses, and phone numbers of at least five references. This service learns about vacancies through word of mouth, ads in *The NCAA News, Chronicle of Higher Education,* and other sources. Primarily they are sources for NCAA schools, conferences, and sporting organizations. You will be contacted about vacancies that are compatible with your interests and experience. You are responsible to contact the prospective employer. This service will also provide the names, resumes, and references of job candidates to organizations with job vacancies. The organization is responsible for contacting the job seeker.

NAFJA Job Registry Resume Bank (Association of International Educators, 1875 Connecticut Ave., Suite 1000, NW, Washington, DC 20009; phone: 202/462–4811) monthly, $18/members only, contact for membership details. Subscribers to the Job Registry periodical are asked to complete a "Job Registry Data Sheet" and submit one copy of their resume. Occasionally employers ask the Job Registry to match subscribers to job openings. When this is done, your resume is given to the employer unless you have specified confidentiality. The employer is responsible for contacting job candidates.

NABTE Business Teacher Education Referral Service (National Association for Business Teacher Education, National Business Education Association, 1914 Association Dr., Reston, VA 22091–1596; phone: 703/860–8300) $10/six–months. Obtain the "Application for Position in Business Teacher Education" form which appears in the October issue of the NBEA's *Business Education Forum* or can be requested from NBEA. You may submit your form October through December only. A list of all available positions and all registrants is sent to all registrants who are then responsible for contacting the hiring institution. Registered institutions may also contact listed job seekers. This list is distributed each year in January to all registrants and hiring schools.

Directories

Peterson's Guides to Graduate and Professional Programs. These five guides provide detailed information on graduate programs in their respective specialties so potential faculty or administrators can get a good idea of what the programs and schools are like, even though they are written for prospective students. All four volumes are published each November. For your convenience, they are available from Planning/Communications by special order; phone: 800/829–5220.

Graduate Programs in the Humanities, Arts, and Social Sciences 1994, $34.95 plus $4.75/shipping, 1,368 pages, covers 10,500 programs in anthropology, architecture, area studies, art and design, communications, criminology, demography, economics, environmental policy, family services, geography, gerontology, history, industrial relations, international affairs, journalism, languages, performing arts, philosophy, political science, psychology, public affairs, social work, sociology, and more.

Graduate Programs in the Physical Sciences and Mathematics 1994, $31.95 plus $3.75/shipping, 664 pages, covers over 2,300 programs in all aspects of the physical sciences and mathematics.

Graduate Programs in Engineering and Applied Sciences 1994, $34.95 plus $4.75/shipping, 1,392 pages, reports on more than 3,500 programs in all aspects of engineering, computer sciences, operations research, technology management, and more.

Graduate Programs in the Biological and Agricultural Sciences 1994, $41.95 plus $5.75/shipping, 2,568 pages, details over 4,500 programs in agronomy, anatomy, animal sciences, biochemistry, biology and biomedical sciences, biophysics, biotechnology, botany, ecology, entomology, environmental sciences, food science, forestry, genetics, horticulture, pathology, pharmacology, physiology, zoology, and more.

Graduate Programs in Business, Education, Health, and Law 1994, $24.95 plus $4.75/shipping, 1,632 pages, profiles 13,000 graduate programs in these fields.

1993–94 AAA Guide (American Anthropological Association, 4350 N. Fairfax Dr., Suite 640, Arlington, VA 22203; phone:.703/528–1902) $50/nonmembers, $35/members. Lists universities, museums, and research departments of anthropology in the U.S. and Canada by faculties and specialties, facilities and programs, and information on financial support.

1993–94 Anthropology Field Schools (American Anthropological Association, 4350 N. Fairfax Dr., Suite 640, Arlington, VA 22203; phone: 703/528–1902) $6/nonmembers, $4/members, photocopy only, call for new edition. Guide to field schools in all branches of anthropology providing descriptions of activities, details on dates, location, entrance requirements, tuition, and credits.

Peterson's Guide to Four–Year Colleges (Peterson's Guides; available from Planning/Communications by special order; phone: 800/829–5220) $18.95 plus $3.75/shipping, 2,744 pages, published each July. Profiles 1,950 accredited institutions in the U.S. that grant baccalaureate degrees. Eight hundred of these schools are described in depth.

Peterson's Guide to Two–Year Colleges (Peterson's Guides; available from Planning/Communications by special order; phone: 800/829–5220) $16.95 plus $3.75/shipping, 752 pages, published each August. Profiles 1,450 accredited institutions in the U.S. that grant the associate degree as their highest degree.

1994 Higher Education Directory (Higher Education Publications, 6400 Arlington Blvd., Suite 648, Falls Church, VA 22042; phone: 703/532–2300) $45, deduct $2 for standing order, published each October. Regarded as one of the most authoritative directories of degree–granting, post–secondary institutions accredited by agencies recognized by the U.S. Secretary of Education. They say they are the only directory that follows the U.S. Department of Education guidelines for inclusion.

1992–93 Accredited Institutions of Postsecondary Education (Oryx Press, Suite 700, 4041 N. Central, Phoenix, AZ 85012; phone: 800/279–6799) $35, 736 pages, 1993. Describes over 5,500 public, private, two–year and four–year colleges and universities, and vocational institutions of higher learning throughout the U.S. plus U.S. sponsored schools in 14 countries. All schools are accredited by national or regional accrediting agencies recognized by the Council on Postsecondary Accreditation.

National Faculty Directory 1994 (Gale Research, Inc., 835 Penobscot Bldg., Detroit, MI 48226; phones: 800/877–4253, 313/961–2242) $605, 3,920 pages in three volumes, July 1993. You can track down any of 600,000 teaching faculty at 3,430 American colleges and universities and 240 Canadian institutions that use English–language instructional materials. The 300 page *1994 Supplement* costs $205 (December 1993).

Washington Education Association Directory (Council for Advancement and Support of Education, 11 Dupont Cr., Suite 400, Washington, DC 20036; phones: 800/554–8536, 202/328–5979) $12, 20 pages, published in winter of even–numbered years. This directory profiles 50 associations that serve and support American higher education, including K–12.

National Guide to Funding in Higher Education (The Foundation Center, 79 Fifth Ave., New York, NY 10003–3076; phones: 800/424–9836, 212/620– 4230) $125 plus $4.50/shipping, May 1992. Covers nearly 3,650 foundations that have awarded grants to colleges, universities, graduate programs, and research institutes.

AERA Biographical Membership Directory (American Educational Research Association, 1230 17th St., NW, Washington, DC 20036–3078; phone: 202/223–9485) $35/nonmembers, $15/members, annual. Members are engaged in educational research.

Academic Job Digest (Taylor Incorporated, 945 S. Rochester Rd., Rochester, MI 48307; phone: 313/651–0286) $29.99 plus $4.99/shipping, annual. Information on whom to contact for faculty and staff positions at about 100 universities and colleges is presented. Includes information on the institution as well as on periodicals it may publish that list job openings.

The K & W Guide to Colleges for the Learning Disabled (HarperReference; hard to find in bookstores, this book is available as a special order from Planning/Communications; phone: 800/829–5220) $20, 592 pages, August 1993. Although written for students who have learning disabilities, this directory can also help the teacher or administrator learn a lot about the colleges that offer these programs.

NUCEA Membership Directory (National University Continuing Education Association, 1 Dupont Cr., Suite 615, Washington, DC 20036; phone: 202/659–3130) $20/nonmembers, free/members, published every October. Essentially a "who's who" in continuing education.

NAFSA Member Directory (Association of International Educators, 1875 Connecticut Ave., Suite 1000, NW, Washington, DC 20009; phone: 202/462– 4811) $50/nonmembers, $25/members, annual. Directory of NAFSA association members.

Black Professionals in Continuing Education (National University Continuing Education Association, 1 Dupont Cr., Suite 615, Washington, DC 20036; phone: 202/659–3130) $10. Lists individuals who wish to be identified for networking purposes.

NCAA Directory (National Collegiate Athletic Association, P.O. Box 7347, Overland Park, KS 66207–0347; phone: 913/339–1900) $6/nonmembers, $3/members, 250 pages, published every October. Lists addresses and phone numbers of NCAA member institutions. Includes the institution's president, director of athletics, senior woman athletics administrator, and more.

Directory of Engineering Graduate Studies and Research (American Society for Engineering Education, 11 Dupont Circle, Suite 200, Washington, DC 20036; phone: 202/986–8500) $69.95/nonmembers, $34.95/members and students, plus $3 shipping, annual, issued each September. Lists schools by type of program, dean's names, address, phone number, accredited or not, and specific types of engineering.

ACSA Annual Directory (Association of Collegiate Schools of Architecture, 1735 New York Ave., NW, Washington, DC 20006; phones: 800/232–2724, 202/786–2324) $14.95, published every September. Includes schools of architecture with the names of their deans and faculty members. Also available as mailing labels: General School Address list (115 schools) for $50, Administrators (190 names) for $75, Full–Time Faculty (3,000) for $300, and Full– and Part–Time Faculty (4,000+) for $400.

Directory of Music Faculties in Colleges and Universities, U.S. and Canada (CMS Publications, P.O. Box 8208, Missoula, MT 59807; phones: 800/729–0235, 406/728–2002) $55, 1993–94 edition. Reports on 30,202 music faculty and 1,808 post–secondary institutions.

Art & Design Facilities Directory (CMS Publications, P.O. Box 8208, Missoula, MT 59807; phones: 800/729–0235, 406/728–2002) $20, 1993–94 edition, annual. Reports on art programs and schools throughout the U.S.

Anderson's 1991 Directory of Criminal Justice Education (Anderson Publishing Company, P.O. Box 1576, Cincinnati, OH 45201; phone: 800/582–7295) $59.95. Features information on all levels of criminal justice education, including 1,100 colleges and universities. Includes department chairs (address and phone), faculty characteristics, enrollment, and course offerings.

American Society of Criminology Membership Directory (American Society of Criminology, 1314 Kinnear Rd., Suite 212, Columbus, OH, 43212; phone: 614/292–9207) free/members only, published in even–numbered years.

ACJS Membership Directory (Academy of Criminal Justice Sciences, Northern Kentucky University, 402 Nunn Hall, Highland Heights, KY 41099–5998; phone: 606/572–5634) $10, published each spring. Members are primarily in academia.

Geotimes (American Geological Institute, 4220 King St., Alexandria, VA 22303; phone: 800/336–4764, 703/0379–2480) $3.50, October issue only. Contains a directory of members of the world's geoscience community.

Guide to Graduate Study in Botany for the United States and Canada (Botanical Society of America, 1735 Neil Avenue, Columbus, OH 43210–1293; phone: 614/292–3519) $10/nonmembers, free/members, published every five to seven years. Call for latest edition. Lists 82 plant science departments in the U.S. and Canada which offer Ph.D. degrees in some area of the plant sciences. Included are: name and address of institution, name of department, fields of specialization, and titles of recent Ph.D. theses directed for all botanical faculty in the department.

Institute of Mathematical Statistics Membership Directory (IMS, 3401 Investment Blvd., Suite 7, Hayward, CA 94545; phone: 510/783–8141) free/members only, most recently published in 1991. Lists member mathematics and statistics professors.

AACTE Directory (American Association of Colleges of Teacher Education, 1 Dupont Cr., NW, Suite 610, Washington, DC 20036; phone: 202/293–2450) $50/nonmembers, $35/members, annual. Describes programs at colleges of teacher education.

AHEA Membership Directory (American Home Economics Association, 1555 King St., Alexandria, VA 22314; phones: 800/424–8080, 703/706–4600) $12/nonmembers, last published in 1990.

A Guide to College Programs in Hospitality and Tourism (John Wiley and Sons; available from Planning/Communications by special order, phone: 800/829–5220) $19.95, 1993. This book by the Council on Hotel, Restaurant, and Institutional Education describes two–year community college, four–year college, and graduate programs in culinary arts; hotel/motel management, restaurant and food service, and travel and tourism. While it's written for the prospective student, it gives prospective faculty and administrators useful information about the schools and their programs.

AIB Directory of Members (School of Business Administration, c/o Dr. Attila Yaprak, Wayne State University, Detroit, MI 48202; phone: 313/577–4487) free/members only, published every two years, last published 1993–94. Lists member business school faculty and administrators.

Directory of Historical Organizations in the United States and Canada
(American Association for State and Local History, 530 Church St., Suite
600, Nashville, TN 37219–2325; phone: 615/255–2971) $79.95/nonmem-
bers, $71.95/members, most recently published in 1990. Includes history–
related organizations with brief descriptions of staff.

NCRE Membership Directory (National Council on Rehabilitation Education, c/o Dr. Garth Eldredge, Department of Special Education, Utah State
University, Logan, UT 84122–2865; phone: 801/750–3241) $25/nonmem-
bers, free/members, printed each December.

Grants for Higher Education (The Foundation Center, 79 Fifth Ave., New
York, NY 10003–3076; phones: 800/424–9836, within New York State call
212/620–4230) $65 plus $4.50/shipping, October 1993. Describes recent
foundation grants of at least $10,000 given to higher education and gradu-
ate/professional schools for programs in all disciplines, as well as to academic
libraries and student services and organizations. This directory is useful for
identifying foundations and grant recipients for which you may wish to work.

Salary surveys

***Comparative Costs and Staffing Report for College and University Facili-
ties*** (Association of Higher Education Facilities Officers, 1446 Duke St.,
Alexandria, VA 22314; phone: 703/684–1446) $90/nonmembers, $35/mem-
bers, plus $8/shipping, published biennially. Study is based on data from
over 500 institutions.

APSA Survey of Political Science Departments (American Political Science
Association, 1527 New Hampshire Ave., NW, Washington, DC 20036;
phone: 202/483–2512) $20, annual. Last published April 1993. Gives salary
information and enrollment trends of four–year institutions offering political
science.

The Annual Report on the Economic Status of the Profession (American Association of University Professors, 1012 14th St., NW, Suite 500, Washington, DC 20005; phone: 202/737–5900) $45, published every April. This survey is included in an issue of *Academe* magazine, but is available as a single issue. Reports on wages and benefits by school, state, gender, number of faculty, and number of tenured faculty.

Careers in Architecture: A Salary Survey of Architects Working in Settings Other Than Private Practice (American Institute of Architects Order Department, P.O. Box 753, Waldorf, MD 20604; phones: 800/365–2724, 410/626–7509) $20/nonmembers, $19/AIA members, plus $5/shipping, 15 pages, 1993. Reports on compensation and benefits for architects who work for colleges, and universities as well as for corporations, developers, builders or contractors, government.

International education

A number of job sources described earlier in this chapter include foreign positions. See the Index listings under "Foreign jobs, Education." Also see Chapter 16, "International jobs."

Job ads in print

PDRC Placement Hotline (Professional Development Resource Center, School for International Training, P.O. Box 676, Kipling Rd., Brattleboro, VT 05302; phone: 802/258–3397) monthly, $25/annual subscription (U.S.), $35/foreign, $15/six–month subscription (U.S.), $20/foreign. Each 14–20 page issue contains 150 ads for teaching, language training, cross–cultural counseling positions, foreign student advising, student life and affairs services, conflict management and negotiation, cultural orientation, and admissions officers in all levels of education. Includes positions in the U.S. and abroad.

The International Educator (P.O. Box 513, Cummaquid, MA 02637; phone: 508/362–1414) quarterly, $25/annual subscription (U.S.), $35/elsewhere. Lists around 100 positions in privately–owned American and International schools in English–speaking countries. Each issue usually includes a report on salaries and benefits.

Teaching Opportunities Overseas Bulletin (Overseas Academic Opportunities, P.O. Box 368, Merrick, NY 11566; phone: 718/706–4898) monthly, $22/six–month nonmember subscription, $34/annual nonmember subscription. About 40 job ads appear under "Education."

TESOL Placement Bulletin (Teachers of English to Speakers of Other Languages, Inc., 1600 Cameron St., Suite 300, Alexandria, VA 22314–2751; phone: 703/836–0774) bimonthly, $20/members only (U.S., Mexico, and Canada), $30/elsewhere (air mail); annual dues range from $38 to $69 depending on category; contact TESOL for membership application; free if you subscribe to the *TESOL Placement Service* described below under "Job Services." Each issue features 60 or so ads for positions to teach English in the U.S. and abroad, and for curriculum developers and materials writers.

Inter Ed (Association for the Advancement of International Education, Thompson House, Westminster College, New Wilmington, PA 16172; phone: 412/946–7192) quarterly, $50/annual nonmember subscription, free/members. Lists many positions for teachers and administrators in American international schools.

Job services

The Placement Service (International Technology Education Association, 1914 Association Dr., Reston, VA 22091–1502; phone: 703/860–2100) free/members only, $50/annual dues. Places high school teachers and people in the technology education field.

British American Educational Foundation (P.O. Box 33, Larchmont, NY 10538; phone: 212/340–8901). Operates a clearinghouse for independent school exchanges.

TESOL Placement Service (Teachers of English to Speakers of Other Languages, Inc., 1600 Cameron St., Suite 300, Alexandria, VA 22314–2751; phone: 703/836–0774) $20/annual member only registration fee (U.S., Canada, and Mexico), $30/elsewhere (air mail); annual dues range from $38 to $69 depending on category; contact TESOL for membership application. Complete the "Candidate's Registration Form" which enables you to specify your worldwide geographical preferences and your qualifications. When a match is made, the prospective employer contacts you for an interview. Teaching positions are with units of higher education, public schools, government agencies, international schools, public and private sector in the U.S. and abroad.

AFS International Intercultural Programs (AFS, 220 E. 42nd St., Third Floor, New York, NY 10017; phone: 212/949–4242). Operates three, five, and seven–week cultural exchange programs in Thailand, Russia, and Mexico where you are able to do volunteer teaching. Contact for further details.

Council for International Exchange of Scholars (3400 International Dr., NW, Suite M–500, Washington, DC 20008). Offers post–doctoral opportunities.

International Schools Service (ISS, P.O. Box 5910, 15 Roszel Road, Princeton, NJ 08543; phone: 609/452–0990). Offers opportunities to teach abroad.

Fulbright Teacher Exchange Program (United States Information Agency, 600 Maryland Ave., SW, Room 235, Washington, DC 20024; phone: 800/726–0479) free. These are exchange opportunities for college/university faculty and secondary and elementary school teachers and administrators to teach in colleges and schools abroad. You must be a U.S. citizen, fluent in English, have a bachelor's degree or higher, three years of full–time teaching/administrative experience, be currently employed full–time in the appropriate subject areas and at the appropriate teaching level, and be fluent in the language of the country in which you wish to teach. The program conducts exchanges with 34 countries in eastern and western Europe, Latin America, Africa, Canada, Russia, and Ukraine. (List of countries is subject to change.) Most exchanges are for the full academic year; however, some are for a semester or six weeks.

The "Direct Exchange" program enables U.S. and foreign teachers to exchange teaching positions for an academic year (semester Argentina and Mexico, six–weeks in Morocco and Egypt). You continue to receive your salary from your home institution.

A "One–Way Assignment" places you in Denmark and a few eastern European countries. You take a leave of absence without pay and receive a maintenance allowance in the currency of the host country.

Applications for all programs must be received by October 15 of the year prior to the summer or academic year for which you are applying.

International School Internship Program (P.O. Box 513, Cummaquid, MA 02637; phone: 508/362–1414) free. Contact for information about international internship placement programs for teachers.

Directories

Private Schools with U.S. Department of State Affiliation (Office of Overseas Schools, Room 234, SA–6, U.S. Department of State, Washington, DC 20520; phone: 703/875–6220). Although pretty much independent of the U.S. government, these schools receive some assistance from the State Department. Each school hires its own staff. This directory lists private and international schools.

Overseas Employment for Educators (Office of Dependents Schools, Room 112, U.S. Department of Defense, 2461 Eisenhower Ave., Alexandria, VA 22331; phone: 703/325–0885) free. Teachers in U.S. Department of Defense Dependents Schools work for the U.S. government. This booklet provides information on working for these schools.

The ISS Directory of Overseas Schools (International Schools Service, P.O. Box 5910, 15 Roszel Road, Princeton, NJ 08543; phone: 609/452–0990) $34.95 plus $6.75/shipping, 1993. Order from Peterson's Guides (P.O. Box 2123, Princeton, NJ 08543; phone: 800/338–3282). Furnishes names and addresses of American schools outside the U.S.

Trades and vocational education

Job ads in print

The Community College Times (American Association of Community Colleges, P.O. Box 1737, Salisbury, MD 21802; phone: 410/546–0391) semiweekly, $46/annual nonmember subscription, free/members. "Careerline" has 5 to 6 pages of ads for teaching and administrative positions at junior and community colleges.

Vocational Education Journal (American Vocational Association, 1410 King St., Alexandria, VA 22314; phones: 800/826–9972, 703/683–3111) eight issues/year, $32/annual nonmember subscription, free/members. "Marketplace" carries ads for three or four vocational educators, administrators, and teacher educators at secondary and post–secondary institutions.

NAABAVE news & notes (National Association for the Advancement of Black Americans in Vocational Education, c/o Dr. Warner Dickerson, 3476 Renault, Memphis, TN 38118; phone: 313/494–1660, ask for Dr. Ethel Washington) semiannual, free/members only. "Job Opportunity" will have one to five notices of job vacancies in vocational teaching and administration. Jobs do not appear in every issue and when they do, the ads are sometimes out of date.

Directories

Who's Who in Community Colleges (American Association of Community Colleges, P.O. Box 1737, Salisbury, MD 21802; phone: 410/546–0391) $57.50/nonmembers, $43/members; 491 pages, published each April. For each institution, this directory gives basic information plus the names of the top twelve administrators.

Forty–Nine State Systems, 1992 Edition (American Association of Community Colleges, P.O. Box 1737, Salisbury, MD 21802; phone: 410/546–0391) $20/nonmembers, $15/members. Provides information on each of the 49 state community college systems.

Corporation and Foundation Giving to Community Colleges (American Association of Community Colleges, P.O. Box 1737, Salisbury, MD 21802; phone: 410/546–0391) $12.50/nonmembers, $10/members. Describes 190 corporations and foundations that make grants to community, technical, and junior colleges.

AACC Membership Directory (American Association of Community Colleges, P.O. Box 1737, Salisbury, MD 21802; phone: 410/546–0391) $44/nonmembers, $33.50/members, annual. Lists all institutional and association members of AACJC.

AACC Statistical Yearbook (American Association of Community Colleges, P.O. Box 1737, Salisbury, MD 21802; phone: 410/546–0391) $44/nonmembers, $33.50/members, last published January 1993. Reports on two–year institutions: number of full– and part–time faculty, number of administrators, name of chief executive officer.

American Trade Schools Directory (Croner Publications, 34 Jericho Turnpike, Jericho, NY 11753; phones: 800/441–4033, 516/333–9085) $99.95 includes monthly updates, over 600 pages. Briefly profiles over 12,000 trade, technical, and vocational schools in the U.S. and Puerto Rico. Includes more than 320 occupational categories.

Directory of Educational Institutions (Association of Independent Colleges and Schools, 1 Dupont Cr., Suite 350, Washington, DC 20036; phone: 202/659–2460) $5/nonmembers, free/members, 70 pages, published each January. Lists hundreds of trade and vocational colleges and junior colleges accredited by AICS.

1993 Directory of Private Accredited Career Colleges and Schools (Career College Association, 750 First Street, NE, Suite 900, Washington, DC 20002–4242; phone: 202/336–6700) free, annual. Lists trade, technical, and vocational schools accredited by ACICS and ACTIS.

The VICA Network (Vocational Industrial Clubs of America, P.O. Box 3000, Leesburg, VA 22075; phone: 703/777–8810) free, last published in January 1991. This organization mentioned that they were planning to implement a computer program to be accessed via modem sometime this year. Call for further details. Gives information about vocational schools.

Chapter 9

Emergency management

Job ads in print

The NCCEM Bulletin (National Coordinating Council on Emergency Management, Unit N, 7297 Lee Highway, Falls Church, VA 22042; phone: 703/533–7672) monthly, free/members only, $75/annual dues. Jobs listed under "Personnel Corner." About one job ad every three months.

Directory

The NCCEM Membership Directory (National Coordinating Council on Emergency Management, Unit N, 7297 Lee Highway, Falls Church, VA 22042; phone: 703/533–7672) $10, published every January.

Chapter 10

Environment

*Also see the chapters on "Science," "Forestry and horticulture," and "Parks and recreation." Additional job sources that focus on environmental positions in government and the private sector appear in the **Government Job Finder** and the **Professional's Private Sector Job Finder**.*

Job ads in print

The Job Seeker (Route 2, Box 16, Warrens, WI 54666; phone: 608/378–4290) biweekly, $60/annual subscription, $36/six–month subscription, $19.50/three–month subscription. Lists 200 environmental and natural resource vacancies in every aspect of these fields, including environmental education. For an additional $10, you can get nine special supplementary issues, December through April, that feature summer jobs not listed in the *Job Seeker.*

Environmental Career Opportunities (Brubach Publishing Company, P.O. Box 15629, Chevy Chase, MD 20825) $29/two–month subscription, $49/four months, $69/six months, $129/annual, $7.95/single issue. You'll find announcements of over 300 positions in all aspects of the environmental field: advocacy, communications, and fundraising; research and education; legislative assistants; environmental policy, legislation, and regulation; conservation and resource management; environmental engineering, risk assessment, and impact analysis; government agencies; and internships. The job announcements include jobs advertised exclusively in this periodical as well as jobs advertised elsewhere.

Environmental Opportunities (P.O. Box 747, Mendocino CA 95460; phone: 707/937–1529) monthly, $44/annual subscription, $24/six–month subscription, $50/annual subscription (Canada), $55/annual subscription elsewhere. Over 125 jobs, internships, seasonal work, educational offerings, and conferences. Includes administrative positions, fisheries, wildlife, forestry, research, parks, outdoor recreation, and ecology. Write for free sample copy.

Opportunities (Natural Science for Youth Foundation, 130 Azalea Dr., Roswell, GA 30075; phones: 800/992–6793, 404/594–9367) bimonthly, $35/annual subscription, $10/single issue, included in membership package. "Positions available" lists details on 45 to 70 jobs for naturalists, curators, raptor rehabilitators, and administrative positions, largely at nature centers.

EarthWorks includes ***Job Scan*** (Student Conservation Association, P.O. Box 550, Charlestown, NH 03603; phone: 603/543–1700) monthly, $29.95/non-member annual subscription, $24.95/member annual subscription. About 70 jobs in a typical issue plus 20 to 30 internships.

The Caretaker Gazette (P.O. Box 342, Carpentersville, IL 60110) quarterly, $8/three–issue subscription. Among its 60 job announcements are jobs and internships in forestry, fisheries, environment, and caretaking.

Jobs Clearinghouse (Association for Experiential Education, 2885 Aurora Ave., Suite 28, Boulder, CO 80303–2252; phone: 303/440–8844) monthly, $40/annual nonmember subscription, $25/members. Lists mostly internships and outdoor education instructorships, counselors, camp staff, program directors, and environmental educators, with an emphasis on wilderness experience, under "Job Openings." From 60 to 125 job vacancies per issue.

Environmental Careers Bulletin (11693 San Vicente Blvd., Suite 327, Los Angeles, CA 90047; phone: 213/399–3533, no phone orders) monthly, free, but when you write for a subscription you must provide your job title, college major, college degree, and year degree was received. From 150 to 200 display ads for environmental positions, largely private sector, but with some in the non–profit sector, appear in the typical issue. Details on this company's environmental job fairs held around the country are included.

Employment Opportunity Service (National Association of Interpretation, P.O. Box 1892, Ft. Collins, CO 80522; 303/491–6434) $3.00/week. This is a printout of the *Dial–a–Job* and *Dial–an–Internship* jobs listed by phone as described below under "Job services." Be sure to indicate the week or weeks for which you want a printout.

The Wildlifer (The Wildlife Society, 5410 Grosvenor Ln., Bethesda, MD 20814; phone: 301/897–9708) bimonthly, free/members only; $36/annual dues, $18/students. About 20 positions in conservation, wildlife, and natural resources appear under "Positions Available."

National Technical News (Black Collegiate Services, Inc., 1240 Broad St., New Orleans, LA 70125; phone: 504/821–5694) biweekly, $26/annual subscription. Eleven job ads appear in "Job Opportunities Bulletin" for health physicists, biologists, and environmental scientists.

Journal of the National Technical Association (Black Collegiate Services, Inc., 1240 S. Broad St., New Orleans, LA 70125; phone: 504/821–5694) biannually, $30/annual subscription, $15/qualified professionals, $35/foreign. About 40 vacancies for health physicists, biologists, and environmental scientists appear in display ads.

Environmental Protection Magazine (Stevens Publishing Company, Customer Service, P.O. Box 2604, Waco, TX 76702; phones: 800/727–7573 [outside of Texas], 817/776–9000) monthly, $77.90/annual subscription (U.S.), $99.90/Canada, $95.90/Mexico, $107.90/elsewhere. Between eight and ten job ads appear per issue.

Journal of Soil and Water Conservation (Soil and Water Conservation Society, 7515 NE Ankeny Rd., Ankeny, IA 50021–9764; phone: 515/232–1080) bimonthly, $39/annual subscription (U.S. and Canada), $45/elsewhere. Jobs listed under "Classified Advertising." About five job ads per issue.

E Magazine (Earth Action Network, 28 Knight St., Norwalk, CT 06851; phone: 203/854–5559) bimonthly, $20/annual subscription (U.S.), $25/Mexico and Canada, $30/elsewhere. Five to ten job openings are in "Classified–Job Opportunities."

Newsletter of the Ecological Society of America (ESA, 2010 Massachusetts Ave., NW, Suite 420, Washington, DC 20036; phone: 202/833–8773) five issues/year, free. 15 to 25 ads for ecotoxicologists, plant ecologists, and ecologists appear under "Job Announcements."

Resource Recycling (P.O. Box 10540, Portland, OR 97210; phone: 503/227–1319) monthly, $42/annual subscription. About two recycling and solid waste management positions are listed under "Positions Available."

Job services

The Nature Conservancy Job Hotline (The Nature Conservancy, 1815 N. Lynn St., Arlington, VA 22209) free, updated every Friday. Call 703/247–3721 any ol' time (does not require a touch–tone phone) and you'll hear the following: how jobs are on the hotline today, the job titles on the hotline, and a detailed description of each job's requirements plus to whom you

should send your resume and cover letter. Jobs include research, field work, administration, science positions, land conservation, and everything else involved in the environmental field.

Dial–a–Job and ***Dial–an–Internship*** (National Association for Interpretation, P.O. Box 1892, Ft. Collins, CO 80522; 303/491–6434) Call 303/491–7410 24 hours a day for a recording of full–time, seasonal, and temporary jobs in environmental education, interpretation, and related fields: naturalists, park rangers, outdoor education, biologists, museum personnel, and publication designers. The tape runs from 10 to 30 minutes. Updated every Wednesday. For internships, call 303/491–6784 24 hours a day. The tape runs from 5 to 20 minutes. Updated each Wednesday.

Environmental Action Job Book (Environmental Action, Inc., 6930 Carroll Ave., Suite 600, Takoma Park, MD 20912; phone: 301/891–1100) free. This up–to–date book of environmental jobs and internships can be seen only at Environmental Action Inc.'s office.

Environmental Careers Organization Placement Service (286 Congress St., Boston, MA 02218–1009; phone: 617/426–4375) $15/one region, $25/more than one region. Geared towards college graduates (you must be at least a junior in college) and career changers, this service finds you temporary employment that ranges from six months to a year. There is also a possibility of permanent placement. Send in their completed application form to the national office in Boston. The national office sends it to a regional office where you are placed into the applicant pool. This service claims to place at least one out of every seven registrants. Positions are with non–profit organizations, government agencies, corporations, and consulting firms.

Diversity Initiative Program Placement Service (Environmental Careers Organization, 286 Congress St., Boston, MA 02218–1009; phone: 617/426–4375) free/one year. This service places minority college students and graduates in permanent positions. Send in a completed application form to the national office in Boston. The national office sends it to a regional office where you are placed into the applicant pool. This service claims to place at least one out of every seven registrants. Positions are with non–profit organizations, government agencies, corporations, and consulting firms.

Resource Assistant Program (The Student Conservation Association, P.O. Box 550, Charlestown, NH 03603; phone: 603/543–1700) free. Although this program places you in a nonpaying three–month volunteer position, you can use the contacts you make to gain an advantage when applying for a paying job from one of these employers. You do receive free travel, lodging, food, and basic living expenses. The program places volunteers with the National Park Service, U.S. Forest Service, U.S. Fish and Wildlife Service, Bureau of Land Management, State Park and Wildlife Agencies, and Private Natural Resource Agencies. Positions include: wildlife and fisheries, forestry, recreation management, geology, archaeology, engineering and surveying, interpretation, visitor assistance, back country and wilderness management, trail maintenance and construction, hydrology and water resources, range management and plant taxonomy, and environmental education. Contact the SCA for an application and more information.

Directories

World Directory of Environmental Organizations (California Institute of Public Affairs, P.O. Box 189040, Sacramento, CA 95818; phone: 916/442–2472) $45 plus 7.25 percent sales tax for California residents, foreign: $63/surface mail, $70/air mail, 232 pages, most recent edition published in 1992. Includes hundreds of government agencies, research institutes, and citizens' and professional associations in the U.S. and around the globe. Divided into 50 topics with index, glossary, and bibliography of related directories and databases.

NAI Membership Directory (National Association of Interpretation P.O. Box 1892, Ft. Collins, CO 80522; 303/491–6434) free/members only, issued each spring. Lists members and institutional members.

Directory of Environmental Information Sources (Government Institutes, 4 Research Plaza, Suite 200, Rockville, MD 20850; phone: 301/921–2355) $74, published in November of even–numbered years. Includes federal and state government resources, professional, scientific, and trade organizations; newsletters, magazines, and databases.

The Air, Waste and Environmental Management Research Faculty Profile (Air & Waste Management Association, P.O. Box 2861, Pittsburgh, PA 15230) $79.95/nonmembers book format, $64/members, $495/nonmember data file, $415/members. Information on 1,200 researchers, representing over 350 colleges and universities. Catagorized by name and address, title, phone and fax, general and specific research interests, waste treatment/control sub–specialties, funding sources, courtroom/litigation experience, staff size and qualifications, collaboration interest with industry, and commercial readiness. Data file information is MAC and PC compatible and can be used with many data management systems.

Gale Environmental Sourcebook (Gale Research, Inc., 835 Penobscot Bldg., Detroit, MI 48226; phone: 800/877–4253) $75, 688 pages, 1992. Gives you full descriptions and contact information on 8,634 environmental organizations, publications, programs, and information services. Includes alphabetical and subject indexes.

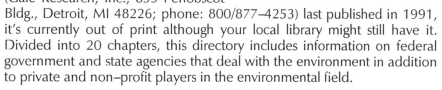

Environmental Information Directory (Gale Research, Inc., 835 Penobscot Bldg., Detroit, MI 48226; phone: 800/877–4253) last published in 1991, it's currently out of print although your local library might still have it. Divided into 20 chapters, this directory includes information on federal government and state agencies that deal with the environment in addition to private and non–profit players in the environmental field.

Job Opps '94: Job Opportunities in the Environment (Peterson's Guides; available from Planning/Communications' catalog at the end of this book) $16.95, 229 pages, published each September. Among its brief descriptions of 1,200 high–growth companies in the environmental field are many non–profit organizations. Briefly describes each organization, number of employees, expertise needed, and person to contact about job vacancies. Many of these agencies need civil engineers, biologists, and air quality control experts. Actual vacancies cannot be guaranteed, but this serves as a good directory of government agency descriptions.

Directory of Natural Science Centers (Natural Science for Youth Foundation, 130 Azalea Dr., Roswell, GA 30075; phones: 800/992–6793, 404/594–9367) $78.50, $58.50/members, 600 pages, 1990, new edition expected in 1994. This tome gives details on over 1,350 nature centers.

The Wildlife Society Membership Directory and Certification Registry (The Wildlife Society, 5410 Grosvenor Ln. Bethesda, MD 20814; phone: 301/897–9770) $3/nonmembers, free/members, published each September.

The Northeast Directory of Programs (Association for Experiential Education, 2885 Aurora Ave., Suite 28, Boulder, CO 80303–2252; phone: 303/440–8844) $7.50/nonmembers, $5/members, add $3.50/shipping. This 35–page directory lists over 100 experiential education programs and agencies in the northeast.

The Northwest Directory of Experiential Programs (Association for Experiential Education, 2885 Aurora Ave., Suite 28, Boulder, CO 80303–2252; phone: 303/440–8844) $7.50/nonmembers, $5/members; add $3.50 shipping. This directory lists 36 programs in seven states and British Columbia.

West Directory of Programs (Association for Experiential Education, 2885 Aurora Ave., Suite 28, Boulder, CO 80303–2252; phone: 303/440–8844) $7.50/nonmembers, $5/members, add $3.50/shipping. A 32–page index that lists 30 organizations and 46 individuals exploring the field of experiential education in seven states in the West.

The New Careers Directory: Internships and Professional Opportunities in Technology and Social Change (Student Pugwash USA, 1638 R St., NW, Suite 32, Washington, DC 20009; phone: 202/328–6555) $18, $10/students, add $3/shipping, 1993. Offers full details on where and how to apply for internships and entry–level jobs with non–profits and government agencies in the environment and energy, development, communications, peace/security, health, law, and general science.

Summer Jobs '94 (Peterson's Guides; available from Planning/Communications' catalog at the end of this book) $15.95, 320 pages, annual. Describes over 20,000 summer job openings in the United States and Canada with environmental programs, resorts, camps, amusement parks, expeditions, theaters, national parks, and government. Each detailed employer description includes salary and benefits, employer background, profile of employees, and whom to contact to apply.

Grants for Environmental Protection & Animal Welfare (The Foundation Center, 79 Fifth Ave., New York, NY 10003–3076; phones: 800/424–9836, within New York State call 212/620–4230) $65 plus $4.50/shipping, October 1993. Describes recent foundation grants of at least $10,000 given for environmental protection and legal agencies, for pollution abatement and control, conservation, and environmental education. This directory is useful for identifying foundations and grant recipients for which you may wish to work.

California Environmental Directory: A Guide to Organizations and Resources (California Institute of Public Affairs, P.O. Box 189040, Sacramento, CA 95818; phone: 916/442–2472) $40, May 1993, 128 pages. A guide to nearly 1,000 government agencies, university programs, and major associations concerned with air quality, soil, law, health, the desert, the coast, and much more.

California Water Resources Directory: A Guide to Organizations and Information Resources (California Institute of Public Affairs, P.O. Box 189040, Sacramento, CA 95818; phone: 916/442–2472) $25, 1991, 120 pages. Includes nearly 1,000 governmental and non–governmental organizations that deal with water policy, development, supply, and conservation as well as related health, environmental quality, energy, and economic aspects.

Chapter 11

Financial

Job ads in print

In Search Of (American Academy of Actuaries, 1720 I St., NW, 7th Floor, Washington, DC 20006; phone: 202/223–8196) bimonthly, $295/members only. Fifty job ads for actuarial positions appear throughout.

Credit Union Magazine (Credit Union National Association, P.O. Box 431 Madison, WI 53701–0431; phones: 800/356–9655, 608/231–4000) monthly, $32/annual subscription. "Classified–Career Opportunities" features announcements for ten or more positions of all types with credit unions.

Credit Union Management (Credit Union Executives Society, P.O. Box 14167, Madison, WI 53714–0167; phones: 800/252–2664, 608/271–2664) monthly, $54/annual nonmember subscription, $40/members. The "Classifieds" feature about five ads for financial CEOs, marketers, operations, data processing, and accountants.

The Accounting Review (American Accounting Association, 5717 Bessie Dr., Sarasota, FL 34233; phone: 813/921–7747) quarterly, $90/annual subscription. Under "Placement Ads," you'll find job descriptions for around 60 university faculty positions.

Directories

American Academy of Actuaries Yearbook (American Academy of Actuaries, 1720 I St., NW, 7th Floor, Washington, DC 20006; phone: 202/223–8196) $25/nonmembers, free/members, published every January.

Directory of Actuarial Membership (American Academy of Actuaries, 1720 I St., NW, 7th Floor, Washington, DC 20006; phone: 202/223–8196) annual, $100/nonmembers, free/members included in dues, published each March.

Credit Union Executive Society Annual Membership Directory (Credit Union Executives Society, P.O. Box 14167, Madison, WI 53714; phones: 800/252–2664, 608/271–2664) free/members only, published annually.

Financial Operation Association Directory (Credit Union Executives Society, P.O. Box 14167, Madison, WI 53714; phones: 800/252–2664, 608/271–2664) free/members only, published annually. Details on operations managers of credit unions.

Financial Marketing Association Directory (Credit Union Executives Society, P.O. Box 14167, Madison, WI 53714; phones: 800/252–2664, 608/271–2664) free/members only, issued annually. Details on marketing directors of credit unions.

Complete Guide to the Real Estate Investment Trusts Industry (NAREIT, 1129 20th St., NW, Washington, DC 20036; phone: 202/785–8717) $695/nonmembers, first copy free/members, $35/additional copies, Issued annually. Detailed information on over 500 NAREIT and REIT members including key contact, address, phone number, investment objective, legal counsel, auditor, advisory firm, trustees, balance sheet, exchange listing, and security offerings. Alphabetic listing of each associate member gives type of firm, contact address, and phone number.

Salary surveys

Compensation in the Accounting/Financial Field (Abbott, Langer & Associates, 548 First St., Crete, IL 60417; phone: 708/672–4200) $450, annual. In–depth analysis of salary and benefits for 18 different positions from junior accountants to chief corporate financial officers in business, industry, education, government, and non–profit organizations.

REIT Executive Compensation Survey (National Association of Real Estate Investment Trusts Membership Directory, 1129 20th St., NW, Washington, DC 20036; phone: 202/785–8717) $500/nonmembers, $300/members, free/participants in survey, issued biannually. Covers executive compensation within the real estate investment trust industry for the top five positions.

Chapter 12

Forestry and horticulture

Forestry and horticulture

*Also see listings in the "Environment" and "Parks and recreation" chapters. The **Professional's Private Sector Job Finder** and **Government Job Finder** contain a substantially more extensive set of job sources in these fields.*

Job ads in print

AABGA Newsletter (American Association of Botanical Gardens and Arboreta, 786 Church Rd., Wayne, PA 19087; phone: 215/688–1120) monthly, free/members only, $50/annual dues, $25/students. About 15 positions in public horticulture ranging from gardener to director appear under "Positions Available."

Internship Directory (American Association of Botanical Gardens and Arboreta, 786 Church Rd., Wayne, PA 19087; phone: 215/688–1120) $5/nonmember, $4/members, published each October. This is a very extensive state–by–state listing of summer internships available in public horticulture and private estates.

ASHS Newsletter (American Society for Horticultural Science, 113 S. West St., Suite 400, Alexandria, VA 22314; phone: 703/836–4606) monthly, free/members only. About 20 research or teaching positions in horticultural science are under "Opportunities."

Job services

Jobs Hotline (American Association of Botanical Gardens and Arboreta, 786 Church Rd., Wayne, PA 19087; phone: 215/688–1120) free. Call 215/688–9127 weekdays 5 p.m. to 8 a.m. (eastern time) and 24 hours on weekends for a tape recording that describes four to eight jobs in public horticulture.

Florapersonnel (2180 W. State Rd. 434, Suite 6152, Longwood, FL 32779–5008; phone: 407/682–5151) free. The job seeker completes Floraperson-nel's form and submits it along with her resume. Resumes are kept on file indefinitely. When a match is made, Florapersonnel contacts the job seeker and, if the job seeker gives the okay, Florapersonnel gives her name and resume to the potential employer who then contacts the employer. (Nor-mally, we don't list "headhunters" in this book, but the horticulture field has so few job sources that it seems essential to include this listing.) Jobs range from greenhouse growers to directors. Includes nursery, floral, landscape, and irrigation.

ASHS Placement Service (American Society for Horticultural Science, 113 S. West St., Suite 400, Alexandria, VA 22314; phone: 703/836–4606) $25/nonmembers, free/members, three–month listing. You complete a "Candidate for Position" resume form which is then sent to prospective employers who have positions for which you may qualify. You are assigned a "C" code so your name does not appear on the resume sent to employers. You may renew after three months.

Directories

AABGA Membership Directory (American Association of Botanical Gardens and Arboreta, 786 Church Rd., Wayne, PA 19007; phone: 215/688–1120) members/only, annual dues: $50, $25/students. Lists institutional members of AABGA.

ASHS Membership Directory (American Society for Horticultural Science, 113 S. West St., Suite 400, Alexandria, VA 22314; phone: 703/836–4606) $30/nonmembers, free/members, published each April. Lists information about ASHS's 5,000 members.

Professional Plant Growers Association Membership Directory (PPGA, P.O. Box 27517, Lansing, MI 48909; phone: 517/694–7700) free/members only, issued each April.

Salary survey

1992 AABGA Salary Survey (American Association of Botanical Gardens and Arboreta, 786 Church Rd., Wayne, PA 19087; phone: 215/688–1120) $38/nonmembers, $28/members. Contains salary information for 22 positions in botanical gardens in the U.S. and Canada.

Chapter 13

Foundations and grants

Also see the "Philanthropy" chapter for additional job sources.

Many directories of grant opportunities have been written specifically for individual states. These are described in Chapter 31, "State–by–state job and grant sources." In addition, be sure to check the Index for grant sources that are listed under a specific discipline elsewhere in this book.

The directories described in this chapter and Chapter 31, "State–by–state job and grant sources" serve two purposes. First, you can use them to locate funding sources. Second, if you wish to work for a foundation, you can use these directories to identify foundations to which you might wish to apply for a job.

Foundations and grants

Job ads in print

Foundation News (Council of Foundations, 1828 L St., NW, Washington, DC 20036; phone: 202/466–6512) bimonthly, $29.50/nonmember annual subscription (U.S. and Canada), $60/elsewhere (airmail). About six job ads for executive directors and coordinators with foundations appear in display ads and in the classifieds section. Includes "Positions Wanted."

Minority Funding Report (Government Information Services, 1611 N. Kent St., Suite 508, Arlington, VA 22209; phone: 703/528–1000) monthly, $128/annual subscription. The "Education Grants Week" section reports on four to 14 grants in education, housing, health care, and other fields.

Foundation Giving Watch (Taft Group, 12300 Twinbrook Pkwy., Suite 520, Rockville, MD 20852–9830; phone: 800/877–8238) monthly, $139/annual subscription. This newsletter is a great source of up–to–date foundation funding opportunities with reports on new foundations, new grant programs, changing funding priorities, and community or regional funding news. Eight pages are devoted to new and updated profiles of foundations. This newsletter is also available by computer modem from NewsNet (voice phones: 800/345–1301, 215/527–8030).

Corporate Philanthropy Report (Craig Smith, 2727 Fairview Ave., East, Suite D, Seattle, WA 00102) phone: 206/329–0422) ten issues/year, $165/annual non–profits' subscription, $200/others. "Spotlight" reports details on funders within a specific category.

Directories

Foundation Grants to Individuals (The Foundation Center, 79 Fifth Ave., New York, NY 10003–3076; phones: 800/424–9836, 212/620–4230) $55, 1991. This book offers everything you need to start your grant search: details on over 2,250 independent and corporate foundations that make grants to individuals. For each foundation, you'll find the contact person, application procedures, financial data, and giving preferences. Since relatively few foundations will issue a grant to an individual, this book is *the essential source* for any individual seeking a grant.

The Grants Database (Oryx Press, Suite 700, 4041 N. Central, Phoenix, AZ 85012–3397; phones: 800/279–6799, 602/265–2651). Constantly updated by Oryx Press, this database is one of the most comprehensive sources of information on funding programs on biomedical, health care, and humanities subjects. It includes details on research grants, award competitions, scholarships, arts contests, internships, visiting professorships and lectureships, and more. You can access this database through DIALOG. For information, call 800/334–2564 (800/982–5838 in California).

1991–92 GRINDEX (American Anthropological Association, 4350 N. Fairfax Dr., Suite 640, Arlington, VA 22203; phone: 703/528–1902) $7/nonmembers, $5/members, include self–addressed stamped envelope with .45 postage. Key to grants and support for anthropology students, faculty, and practitioners. GRINDEX cross–indexes 170 agencies by program, geographical area, topic, and users' need.

This database is also available as ***DIALOG OnDisc: The Grants Database***, on CD–ROM compact disks for an $850 annual subscription ($1,500 with CD–ROM drive included). It is updated bimonthly. For details, call Dialog Marketing at 800/334–2564 (800/982–5838 in California).

Annual Register of Grant Support 1994 (R.R. Bowker; available from Reed Reference Publishing, P.O. Box 31, New Providence, NJ 07974; phone: 800/521–8110) $175 plus 7 percent shipping and handling, published each September. Describes over 3,000 sources of grant funding: traditional sources (private, corporate, and public) plus non–traditional sources (educational associations, unions, special interest groups, church organizations, community trusts, and more). Areas covered include: multiple special purpose, humanities, international affairs, special populations, urban and regional affairs, education, sciences, social sciences, physical sciences, life sciences, and technology and industry. Includes all the information you need to write your grant proposal.

The Foundation Directory (The Foundation Center, 79 Fifth Ave., New York, NY 10003–3076; phones: 800/424–9836, 212/620–4230) $160/softcover. Includes entries on over 6,300 foundations that hold assets of at least $2 million or annually distribute $200,000 or more in grants. Each entry includes financial data, purpose and activities, types of support, limitations, and application information.

The Foundation Directory, Part 2 (The Foundation Center, 79 Fifth Ave., New York, NY 10003–3076; phones: 800/424–9836, 212/620–4230) $160/softcover. Includes entries on over 10,000 foundations with grant programs of $50,000 to $200,000. Each entry includes financial data, purpose and activities, types of support, limitations, application information, and a list of sample grants.

The Foundation 1,000 (The Foundation Center, 79 Fifth Ave., New York, NY 10003–3076; phones: 800/424–9836, 212/620–4230) $225. Contains 1,000 extremely detailed profiles of foundations that run several pages. This is probably the most thorough analysis of foundations available anywhere.

America's New Foundations (Taft Group, 12300 Twinbrook Pkwy., Suite 520, Rockville, MD 20852–9830; phone: 800/877–8238) $150, 1100 pages, annual. Profiles over 3,400 private company and community foundations that give over $100,000 annually or have assets over $1,000,000. Includes 500 foundations not previously reported. Each listing includes the foundation's priorities, recipient types, financial information, names of officers and directors and a list of major grant recipients.

Directory of New and Emerging Foundations (The Foundation Center, 79 Fifth Ave., New York, NY 10003–3076; phones: 800/424–9836, 212/620–4230) $95, 1991; currently out of print but may still be purchased from the Foundation Center or found at your local library. Includes detailed informa-

"I'm personally studying the effects of relaxation on
people who receive research grants."

tion on 1,000 foundations: contact person, financial data, purpose and activities, types of support, limitations, application procedures, offices and trustees, and staff size. Another 2,000 foundations that make grants of up to $25,000 per year are also briefly profiled.

Foundation Reporter (Taft Group, 12300 Twinbrook Pkwy., Suite 520, Rockville, MD 20852–9830; phone: 800/877–8238) $335, 1,200 pages, annual. Provides detailed profiles of 600 leading foundations: foundation philosophy, financial summary, typical grant recipients, extensive list of recent grants, new programs supported and programs being phased out, and biographical information on foundation officers and directors. Also available on MS–DOS disks for $650.

Guide to U.S. Foundations (The Foundation Center, 79 Fifth Ave., New York, NY 10003–3050; phones: 800/424–9836, 212/620–4230) $195, April 1993. These two volumes report fundamental information on over 33,000 U.S. foundations. Each entry includes the name and address, contact person, and total grants during the past year. The contents of this book are also available by computer modem via DIALOG File 26 and 27. DIALOG File 27 enables you to generate lists of foundations by grant subject area. Contact DIALOG at 800/334–2564 for information on using these databases. Contact the Foundation Center's Online Support Staff at 212/620–4230 to learn more about which online utilities provide "gateway" access, or for free materials to help you search these database files.

Funding Decision Makers (Taft Group, 12300 Twinbrook Pkwy., Suite 520, Rockville, MD 20852–9830; phone: 800/877–8238) $170, 1,300 pages, annual. Build networking opportunities with a close look at over 23,800 top funding decision makers at organizations with assets of $3 million or more or annual contributions of over $300,000. For each funding official, this directory gives you her education, funding affiliations, and non–profit affiliations.

National Directory of Corporate Giving (The Foundation Center, 79 Fifth Ave., New York, NY 10003–3076; phones: 800/424–9836, 212/620–4230) $195, 1993. Presents profiles on 2,000 corporate foundations plus an additional 500+ direct giving programs: application procedures, key per-sonnel, types of support awarded, giving limitations, and purpose and activity statements. Also includes a "Current Giving" section which lists recent grant recipients by subject area.

Corporate Foundation Profiles (The Foundation Center, 79 Fifth Ave., New York, NY 10003–3076; phones: 800/424–9836, 212/620–4230) $135, March 1992. This book offers four to six–page analyses of 247 of the U.S.'s top corporate foundations and grant makers whose annual giving is at least $1.25 million.

Corporate and Foundation Grants (Taft Group, 12300 Twinbrook Pkwy., Suite 520, Rockville, MD 20852–9830; phone: 800/877–8238) $150, 2,901 pages in two volumes, annual. Learn about over 5,500 corporate and private grant makers: application procedures, deadlines, restrictions, grant recipients, geographic area and interest covered. Includes hard–to–identify corporate givers.

Corporate and Foundation Givers (Taft Group, 12300 Twinbrook Pkwy., Suite 520, Rockville, MD 20852–9830; phone: 800/877–8238) $199, two volumes, 3,500 pages, annual. This tome details over 8,000 organizations that distribute at least $250,000 in grants each year. Included in each entry are contact information, eligibility requirements, giving priorities, grant types, and financial data. Each entry also includes biographies of the officers and directors, and the recipients of the ten largest grants. Nine indexes help you locate potential funders by grant type, recipient type, headquarters state, industry, and company operating location.

Corporate Giving Yellow Pages (Taft Group, 12300 Twinbrook Pkwy., Suite 520, Rockville, MD 20852–9830; phone: 800/877–8238) $82, 420 pages, annual. Lists the contact person (with address and phone number) at each of over 3,900 corporate giving programs and corporate foundations.

Corporate Giving Directory (Taft Group, 12300 Twinbrook Pkwy., Suite 520, Rockville, MD 20852–9830; phone: 800/877–8238) $327, 1,150 pages, annual. Get full details on the 550 most important corporate givers, including contact names, deadlines, total assets and giving, average grant size, and names of recent grant recipients. Learn also which organizations give to your type of cause, which organizations give in your geographic area, and which organizations offer the type and level of grant support you need. Also available on MS–DOS computer disk for $650.

International Foundation Directory (Gale Research, Inc., 835 Penobscot Bldg., Detroit, MI 48226–4094; phone: 800/877–4253) $140, 1991. Covers more than 770 foundations, trusts, and similar non–profit institutions in 49 countries.

Directory of International Corporate Giving in America and Abroad (Taft Group, 12300 Twinbrook Pkwy., Suite 520, Rockville, MD 20852–9830; phone: 800/877–8238) $155, 499 pages, annual. Over 450 foreign and U.S. multinational corporations are profiled. Included in each listing are the contact name for grants, average grant size, names of recent grant recipients, application procedures, and typical grants.

Inside Japanese Support (Taft Group, 12300 Twinbrook Pkwy., Suite 520, Rockville, MD 20852–9830; phone: 800/877–8238) $209, 300 pages, annual. Japanese foundations and corporations donated over $200 million to U.S. non–profits in 1990. This directory reports on 300 of the major Japanese funders: contact person, application procedures, program description, recent grant recipients.

Directory of Biomedical and Health Care Grants 1994 (Oryx Press, 4041 N. Central, Phoenix, AZ 85012–3397; phones: 800/279–6799, 602/265–2651) $84.50, 648 pages, 1993. Furnishes details on over 3,000 funding sources: full program descriptions, contact names (with address and phone number), application procedures, deadlines, and any special restrictions.

National Directory of Grants & Aid to Individuals in the Arts, 8th Edition (Allied Publishing, P.O. Box 12010, Des Moines, IA 50312; phone: 515/255–5577) biannual, April 1993. $30/nonmembers, $22/members. Grant information on the arts, education, and scholarships.

Directory of Financial Aids for Minorities, 1993–1994 (Reference Service Press, 1100 Industrial Road, Suite 9, San Carlos, CA 94070) $47.50/prepaid plus $4 shipping, 668 pages, 1993. Provides details on over 2,000 grants, fellowships, loans, awards, and internships designed primarily or exclusively for members of minority groups.

Grants for Minorities (The Foundation Center, 79 Fifth Ave., New York, NY 10003–3076; phones: 800/424–9836, within New York State call 212/620–4230) $65 plus $4.50/shipping, October 1993. Describes recent foundation grants of at least $10,000 for ethnic groups and minority populations, including African–Americans, Hispanics, Asian–Americans, Gays and lesbians, Native Americans, immigrants, and refugees. This directory is useful for identifying foundations and grant recipients for which you may wish to work.

SYLVIA   **by Nicole Hollander**

Sylvia reprinted by permission of Nicole Hollander. Copyright 1991. All rights reserved.

Directory of Financial Aids for Women, 1993–1995 (Reference Service Press, 1100 Industrial Road, Suite 9, San Carlos, CA 94070) $45/prepaid plus $4 shipping, 468 pages, 1993. Provides details on over 1,700 grants, fellowships, loans, awards, and internships designed primarily or exclusively for women.

Grants for Women & Girls (The Foundation Center, 79 Fifth Ave., New York, NY 10003–3076; phones: 800/424–9836, within New York State call 212/620–4230) $65 plus $4.50/shipping, October 1993. Describes recent foundation grants of at least $10,000 given for education, career guidance, vocational training, equal rights, rape prevention, shelter programs for victims of domestic violence, health programs, abortion rights, pregnancy programs, athletics and recreation, arts programs, and social research. This directory is useful for identifying foundations and grant recipients for which you may wish to work.

Directory of Grants in the Humanities 1993/94 (Oryx Press, Suite 700, 4041 N. Central, Phoenix, AZ 85012–3397; phones: 800/279–6799, 602/265–2651) $84.50, 720 pages, 1993. Includes details on 4,000 corporate, private, and government support for competitions and awards, performances, productions, exhibits, conferences, scholarships, internships, graduate assistantships, and more: full program descriptions, contact names (with address and phone number), deadlines, and any special restrictions.

Grants–at–a–Glance (Association for Women in Science, 1522 K St., NW, Suite 820, Washington, DC 20005; phone: 202/408–0742) $7.50/non-members, $6/members, 100 pages. Lists over 400 awards, fellowships, and scholarships for women in engineering, mathematics, and a wide variety of scientific fields at all levels of undergraduate and graduate studies.

Directory of Building and Equipment Grants (Research Grant Guides, P.O. Box 1214, Loxahatchee, FL 33470; phone: 407/795–6129) $49.50 plus $4/shipping, prepaid, 216 pages, published in even–numbered years. Profiles over 900 foundations and 20 federal programs that issue grants for construction, renovation, and equipment.

Directory of Operating Grants (Research Grant Guides, P.O. Box 1214, Loxahatchee, FL 33470) $42.50 plus $4 shipping, prepaid, last published November 1992. Profiles over 640 foundations that support general ongoing operating expenses. Listed by state, information includes: address, phone number, grant range, contact person, and list of recent organizations funded.

Computer and High Technology Grants (Research Grant Guides, P.O. Box 1214, Loxahatchee, FL 33470) $44.50 plus $4 shipping, prepaid. Includes 3,200 funding entries for obtaining computers, software, copy machines, fax machines, modems, telephone systems, typewriters, and more. Additional information includes corporations offering discounts on their products and detailed information regarding 32 federal funding programs.

Handicapped Funding Directory (Research Grant Guides, P.O. Box 1214, Loxahatchee, FL 33470) $39.50 plus $4 shipping, prepaid. Profiles more than 1,200 foundations, corporations, government agencies, and associations which award grants to non–profit organizations. This directory also includes key federal contacts and 4,600 entries in four indexes.

Chapter 14

Health care

*See the **Professional's Private Sector Job Finder** for a much more exten-sive listing of job sources in private sector health care. The listings here focus on non–profit positions. **Virtually all of the job sources described in this chapter include teaching or research positions even if the description doesn't mention this fact.***

Health care in general

Job ads in print

The Nation's Health (American Public Health Association, 1015 15th St., NW, Washington, DC 20005; phone: 202/789–5600) 11 issues/year, $15/an-nual subscription (U.S.), $18/foreign. Jobs listed under "Job Openings" in the "Classified Advertising" section. Typical issue announces about 50 job openings.

Hospitals and Health Networks (American Hospital Publishing, P.O. Box 92567, Chicago, IL 60675; phones: 800/621–6902, 312/440–6836) bi-monthly, $65/annual nonmember subscription. From five to 15 positions, mostly for hospital administrators, but also for a handful of maintenance, and patient care positions (doctors, nurses, etc.) appear under "Classified."

Rural Health Care (National Rural Health Care Association, 301 E. Armour Blvd., Kansas City, MO 64111; phone: 816/756–3140) bimonthly, free/member only. About 25 physician and nursing positions appear under "Classified."

American Journal of Health Promotion (1812 S. Rochester Rd., Suite 200, Rochester Hills, MI 48307–3532; phone: 313/650–9600) bimonthly, $49.50/annual subscription. About two positions for wellness program administrators and postdoctoral research fellowships appear under "Job Opportunities."

AABB News Briefs (American Association of Blood Banks, (8101 Glenbrook Rd., Bethesda, MD 20814; phone: 301/907–6977) monthly, free/members only, $5/annual dues. "Referral Exchange" runs about 20 ads for medical technologists, donor recruiters, laboratory directors, inventory managers, professors, and all other positions in blood banks and transfusion medicine.

Academic Medicine (Association of American Medical Colleges, 2450 N Street, NW, Washington, DC 20037; phone: 202/028 0416) monthly, $60/annual nonmember subscription (U.S.), $70/foreign, free/members. About 15 display ads in the back of the magazine tout job opportunities for deans and presidents of medical schools, student health center administrators, and university physicians.

Action (American College Health Association, P.O. Box 28937, Baltimore, MD 21240; phone: 301/963–1100) bimonthly, free/members only. "Placement Listings" features 12 to 16 job vacancies for physicians, nurses, and health educators with college health centers.

The Neuroscience Newsletter (Society for Neuroscience, 11 Dupont Circle, NW, Suite 500, Washington, DC 20036; phone: 202/462–6688) bimonthly, free/members only. Thirty to 40 vacancies for faculty and researchers dominate the "Positions Available" section of this attractive newsletter.

Journal of Nuclear Medicine (Society of Nuclear Medicine, 136 Madison Ave., New York, NY 10016; phone: 212/889–0717) monthly, $120/annual nonmember subscription, $130/Canada, $160/elsewhere, free/members. About 25 positions for physicians, technologists, and radiologists are advertised. SNM says it plans to move its offices to Reston, VA (call long idstance directory assistance,1–703/555–1212, to get new number) in October, 1994.

AMHA Newsletter (Association of Mental Health Administrators, 60 Revere Drive, Suite 500, Northbrook, IL 60062; phone: 708/480–9626) semimonthly, $46/six month nonmember subscription, free/members. 4 or 5 job ads appear under "Executive Classified Service" for administrative positions in behavioral health facilities.

Emergency Medical Services (Summer Communications, Inc., 7626 Densmore Ave., Van Nuys, CA 91406–2088) monthly, $18.95/annual subscription (U.S.), $29/foreign. About four positions for paramedics and emergency physicians appear under "Employment Opportunities."

Nationwide Jobs in Dietetics (P.O. Box 3537, Santa Monica, CA 90408–3537; phone: 310/453–5375) monthly, with mid–month job updates, $84/annual subscription, $48/three–month subscription, $36/two–month subscription, $24/one–month subscription. California residents add 8.25 percent sales tax. About ten percent of the 400 dietitian, nutritionist, and food service professional jobs in a typical issue fall under the moniker "Public Health & Community Nutrition." Your first issue will include a sheet that names additional sources of government and non–profit sector positions.

Journal of the American Dietetic Association (ADA, 216 W. Jackson Blvd., Chicago, IL 60606; phone: 312/899–0040) monthly, $98/nonmember annual subscription, free/members. About 40 ads for dietitians appear under "Classified Advertising" each issue.

California Jobs in Dietetics (P.O. Box 3537, Santa Monica, CA 90408–3537; phone: 310/453–5375) biweekly, $48/six–issue subscription. California residents add 8.25 percent sales tax. Almost ten percent of the 230 dietitian and nutritionist jobs in a typical issue are listed under "Public Health & Community Nutrition." Your first issue will include a sheet that names additional sources of government and non–profit sector positions in California and nationally.

Journal of Nutrition Education (Decker Periodicals, 1 James Street South, P.O. Box 620, LCD1, Hamilton, Ontario, L8N3K7; phone: 416/522–7017) bimonthly, $80/annual subscription (U.S. and Canada), $100/elsewhere. Display ads throughout carry ads for about two positions, largely directors of education and faculty positions.

Career Mart (American College of Healthcare Executives, 840 N. Lake Shore Dr., Chicago, IL 60611; phone: 312/943–0544) monthly, available only to members, $35/member six–month subscription. Typical issue includes more than 70 upper–level health care management positions listed under "Career Mart."

ADVANCE for Health Information Professionals (Merion Publications, 650 Park Ave., West, King of Prussia, PA 19406–4025; phones: 800/355–1088, 215/265–7812) biweekly, free to qualified professionals, contact publisher for subscription application. Under "Classified Employment Opportunities" you'll find a handful of faculty positions for instructors of health information technology and medical records technology. You'll also find around 70 job ads for medical records coding specialists, medical records supervisors/directors/assistants, DRG managers, abstracters, oncology data managers, transcriptionists, and tumor registrars.

Journal of the American Health Information Management Association (AHIMA, 919 N. Michigan Ave., Suite 1400, Chicago, IL 60611–1683; phone: 312/787–2672, ext. 253) monthly, $72/nonmember annual subscription, free/members. Around 10 to 15 classified ads for medical record administrators, technicians, coders, and reviewers are in the typical issue. This organization recently changed its name from the American Medical Records Association.

FASEB Newsletter (FASEB, Room 2310, 9650 Rockville Pike, Bethesda, MD 20814; phone: 301/530–7027) eight issues/year, $60/nonmembers, free/members. "Positions and Opportunities" features about six openings for professors and research assistants.

ADVANCE for Respiratory Care Practitioners (Merion Publications, 650 Park Ave., West, King of Prussia, PA 19406–4025; phones: 800/355–1088, 215/265–7812) biweekly, free to qualified professionals, contact publisher for subscription application. Under "Classified Employment Opportunities" you'll find around 120 job ads for respiratory therapists, respiratory technicians, electroencephalograph technicians, home care therapists, pulmonary technologists, directors of respiratory care, neonatal respiratory therapists, and polysomnographic technologists. A handful of ads appear for faculty positions in cardio–respiratory care, directors of clinical education, and respiratory therapy.

Journal of School Health (American School Health Association, 7263 State Route 43, Kent, OH 44240; phone: 216/678–1601) ten issues/year, $85. Two or three vacancies for professors and camp nurses are in the typical issue.

Trends (Association of Schools of Allied Health Professions, 1101 Connecticut Ave., NW, Suite 700, Washington, DC 20036; phone: 202/857–1150) monthly, $55/annual subscription. Three job ads appear for allied health educators or administrators.

Journal of Perentology (Mosby Yearbook, 11830 Westline Industrial Drive, St. Louis, MO 63146; phone: 314/453–4406) quarterly, $50/annual subscription (U.S.), $62.50/foreign. The "Classified" section has around ten positions for nutritionists, perentologists (prenatal), and nurses.

Journal of Environmental Health (National Environmental Health Association, Suite 970, South Tower, 720 S. Colorado Blvd., Denver, CO 80222; phone: 303/756–9090) bimonthly, $75/nonmember annual subscription, included in dues ($60/year, $15/students). Jobs listed under "Opportunities." Five to ten job ads appear in the typical issue for sanitarians, toxicologists, health planners, and related positions.

Career Services Bulletin (American College of Sports Medicine, 401 W. Michigan St., Indianapolis, IN 46202–3233; phone: 317/637–9200) monthly, $20/annual non-member subscription, $10/members. Around 50 positions in sports medicine and exercise science appear throughout, many on university faculties.

American Journal of Obstetrics and Gynecology (Mosby Year Book, Journal Subscription Services, 11830 Westline Industrial Dr., St. Louis, MO 63146; phone: 800/453–4351) monthly, $116/annual subscription (U.S.), $52/student (U.S.), $157.12/Canada, $149/elsewhere. Close to 60 practitioner and faculty positions appear in display ads.

Opportunities in Dermatology (American Academy of Dermatology, 930 N. Meacham Rd., Schaumburg, IL 60168; phone: 708/330–0230) quarterly, $100/annual nonmember subscription, $50/members. Your subscription gets you four different quarterly editions: *Clinical Positions Available, Dermatologists Seeking Clinical Positions, Academic Positions Available,* and *Dermatologists Seeking Academic Positions*. Hundreds of positions are listed state–by–state in each "positions available" edition. Only about 70 dermatologists are listed in the "seeking positions" editions.

The New Careers Directory: Internships and Professional Opportunities in Technology and Social Change (Student Pugwash USA, 1638 R St., NW, Suite 32, Washington, DC 20009; phone: 202/328–6555) $18, $10/students, add $3/shipping, 1993. Offers full details on where and how to apply for internships and entry–level jobs in health care and related fields.

Job services

National Hospice Organization Job Bank (NHO, 1901 N. Moore St., Suite 901, Arlington, VA 22209; phone: 703/243–5900) free. Call 703/243–4348 24–hours a day to hear a recording that briefly describes openings in hospices: administrative, nursing, social workers, spiritual care, etc. You pay only regular long distance phone rates for this job hotline which is updated weekly.

Jobs for Dietitians Job Advice Hotline (P.O. Box 3537, Santa Monica, CA 90408–3537; phone: 310/453–5375) available only to subscribers to either the national or California edition of *Jobs for Dietitians* described above under "Job ads in print." Hotline number is given in the newsletter.

Directories

Directory of Biomedical and Health Care Grants 1994 (Oryx Press, 4041 N. Central, Phoenix, AZ 85012–3397; phones: 800/279–6799, 602/265–2651) $84.50, 648 pages, 1993. Furnishes details on over 3,000 funding sources: full program descriptions, contact names (with address and phone number), application procedures, deadlines, and any special restrictions.

Twenty–Eight Allied Health Careers (American Medical Association, Order Department, P.O. Box 109050, Chicago, IL 60610–9050; phone: 800/621–8335) free/members, nonmembers can receive this item only if they purchase the *Allied Health Education Directory,* described immediately below, for $45 (then this item is included free if you request it), published annually. Includes history, occupational description, job description, employment characteristics, starting salaries, required education, prerequisites, curriculum, and essentials for many physician–support professions.

Allied Health Education Directory (American Medical Association, P.O. Box 109050, Order Department, Chicago, IL 60610; phones: 800/621–8335, 312/464–0183) $30/members, $45/nonmembers, published each April. Covers 3,000 programs in accredited, post–secondary institutions. Describes each occupation, work environment, entry–level salaries, and more.

Medical Research Centres (Gale Research, Inc., 835 Penobscot Bldg., Detroit, MI 48226–4094; phone: 800/877–4253) $470, last published 1990. Details 9,000 medical and biochemical research centers: research laboratories, universities, societies, industrial enterprises, and professional associations engaged in research in medicine and related subjects like dentistry, nursing, pharmacy, psychiatry, and surgery.

Encyclopedia of Medical Organizations and Agencies (Gale Research, Inc., 835 Penobscot Bldg., Detroit. MI 48226–4094; phone: 800/877–4253) $205, 1,200 pages, 1993. Provides information on 12,000 major public and private organizations and agencies concerned with medical information, funding, research, education, planning, advocacy, advice, and service. A good source of information on potential employers as well as identifying desirable places to work.

Medical and Health Information Directory (Gale Research, Inc., 835 Penobscot Bldg., Detroit. MI 48226–4094; phone: 800/877–4253) $485/three–volume set, 1992. *Volume 1: Organizations, Agencies, and Institutions* ($195, 1,331 pages) details over 16,400 national, international, and state professional and voluntary organizations, as well as foundations and grant–issuing organizations, research centers, and medical and allied health schools. It's a good source for finding health care associations for which to work. *Volume 2: Publications, Libraries, and Other Information Sources* ($195, 730 pages) reports on over 9,700 libraries, audiovisual producers and services, publications, publishers, and databases. *Volume 3: Health Services* ($195, 870 pages) gives current data on more than 23,000 clinics, treatment centers, care programs, counseling/diagnostic services, and other health services arranged into 31 subject chapters.

AABB Membership Directory (American Association of Blood Banks, 8101 Glenbrook Rd., Bethesda, MD 20814; phone: 301/907–6977) $50 plus $4/shipping, issued in December of even–numbered years.

American College of Physician Executives Membership Directory (American College of Physician Executives, 4890 W. Kennedy Blvd., Suite 200, Tampa, FL 33609; phone: 813/287–2000) free/members only, annual.

American Health Information Management Association Membership Directory (AHIMA, 919 N. Michigan Ave., Suite 1400, Chicago, IL 60611–1683; phone: 312/787–2672, ext. 253) $18, last published in 1993. This organization changed its name from the American Medical Records Association.

Membership Directory of the American College Health Association (ACHA, P.O. Box 28937, Baltimore, MD 21240; phone: 301/963–1100) free/members only, annual. Last published 1992.

AHA Guide to the Health Care Field (American Hospital Association, ATTEN: AHA Services, P.O. Box 92683, Chicago, IL 60675–2683; phone: 800/242–2626) $195/nonmembers plus $12.95 shipping and handling, $75/members plus $7.95 shipping and handling, annual each August. Provides details on hospitals, health care systems, health care organizations, agencies, and providers. Also available on computer disk, $2000/nonmembers, $1800/members.

HCIA Directory of Health Care Professionals (HCIA, 300 E. Lombard St., Baltimore, MD 21202; phone: 800/568–3282) $299/nonmembers plus $7.95 shipping and handling, $259/members plus $7.95 shipping and handling, annual.

National Guide to Funding in Health (The Foundation Center, 79 Fifth Ave., New York, NY 10003–3076; phones: 800/424–9836, 212/620–4230) $135, 1990. Entries for each of the 3,000 foundations and corporate giving programs include application information, list of recent grant recipients, and over 8,000 sample grants.

AIDS Funding: A Guide to Giving by Foundations and Charitable Organizations (The Foundation Center, 79 Fifth Ave., New York, NY 10003–3076; phones: 800/424–9836, 212/620–4230) $60, July 1991. Entries for each of the 500 foundations, public charities, and corporate giving programs include application information and a list of recent grant recipients.

Association of Academic Health Centers Directory (AAHC, 1400 16th St., NW, Washington, DC 20036; phone: 202/265–9600) $10/nonmembers, free/members, issued each January.

Membership Directory for the Society of Nuclear Medicine (Society of Nuclear Medicine, 136 Madison Ave., New York, NY 10016; phone: 212/889–0717) $50/nonmembers, free/members; last published in July 1993. SNM tells us it intends to move Reston, VA in October,1994. If it really moves then and mail or phone calls are not forwarded, call long distance directory assistance in Reston (1–703/555–1212) for the new phone number.

FASEB Directory (FASEB, Room 2310, 9650 Rockville Pike, Bethesda, MD 20814; phone: 301/530–7027) $50/nonmembers, prepaid, free/members, published annually. Includes members of the Federation of American Societies for Experimental Biology.

Grants for Health Programs for Children and Youth (The Foundation Center, 79 Fifth Ave., New York, NY 10003–3076; phones: 800/424–9836, within New York State call 212/620–4230) $65 plus $4.50/shipping, October 1993. Describes recent foundation grants of at least $10,000 given to hospitals and health care facilities, social service agencies, and education institutions for research, program development, general operating support, education programs, treatment for drug and alcohol abuse, pregnancy, and children with disabilities. This directory is useful for identifying foundations and grant recipients for which you may wish to work.

Grants for Public Health & Diseases (The Foundation Center, 79 Fifth Ave., New York, NY 10003–3076; phones: 800/424–9836, within New York State call 212/620–4230) $65 plus $4.50/shipping, October 1993. Describes recent foundation grants of at least $10,000 for public health programs and diseases including genetic diseases; birth defects; cancer; AIDS; nerve, muscle, and bone diseases, allergies, and other diseases; prevention of sexually transmitted diseases; and epidemology. This directory is useful for identifying foundations and grant recipients for which you may wish to work.

Grants for Hospitals, Medical Care & Research (The Foundation Center, 79 Fifth Ave., New York, NY 10003–3076; phones: 800/424–9836, within New York State call 212/620–4230) $65 plus $4.50/shipping, October 1993. Describes recent foundation grants of at least $10,000 given to hospitals, clinics, nursing homes, health care facilities, health support services, public health programs, reproductive health care, and medical research centers. This directory is useful for identifying foundations and grant recipients for which you may wish to work.

Grants for Medical & Professional Health Education (The Foundation Center, 79 Fifth Ave., New York, NY 10003–3076; phones: 800/424–9836, within New York State call 212/620–4230) $65 plus $4.50/shipping, October 1993. Describes recent foundation grants of at least $10,000 given to graduate and professional schools of medicine, dentistry, nursing, and public health for general support, faculty development, symposiums, and conferences. This directory is useful for identifying foundations and grant recipients for which you may wish to work.

Salary survey

1991 Salary Survey Report (American College Health Association, P.O. Box 28937, Baltimore, MD 21240; phone: 410/963–1100) free/members only.

Dentists

Job ads in print

Journal of Dental Education (American Association of Dental Schools, 1625 Massachusetts Ave., NW, Suite 502, Washington, DC 20026; phone: 202/667–9433) monthly, $60/annual subscription (U.S. and Canada), $75/elsewhere. Around 20 vacancies for dental school faculty appear under "Classified."

Journal of Dentistry for Children (American Society of Dentistry for Children, 211 E. Chicago Ave., Chicago, IL 60611; phone: 312/943–1244) bimonthly, $65/annual nonmember subscription (U.S.), $75/foreign, free/members. About 11 positions and practices for sale appear under "Opportunities for Pedodontists." Also "positions wanted."

Journal of Dental Research (International Association for Dental Researchers, 1111 14th St., NW, Suite 1000, Washington, DC 20005; phone: 202/898–1050) 16 issues/year, $350/annual nonmember subscription, $41/members, $16/student members. The inside front cover runs one to three classified ads for dental researchers.

Directory

Directory of Institutional Members (American Association of Dental Schools, 1625 Massachusetts Ave., NW, Washington, DC 20026; phone: 202/667–9433) $25/nonmembers, $10/members, annual.

Doctors

Job ads in print

New England Journal of Medicine (Massachusetts Medical Society, 10 Shattuck St., Boston, MA 02115–6094; phone: 617/893–3800) weekly, $96/annual subscription. Among the 300 to 500 physician positions advertised in the "Classifieds" section and in display ads throughout the magazine are many teaching and research positions.

JAMA: The Journal of the American Medical Association (American Medical Association, Order Department, P.O. Box 109050, Chicago, IL 60610–9050; phone: 800/621–8335) weekly, $110/annual nonmember subscription, free/members. "Classified Advertising" offers openings for 275 to 325 physicians of all types. Also available on CD–ROM for $295/nonmembers, $220/members.

Canadian Medical Association Journal (Canadian Medical Association, 1867 Alta Vista Drive, P.O. Box 8650, Ottawa, ON K1G 3Y6 Canada) biweekly, $82/annual subscription (Canada), $100/annual subscription (U.S.), $107/elsewhere. From 150 to 175 positions for physicians appear under "Classifieds."

Canadian Journal of Surgery (Canadian Medical Association, 1867 Alta Vista Drive, P.O. Box 8650, Ottawa, ON K1G 3Y6 Canada) six issues/year, $58/annual subscription (Canada), $63/U.S. and elsewhere. From 10 to 15 positions for physicians appear under "Classifieds."

Canadian Association of Radiologists Journal (Canadian Medical Association, 1867 Alta Vista Drive, P.O. Box 8650, Ottawa, ON K1G 3Y6 Canada) six issues/year, $110/annual subscription (Canada), $100/U.S. and elsewhere. From 12 to 15 positions for physicians appear under "Classifieds."

American Family Physician (American Academy of Family Physicians, 8880 Ward Pkwy., Kansas City, MO 64114; phone: 800/274–2237 ext. 3166) monthly, $65/annual subscription, free/student members. "AFP Classified Information" overflows with over 300 available positions, including around 40 faculty openings.

Annals of Internal Medicine (American College of Physicians, Independence Mall West, 6th St. at Race, Philadelphia, PA 19106; phone: 800/523–1546) $84/annual nonmember subscription (U.S.), $134.82(includes GST)/Canada,$142/elsewhere; $59.25/nonmember physicians, $42/nonmember medical students, included in membership package. From 100 to 150 vacancies for physicians in internal medicine appear under "Classified."

Journal of the American Medical Women's Association (AMWA, 801 N. Fairfax St., Suite 400, Alexandria, VA 22314; phone: 703/838–0500) bimonthly, $35/annual nonmember subscription, free/members. The "Classifieds" carry 30 to 40 job openings for physicians of all types.

Journal of the National Medical Association (SLACK, Inc., 6900 Grove Rd., Thorofare, NJ 08086; phone: 609/848–1000) monthly, $78/annual subscription (U.S.), $96/Canada plus 7 percent GST tax, $114/elsewhere. About 20 openings for pathologists, surgeons, staff, and faculty appear under "Positions Available."

The New Physician (American Medical Student Association, 1890 Preston White Dr., Reston, VA 22091; phone: 703/620–6600) nine issues/year, $22/annual nonmember subscription, free/members. Five to ten residency positions appear under "Classifieds/Opportunities."

ACPM News (American College of Preventive Medicine, 1015 15th St., NW, Suite 403, Washington, DC 20005; phone: 202/789–0003) quarterly, $25/annual nonmember subscription, free/members. The "Classified" section contains two or three job vacancies for faculty, health educators, MPH qualified health professionals, and fellowships.

The Lancet (Williams & Wilkins, 428 E. Preston St., Baltimore, MD 21202–3993; phone: 800/638–6423) weekly, $108/annual personal subscription, $65/physicians in training; add $10/year postage plus 7 percent GST for Canadian subscriptions. Five to six physician vacancies throughout the world appear under "Classified Advertising."

The DO (American Osteopathic Association, 142 Ontario St., Chicago, IL 60611–2864; phone: 312/280–5800) monthly, $40/annual subscription (U.S.), $70/foreign. About 125 openings for osteopaths appear under "Classifieds–Opportunities."

AAO–HNS Bulletin (American Academy of Otolaryngology–Head and Neck Surgery, 1 Prince St., Alexandria, VA 22314; phone: 703/836–4444) free/residents, $25/member annual subscription, $55/nonmembers, $65/foreign. "Employment Classifieds" publish 150 to 200 positions for otolaryngologists.

AGA News (SLACK, Inc., 6900 Grove Rd., Thorofare, NJ 08086; phone: 609/848–1000) monthly, free/members only. "Personnel" describes around 40 positions for gastroenterological physicians, researchers, and assistants.

Archives of Dermatology (American Medical Association, Subscription Dept., 515 N. State St., Chicago, IL 60610; phone: 312/464–5000) monthly, $125/annual subscription (U.S.), $160/foreign. From 50 to 75 job openings for practitioners, businesses, and faculty appear under "Classified Advertising."

The Dendrite (American Academy of Neurology, 2221 University Ave., SE, Minneapolis, MN 55414; phone: 612/623–8115) bimonthly, $70/annual nonmember physician subscription, $25/junior AAN members, $50/AAN members and nonmember residents, $175/hospitals and physician groups, $250/executive search firms. Over 100 positions plus 30 fellowships, 15 placement firms, and "positions wanted" fill each issue.

Archives of Neurology (American Medical Association, Subscription Dept., 515 N. State St., Chicago, IL 60610; phone: 312/464–5000) monthly, $135/annual subscription (U.S.), $170/foreign. Fifty to 100 positions for neurologists, residencies, administration, and faculty are published under "Classified Advertising."

Obstetrics and Gynecology (Elsevers Science, 655 Avenue of the Americas, New York, NY 10010; phone: 212/989–5800) monthly, $115/annual subscription, $79/interns and residents. Sixty to 70 small display ads for job openings appear toward the end of each issue.

American Journal of Clinical Pathology (J.B. Lippincott, P.O. Box 1590, Hagerstown, MD 21741; phone: 800/777–2295) monthly with 2 supplements, $135/annual subscription (U.S.), $195/foreign. About 20 to 25 positions in pathology and laboratory medicine under "Classified."

Archives of Physical Medicine and Rehabilitation (W.B. Saunders Company, Periodicals, 6277 Sea Harbor Drive, Orlando, FL 32887–4800; phone: 800/654–2452) monthly, $118/annual nonmember subscription (U.S. and Canada), $145/foreign, $36/members, $18/student members. Sixty to 80 openings for physicians, rehabilitation practitioners, occupational therapists, psychologists, and speech therapists appear under "Classified Advertising."

CAMS Newsletter (Chinese American Medical Society, 281 Edgewood Ave., Teaneck, NJ 07666; phone: 201/833–1506) quarterly, available only to members; $100/annual dues. Three or four practitioner and academic positions appear under "Positions Available."

Archives of Ophthalmology (American Medical Association, Subscription Dept., 515 N. State St., Chicago, IL 60610; phone: 312/464–5000) monthly, $105/annual subscription (U.S.), $140/foreign. Around 30 openings for practitioners, residencies, faculty, and businesses appear under "Classified Advertising."

Journal of Visual Impairment and Blindness (American Foundation for the Blind, 15 W. 16th St., New York, NY 10011; phone: 212/620–2155) ten issues/year, $45/annual subscription (U.S.), $85/foreign. "Classified" contains ads for practitioners, teachers (elementary school through university), researchers, and administrators interested in working with the blind.

Journal of Perentology (Mosby Yearbook, 11830 Westline Industrial Drive, St. Louis, MO 63146; phone: 314/453–4406) quarterly, $50/annual subscription (U.S.), $62.50/foreign. The "Classified" section has around ten positions for nutritionists, perentologists (prenatal), and nurses.

Job services

National Physicians Register (8 Park Plaza, Suite 422J, Boston, MA 02116; phone: 800/342–1007) free. A physician submits a copy of her resume and gives her geographic preference and type of position sought. NPR creates a synopsis of the resume and assigns a code number to it. These synopses are published with code numbers rather than the physician's name in a bulletin sent bimonthly to 9,300 hospitals, clinics, group practices, and health maintenance organizations. The potential employer tells NPR which doctors interest it and NPR sends the contact information to the employer. Then, the employer can ask for a copy of her resume. (Employers usually ask for 20 to 50 persons per week at this service.) However, if the physician tells NPR that he doesn't want his name given out, NPR sends the job seeker a letter telling him a particular facility is interested in him and that he should contact the potential employer directly. Between 300 and 1,000 physicians are registered at any one time, although that number is growing. Serves both M.D. and osteopathic physicians.

AMA–FREIDA–AMA Fellowship and Residency Electronic Interactive Database (American Medical Association, P.O. Box 109050, Order Department, Chicago, IL 60610; phone: 800/621–8335) $550/members, $1,100/nonmembers, available on 3.5 inch and 5.25 inch MS–DOS disks. The only official listing of residency and fellowship programs accredited by the Accreditation Council for Graduate Medical Education, these disks provide detailed information on over 70 percent of the residency and fellowship programs available.

Women Physicians' Placement Service (American Medical Women's Association, 801 N. Fairfax St., Suite 400, Alexandria, VA 22314; phone: 703/838–0500) free/members, contact for nonmember fee structure. It will match female physicians with job openings.

National Resident Matching Program (2450 N Street, NW, Washington, DC 20037; phone: 202/828–0676) contact for rates. Matches graduating medical students with residencies.

Teratology Society Placement Service (Teratology Society, c/o Dr. Alan Hoberman, Argus Research Lab, Inc., 905 Sheehy Drive, Building A, Horsham, PA 19044; phone: 215/443–8710) $10/annual fee. Complete the service's resume form. This service sends your form to all registered employers. It is kept on file for a year or until you find a new job, whichever comes first. Positions are for physicians and scientists who do clinical, pre–clinical work, or research on birth defects.

Directories

AMWA Membership Directory (American Medical Women's Association, 801 N. Fairfax St., Suite 400, Alexandria, VA 22314; phone: 703/838–0500) $50/nonmembers, free/members, 350 pages, published in January of odd–numbered years. Lists physician members in all specialties.

Yearbook and Directory of Osteopathic Physicians (American Osteopathic Association, 142 Ontario St., Chicago, IL 60611–2864; phone: 312/280–5800) $55, annual. In nearly 700 pages, this directory offers both alphabetical and geographical listings of osteopathic physicians plus osteopathic hospitals, research centers, and postdoctoral training programs.

Optics Education Directory (SPIE, P.O. Box 10, Bellingham, WA 98227; phone: 206/676–3290) annual, free. Lists colleges and universities worldwide offering educational programs in optics and related fields.

CAMS Membership Directory (Chinese American Medical Society, 281 Edgewood Ave., Teaneck, NJ 07666; phone: 201/833–1506) free/members only, issued in even–numbered years.

ACPM Membership Directory (American College of Preventive Medicine, 1015 15th St., NW, Suite 403, Washington, DC 20005; phone: 202/789–0003) $20/nonmembers, free/members, published in the summer of even–numbered years.

Membership Directory for the Society of Nuclear Medicine (Society of Nuclear Medicine, 136 Madison Ave., New York, NY 10016; phone: 212/889–0717) $50/nonmembers, free/members, 1993. SNM intends to move to Reston, VA in October, 1994. If there's no forwarding number or address, call long distance directory assistance in Reston (1–703/555–1212) for the new phone number.

Directory of the American Academy of Orthopedic Surgeons (AAOS, 6300 N. River Rd., Rosemont IL 60018–4262; phone: 708/823–7186) available only to members, annual.

Nursing

Job ads in print

The Nurse Practitioner (Vernon Publications, 3000 Northup Way, Suite 200, Bellevue, WA 98004; phone: 206/827–9900) monthly, $39/annual subscription (U.S.), $45/foreign. You'll find around 50 job openings under "Positions and Opportunities" for nurse practitioners, pediatric, psychiatric, ob/gyn, geriatric, family, public health, occupational medicine, and faculty positions.

The American Nurse (American Nurses Association, 600 Maryland Ave., S.W., Suite 100 West, Washington, DC 20024–2571; phone: 800/274–4262) ten issues/year, $20/annual nonmember subscription, $10/students, free/members. "Positions Available" features about 35 job openings for nursing faculty including positions overseas.

American Journal of Nursing (555 W. 57th St., New York, NY 10019; phone: 212/582–8820) monthly, $35/annual subscription (U.S.), $45/Canada, $51/elsewhere. Over 30 nursing and nursing administrative and academic positions, plus privately operated placement services, appear in the "Classifieds Ads."

Nursing Outlook (Mosby Yearbook, 11830 W. Line Industrial Dr., St. Louis, MO 63146; phone: 800/325–4177) bimonthly, $29/annual subscription (U.S.), $41.03/Canada, $39/elsewhere. "Advertising–Classifieds" includes ten ads for nursing administrators, nurse educators, and deans of nursing schools.

ABNF Journal (Association of Black Nursing Faculty in Higher Education, 5832 Queens Cove, Lisle, IL 60532; phone: 708/969–3809) bimonthly, $50/nonmembers, free/members. The "Classifieds" carry ads for twelve to 22 nursing positions at universities and colleges.

NANPRH Newsletter (National Association of Nurse Practitioners in Reproductive Health (325 Pennsylvania Ave., SE, Washington, DC 20003; phone: 202/466–4825) three issues/year, $50/annual subscription. About 50 openings for nurse practitioners appear under "Job Openings." Most openings are with affiliates of Planned Parenthood.

Nursing Research (American Journal of Nursing Co., 555 W. 57th St., New York, NY 10019; phone: 212/582–8820) bimonthly, $35/annual subscription. About ten research positions appear under "Classified Advertising."

Nurse Educator (J.B. Lippincott Company, P.O. Box 1590, Hagerstown, MD 21741; phone: 800/777–2295) bimonthly, $43/annual subscription (U.S.), $65/foreign. About five university positions appear under "Classified."

The Journal of Nursing Administration (J. B. Lippincott Company, P.O. Box 1590, Hagerstown, MD 21741; phone: 800/777–2295) 11 issues/year, $52/annual subscription (U.S.), $79/foreign. Twenty positions for nurse administrators appear under "Classified."

Nursing and Health Care (National League for Nursing, 350 Hudson St., New York, NY 10014; phone: 800/669–1656) ten issues/year, $40/annual subscription. The "Classified" section features five to 10 pages of ads for hospital nursing staff as well as academic positions.

Journal of Nursing Education (SLACK, Inc., 6900 Grove Rd., Thorofare, NJ 08086–9447; phone: 800/257–8290) nine issues/year, $44/annual subscription (U.S.), $62/Canada plus 7 percent GST tax, $80/elsewhere. About six job openings appear under "Classified Marketplace."

Directory

Toll–Free Instant RSVP Nursing Career Directory (Springhouse Corp., 1111 Bethlehem Pike, Springhouse, PA 19477; phone: 215/646–8700) free. Published each January, this directory lists over 600 hospitals and health centers that are looking for nursing professionals. Job openings are listed under "Nurse Recruitment." You can be put directly in touch with a facility's nurse recruiter by calling 800/633–2648 (in Pennsylvania, call 800/633–2649) and giving your qualifications and specialty interests or sending in the reader service card from the directory. The RSVP line calls the nurse recruiter at the facilities of your choice. The nurse recruiter sends you an application form.

Pharmaceuticals

Job ads in print

American Association of Colleges of Pharmacy News (AACP, 1426 Prince St., Alexandria, VA 22314; phone: 703/739–2330) 11 issues/year, $25/annual subscription. Half of the newsletter is devoted to ten to 20 job vacancy notices for pharmacy educators and instructors.

Directories

Profile of Faculty (American Association of Colleges of Pharmacy, 1426 Prince St., Alexandria, VA 22314; phone: 703/739–2330) $25/nonmembers, free/members, published each February.

FASEB Directory of Members (Federation of American Societies for Experimental Biology, 9650 Rockville Pike, Bethesda, MD 20814; phone: 301/530–7000) $50/nonmembers, free/members of American Society for Pharmacology and Experimental Therapeutics; over 450 pages, annual.

Research

Also see the "Research" chapter.

Job ads in print

Cancer Research Journal (American Association for Cancer Research, 620 Chestnut St., Suite 816, Philadelphia, PA 19106–3483; phone: 215/440–9300) semimonthly, $415/annual nonmember subscription (U.S.), $475/foreign, free/members. The March 1, July 1, September 1, and November 1 issues include an "Employment Register" where 130 job seekers advertise themselves and around 100 research positions, generally post–doctoral, are advertised.

Directory

Directory of Members: American Association for Cancer Research (AACR, 620 Chestnut St., Suite 816, Philadelphia, PA 19106–3483; phone: 215/440–9300) $50/nonmembers, free/members, annual.

Technical and support staff

Job service

New England Technologists Section Job Hotline (Society of Nuclear Medicine, 136 Madison Ave., New York, NY 10016; phone: 212/889–0717) free. Medical technologists can call 800/562–6387 to register. You'll be sent a list of vacancies from Tom Starno who operates this service which is funded by the Tech Physicians of New England. To reach Tom Starno for more information, call 207/945–7186. Vacancies are kept on the list for three months.

Therapy–mental

Also see the "Social services" chapter.

Job ads in print

The APA Monitor (American Psychological Association, 750 First St., NE, Washington, DC 20002–4242; phone: 202/336–5500) $25/nonmember annual subscription (U.S.), $37/foreign, free/members. Jobs listed under "Position Openings." From 400 to 800 job ads for psychologists and support staff grace the pages of a typical issue.

Psychiatric News (American Psychiatric Association, 1400 K. St., NW, Washington, DC 20005; phone: 202/682–6250) semimonthly, $40/annual nonmember subscription (U.S.), $60/foreign, free/members. Display ads and the "Classified Notices" feature 300 to 350 job vacancies for staff psychiatrists and psychologists, administrative staff, and support staff.

National Council News (National Council of Community Mental Health Centers, Suite 320, 12300 Twinbrook Pkwy, Rockville, MD 20852; phone: 301/984–6200) 11 issues/year, $25/nonmember annual subscription, free/members. Jobs listed under "JOBank." Typical issue features 20 to 30 job ads for social workers and counselors, psychiatrists, psychologists, clinical workers, and administrative positions.

Communiqué (National Association of School Psychologists, 8455 Colesville Rd., Suite 1000, Silver Spring, MD 20919; phone: 301/608–0500) monthly, $30/annual nonmember subscription, free/members. About 20 job vacancies for psychologists in elementary schools through colleges appear under "Employment Notices." You are instructed to contact these employers to learn of any job openings they currently have.

Journal of the American Academy of Child & Adolescent Psychiatry (Williams & Wilkins Publisher, 428 E. Preston St., Baltimore, MD 21202; phones: 410/528–4294, 800/628–6423) nine issues/year, $85/annual subscription (U.S.), $110/foreign, $25/single issue price. Eight to ten ads appear for child and adolescent psychiatrists including: medical directors, division chiefs, and residency programs.

Psych Discourse (The Association of Black Psychologists, P.O. Box 55999, Washington, DC 20040–5999; phone: 202/722–0808) monthly, $95/nonmembers, free/members of ABP, $15/single issue. A handful of job ads appear for faculty positions.

AMHCA Advocate (American Mental Health Counselors' Association, 5999 Stevenson Ave., Alexandria, VA 22304; phones: 800/326–2642, 703/823–9800) ten issues/year, $25/nonmember annual subscription, free/members. Jobs listed under "Classifieds." About four job ads in the usual issue.

AACAP News (American Academy of Child and Adolescent Psychiatry, 3615 Wisconsin Ave., NW, Washington, DC 20016; phones: 800/333–7636, 202/966–7300) bimonthly, contact for availability and subscription rates. You'll generally find about six ads under "Positions" for practitioner and academic positions.

Family Therapy News (American Association for Marriage and Family Therapy, 1100 17th St., NW, Washington, DC 20036; phone: 202/452–0109) bimonthly, $25/annual subscription (U.S.), $35/foreign. "Classified Ads" has about 25 openings for marriage and family therapists including practitioners, researchers, pastoral counselors, faculty, and practices for sale.

ABA Newsletter (Association for Behavior Analysis, ATTEN: Patty DeLoach, 258 Wood Hall, Western Michigan University, Kalamazoo, MI 49008–5052; phone: 616/387–4495) quarterly, $20/annual nonmember subscription, free/members. "Positions available" lists from five to ten openings for psychologists, therapists, consultants, and faculty.

Job service

Psychiatric Placement Service (American Psychiatric Association, 1400 K St., NW, Washington, DC 20005; phone: 202/682–6000) free. Obtain an application form and submit it with your resume. After being matched with a vacancy, both the job seeker and the potential employer are notified. Resumes are kept on file indefinitely.

Directories

APA Membership Register (American Psychological Association, 750 First St., NE, Washington, DC 20002–4242; phone: 202/336–5500) $35/nonmembers, $22.50/members, published every year, except in years that the *APA Membership Directory,* described immediately below, is published. Most recent edition, 1994. Provides names and phone numbers of APA members.

APA Membership Directory (American Psychological Association, 750 First St., NE, Washington, DC 20002–4242; phone: 202/336–5500) $70/nonmembers, $50/members, published every four years. Most recent edition, July 1993. Provides names, phone numbers, and educational backgrounds of APA members.

AMHA Membership Directory (Association of Mental Health Administrators, 60 Revere, Suite 500, Northbrook, IL 60062; phone: 708/480–9626) contact them for price. This directory of mental health administrators was first published in August 1991.

Mental Health Directory (Superintendent of Documents, Government Printing Office, P.O. Box 371954, Pittsburgh, PA 15250; phone: 301/443–2792) $23. Stock number 017–024–01419–2. Prepared by the National Institute of Mental Health, this directory includes hospitals, group homes, and halfway houses by city and state.

National Registry of Community Mental Health Services (National Council of Community Mental Health Centers, Suite 320, 12300 Twinbrook Pkwy, Rockville, MD 20852; phone: 301/317–8912) $59/nonmembers, $29/members, December 1991. This directory contains information on over 1,900 agencies in the U.S. and possessions.

AMHA Membership Directory (Association of Mental Health Administrators, 60 Revere, Suite 500, Northbrook, IL 60062; phone: 708/480–9626) contact them for price. This directory of mental health administrators was first published in August 1991.

Association of State and Provincial Psychology Boards Membership Roster (Association of State & Provencial Psychology Boards, P.O. Box 4389, Montgomery, AL 36103; phone: 205/832–4580) $4, prepaid. Lists addresses and phone numbers of state and provincial psychology licensing boards in the U.S. and Canada.

Association for Behavior Analysis Membership Directory (ABA, 258 Wood Hall, Western Michigan University, Kalamazoo, MI 49008–5052; phone: 616/387–4495) $10, 80 pages, issued each February. Lists the names, addresses, phones, fax numbers, and specialty for 2,300 members.

Grants for Mental Health, Addictions & Crisis Services (The Foundation Center, 79 Fifth Ave., New York, NY 10003–3076; phones: 800/424–9836, within New York State call 212/620–4230) $65 plus $4.50/shipping, October 1993. Describes recent foundation grants of at least $10,000 given to hospitals, health centers, residential treatment facilities, group homes, and mental health associations for addiction prevention and treatment, for hotline/crisis intervention services, and for public education and research. This directory is useful for identifying foundations and grant recipients for which you may wish to work.

Salary survey

Survey of Salary Benefits and Staffing Patterns of Community Mental Health Providers (National Council of Community Mental Health Centers, Suite 320, 12300 Twinbrook Pkwy, Rockville, MD 20852; phone: 301/317–8912) $69/nonmembers, $49/members, published in December 1991. Based on a sample of over 500 community mental health providers, this survey gives salary and fringe benefit figures by region, service area type, and nationally.

Therapy–physical

Also see the "Social services" chapter.

Job ads in print

ASHA (American Speech–Language–Hearing Association, 10801 Rockville Pike, Rockville, MD 20852; phones: 800/638–8255, 301/897–5700) 11 issues/year, $90/annual nonmember subscription, free/members. Around 200 ads in the "ASHA Classifieds" describe openings for speech–language pathologists, audiologists, speech scientists, and speech and hearing professors.

Guidepost (American Rehabilitation Counseling Association, 5999 Stevenson Ave., Alexandria, VA 22304–3300; phone: 703/823–9800, ext. 244) 12 issues/year, $30/annual subscription. "Employment Classifieds" describe around 35 vacancies for psychologists and counselors in private practice, agencies, and universities.

Physical Therapy (American Physical Therapy Association, 1111 N. Fairfax St., Alexandria, VA 22314; phones: 800/999–2782, 703/684–2782) monthly, $60/annual nonmember subscription ($80 via first class mail), free/members. About 40 ads for physical therapists and assistants, faculty, and related positions appear under "Classified Advertising."

PT Bulletin (3700 Wheeler Ave., Alexandria, VA 22304; phone: 900/826–4150) weekly, $80/members of the American Physical Therapy Association or physical therapists only. About 400 ads for physical therapists, PT assistants, rehab directors, and physical medicine in the fields of: acute care, long–term care, geriatrics, orthopedics, sports medicine, industrial rehab, home health care, and hand therapy.

Occupational Therapist Weekly (164 Rollins Ave., Suite 301, Rockville, MD 20852; phone: 301/881–2490) weekly, free to qualified occupational therapists. Around 225 job openings for occupational therapists fill this tabloid.

Newsletter of the American Art Therapy Association (AATA, 1202 Allanson Rd., Mundelein, IL 60060; phone: 708/949–6064) quarterly, $16/annual nonmember subscription (U.S. and Canada), $28/elsewhere, free/members. Positions for art therapists in rehabilitation medical facilities and universities appear under "Opportunities" when available.

Update (American Alliance for Health, Physical Education, Recreation and Dance, 1900 Association Dr., Reston, VA 22091; phone: 703/476–3400) eight issues/year, $45/annual nonmember subscription, free/members. "Job Exchange" features 30 or more jobs largely with universities as well as numerous graduate assistantships and grants.

Journal PERD (American Alliance for Health, Physical Education, Recreation and Dance, 1900 Association Dr., Reston, VA 22091; phone: 703/476–3400) monthly, $65/annual nonmember subscription, free/members. The "Classifieds" feature about five positions with camps and universities.

Journal of Cognitive Rehabilitation (NeuroScience Publishers, 6555 Carrollton Ave., Indianapolis, IN 46220; phone: 317/257–9672) bimonthly, $35/annual subscription (U.S.), $40/Canada, $50/elsewhere. You'll find about five ads for administrators and speech pathologists, psychologists, physical therapists, and occupational therapists under "Job Positions."

NCRE Newsletter (National Council on Rehabilitation Education, Department of Special Education, Utah State University, Logan, UT 84322–2870; phone: 801/750–3241) bimonthly, free/members only. About two or three ads for rehabilitation personnel appear under "Display Ads."

Job service

The Job Bank (164 Rollins Ave., Suite 301, Rockville, MD 20852; phone: 301/881–2490) contact for details. If you have a computer modem you can access this database to see about 650 job vacancies for occupational therapists.

Directories

ASHA Membership Directory (American Speech–Language–Hearing Association, 10801 Rockville Pike, Rockville, MD 20852; phones: 800/638–8255, 301/897–5700) $60/nonmembers, $40/members, published in odd–numbered years.

National Directory of Services in Audiology and Speech–Language Pathology (American Speech–Language–Hearing Association, 10801 Rockville Pike, Rockville, MD 20852; phones: 800/638–8255, 301/897–5700) biannual each January, last issued 1993. Gives names, addresses, phone numbers, and contact person at facilities offering audiology and/or speech–language pathology services.

Membership Directory of the American Art Therapy Association (AATA, 1202 Allanson Rd., Mundelein, IL 60060; phone: 708/949–6064) $50/individual nonmembers, $100/nonmember institutions, $10/members, new edition after December of even–numbered years.

American Horticultural Therapy Association Annual Membership Directory (AHTA, 362–A Christopher Ave., Gaithersburg, MD 20879; phone: 301/948–3010) free/members only, issued each January.

Salary surveys

1990 Member Data Survey: Summary Report (Occupational Therapy Association, Research and Evaluation Division, 1383 Piccard Dr., Rockville, MD 20850; phone: 301/948–9626) contact for price, published every three or four years. Based on returns from 50 percent of its 40,000 members, this report discloses details on member salaries, demographics, education, and types of jobs.

Membership Survey Report (American Art Therapy Association, 1202 Allanson Rd., Mundelein, IL 60060; phone: 708/949–6064) $2.75/nonmembers, 75¢/members, issued in June of odd–numbered years. Lists areas of specialization, educational degrees, work settings, ages of populations, and salaries.

Chapter 15

Housing, planning, and development

*Also see the entries for each of these specialties in
the **Government Job Finder**.*

Housing, planning, and development

Job ads in print

Planners Network (Planners Network, 5th Floor, 1601 Connecticut Ave.,
NW, Washington, DC 20009; phone: 202/347–1457) bimonthly, free/mem-
bers only; annual dues: $15/unemployed and students, all others: $25 +
$1 per $1000 earned over $10,000. Jobs listed under "Job." Typical issue
features about five to 20 jobs in housing, community development, organizing, and university faculty and research.

The NonProfit Times (190 Tamarack Cr., Skillman, NJ 08558; phone:
609/921–1251) monthly, free to qualified non–profit organization executives, $49/annual subscription for others. Jobs listed under "National Em-
ployment Non–Profit Marketplace." Around 30 jobs per issue in planning,
economic development, public administration, and non–profit associations.

Shelterforce (National Housing Institute, 439 Main St., Orange, NJ 07050;
phone: 201/678–3110) bimonthly, $18/annual individual subscription, $28/li-
braries, institutions, and law firms; add $15 for delivery to foreign countries.

131

Under "Jobs" you'll find five to ten positions largely with non–profit economic/community development agencies, housing authorities, and in organizing.

Roundup (National Low–Income Housing Information Service, 1012 14th St., NW, Suite 1200, Washington, DC 20005; phone: 202/662–1530) ten issues/year, $35/annual subscription, $10/low–income subscribers. "Job Openings" carries ads for about eight positions in community and economic development, housing, organizing, and rural development.

Historic Preservation News (National Trust for Historic Preservation, 1785 Massachusetts Ave., NW, Washington, DC 20036; phone: 202/673–4075) free/members only, $15/year annual dues. Five job ads listed under "Marketplace" for positions in the preservation field.

Council News (American Economic Development Council, 9801 W. Higgins, Suite 540, Rosemont, IL 60018; phone: 708/692–9944) 10 issues/year, available to members only, annual membership: $265, plus $15 processing fee first year only; $140, plus $15 processing fee first year only, when another person in your office is already a member. Jobs listed under "Career Opportunities." About 6 job ads per issue.

Economic Developments (National Council for Urban Economic Development, 1730 K St., NW, Suite 915, Washington, DC 20006; phone: 202/223–4735) 24 issues/year, free/members only; annual dues: $275. Jobs listed under "Job Mart." Typical issue sports three to ten job ads.

City Limits (40 Prince St., New York, NY 10012; phone: 212/925–9820) ten issues/year; $20/annual subscription for individuals and community groups, $35/all others. About ten positions ranging from grant writers to administrators for housing, social work, community development, and neighborhood organizations in New York City are listed under "Job Ads."

AAG Newsletter (Association of American Geographers, 1710 16th St., NW, Washington, DC 20009; phone: 202/234–1450) monthly, available only to members. From 25 to 50 positions, primarily academic, are listed under "Jobs in Geography."

Job Openings for Economists (American Economic Association, 2014 Broadway, Suite 305, Nashville, TN 37203; phone: 615/322–2595) bimonthly, $25/annual nonmember subscription (U.S.), $34/foreign, $15/AEA regular members, $7.50/AEA junior members. Among the 150 plus jobs in a typical issue are a number in the non–profit sector including university faculty.

Job Placement Bulletin (National Economics Association, School of Business, University of Michigan, Ann Arbor, MI 48109–1234; phone: 313/763–0121) available only to members. About eight jobs for economists appear in the typical issue.

Public Sector Job Bulletin (P.O. Box 1222, Newton, IA 50208–1222; phone: 515/791–9019) biweekly, $19/annual subscription, $12/six months. Among the 30 to 50 job openings in each issue are a growing number of positions in economic development and housing with non–profit entities.

AIC Newsletter (American Institute of Constructors, 9887 N. Gandy Blvd., Suite 104, St. Petersburg, FL 33702; phone: 813/578–0317) bimonthly, free/members only. Some faculty positions and "constructors" (estimators, project managers, project engineers, etc.) are sometimes scattered throughout.

Urban Affairs (University of Delaware, Newark, DE 19716; phone: 302/831–2394) five issues/year, free/members, contact for nonmember price. Jobs listed under "Positions Available." About three to ten job ads are printed in a typical issue. Lists university teaching positions in urban affairs and related areas.

The New Careers Directory: Internships and Professional Opportunities in Technology and Social Change (Student Pugwash USA, 1638 R St., NW, Suite 32, Washington, DC 20009; phone: 202/328–6555) $18, $10/students; add $3 shipping, last published in 1993. Offers full details on where and how to apply for internships and entry–level jobs in development.

Job service

Resume Referral Service (American Economic Development Council, 9801 W. Higgins, Suite 540, Rosemont, IL 60018; phone: 708/692–9944) $100/nonmembers for 12 months, free to members. Return form with 10 copies of your resume. AEDC lets you know when it matches your qualifications with a potential employer, but it is up to the employer to contact you for the interview. Once you are in the resume referral service you will be sent by first class mail job listings from hiring organizations as they come into the AEDC office. You are responsible for contacting prospective employers. Ads will be mailed within a week of receipt.

Directories

Directory of State Housing Coalitions (National Low–Income Housing Information Service, 1012 14th St., NW, Suite 1200, Washington, DC 20005; phone: 202/662–1530) $5, most recent edition published May 1991, 26 pages. Includes 87 organizations with synopses of 41 of them.

American Planning Association Membership Directory (American Planning Association, 1313 E. 60th St., Chicago, IL 60637; phone: 312/955–9100) $36.95 plus $4.95 shipping, published in even–numbered years, although it is unknown at this time if APA will publish this again after 1992. Alphabetical listing of 26,000 professional planners and planning commissioners plus geographical index and specialty index.

AICP Roster (American Institute of Certified Planners, c/o American Planning Association, 1776 Massachusetts Ave., NW, Washington, DC 20036; phone: 202/872–0611) $30/nonmember, $20/APA member, free/AICP members, published in even–numbered years. AICP is an institute within the American Planning Association. This directory lists the 7,000+ AICP members alphabetically and by city within each state. Although AICP membership is achieved by passing a demanding test, it does not indicate that AICP members are better qualified nor more competent than other professional planners. Since titles are listed, this is a good source to identify directors of municipal and county planning departments and related departments.

CUED Directory (National Council for Urban Economic Development, 1730 K St., NW, Suite 915, Washington, DC 20006; phone: 202/223–4735) free/members only, published annually. Lists all private corporate members of National Council for Urban Economic Development.

Trends & Economic Development Organizations: A Directory (National Council for Urban Economic Development, 1730 K St., NW, Suite 915, Washington, DC 20006; phone: 202/223–4735) $225/nonmembers, $145/members. Profiles 114 economic development organizations from 35 metropolitan areas

Who's Who in Economic Development (American Economic Development Council, 9801 W. Higgins, Suite 540, Rosemont, IL 60018; phone: 708/692–9944) available only to members, included in dues. Published each August. Geographical and alphabetical listings of members throughout the world. Also includes geographical and alphabetical lists of certified economic developers.

Membership Directory (American Institute of Constructors, 9887 N. Gandy Blvd., Suite 104, St. Petersburg, FL 33702; phone: 813/578–0317) free/members only, issued every June.

Grants for Community Development, Housing & Employment (The Foundation Center, 79 Fifth Ave., New York, NY 10003–3076; phones: 800/424–9836, within New York State call 212/620–4230) $65 plus $4.50/shipping, October 1993. Describes recent foundation grants of at least $10,000 given to community organizations, government agencies, and universities for a wide range of social services, housing and urban development programs, including business services and federated giving programs. This directory is useful for identifying foundations and grant recipients for which you may wish to work.

Grants for Homeless (The Foundation Center, 79 Fifth Ave., New York, NY 10003–3076; phones: 800/424–9836, within New York State call 212/620–4230) $65 plus $4.50/shipping, October 1993. Describes recent foundation grants of at least $10,000 given to shelters and temporary housing services, legal rights and advocacy programs, food services and health care, and to services for homeless families, youth, and children. This directory is useful for identifying foundations and grant recipients for which you may wish to work.

Grants for Public Policy and Public Affairs (The Foundation Center, 79 Fifth Ave., New York, NY 10003–3076; phones: 800/424–9836, within New York State call 212/620–4230) $65 plus $4.50/shipping, October 1993. Describes recent foundation grants of at least $10,000 for government and public administration, public affairs, leadership development, foreign policy, international peace and security, and a wide range of public policy studies. This directory is useful for identifying foundations and grant recipients for which you may wish to work.

Salary surveys

CUED Salary Survey (National Council for Urban Economic Development, 1730 K St., Suite 915, NW, Washington, DC 20006; phone: 202/223–4735) $75/nonmembers, $45/members, published every two years.

1992–1993 Compensation and Benefits Survey (American Economic Development Council, 9801 W. Higgins Rd., Suite 540, Rosemont, IL 60018; phone: 708/692–9944) $75/nonmembers, $50/members, issued every three years. Profiles organization background, base salary, and benefits for economic development professionals.

Annual Graduating Senior Placement Survey (American Institute of Constructors, 9887 N. Gandy Blvd., Suite 104, St. Petersburg, FL 33702; phone: 813/578–0317) $25/nonmembers, free/members, published each October. Reports on the salaries of seniors in construction who graduated the previous spring.

Chapter 16

International jobs

International jobs

To avoid being labeled an "ugly American" when looking and applying for work outside the U.S., you will have to adapt your notions of job hunting to the cultures of the countries in which you wish to work as well as to any different hiring procedures or customs they may have.

In addition to introducing you to periodicals and directories that will facilitate your job search abroad, this chapter presents information on a number of books that describe the different hiring procedures and customs you will encounter in other countries. Also, be sure to look under "Foreign jobs" in the index of this book to identify sources of foreign positions noted in chapters two through 30.

Before you begin your search for non–profit sector positions outside the United States, you should first develop a pretty good idea where you would like to work. It may help your decision to know the political, social, and economic characteristics of the countries you are considering for your next home.

A good place to start is at your local library with a copy of the ***Worldwide Government Directory*** (Belmont Publications, sold by Gale Research, Inc., 835 Penobscot Bldg., Detroit, MI 48226; phone: 800/877–4253; $325, published annually). This rather thorough tome proffers detailed information on the governments of over 195 countries. Most valuable for you, however, are the detailed listings of each country's embassies and consulates, including United Nation's missions; addresses, phones, and officers of central banks; and basic facts on each country such as the capital city, official and business languages, religious affiliations of the population, local currency and rate of exchange against the U.S. dollar, international telephone dialing code, national holidays, and the next scheduled presidential election and political parties, if any.

This directory also furnishes information on over 100 international organizations and the United Nations.

Another similar volume is *Countries of the World and Their Leaders Yearbook 1993* (Gale Research, Inc., 835 Penobscot Bldg., Detroit, MI 48226; phone: 800/877–4253; $160, 1,900 pages, published annually; *Supplement* published in June between annual editions costs $81) which includes the U.S. State Department's "Background Notes on the Countries of the World;" basic social, economic, and political data on 170 countries; current travel warnings from the State Department; and U.S. embassies and consulates and their personnel. The "Travel Notes" section describes the immigration and customs requirements of each country. This is a very useful source for determining which countries should be part of your overseas job search.

The *Handbook of the Nations* (Gale Research, Inc., 835 Penobscot Bldg., Detroit, MI 48226; phone: 800/877–4253; $105, 420 pages, 1993) contains timely information on the governments, politics, sociology, and economies of nearly 250 nations.

Specialty associations in foreign countries provide many of the same job services offered by associations of government professionals in the United States. We've included job sources offered by some of those associations. You can identify other professional associations outside the U.S. by using the *Encyclopedia of Associations: International Organizations 1994* (Gale Research, Inc., 835 Penobscot Bldg., Detroit, MI 48226; phone: 800/877–4253; $455, 3,000 pages; September 1993) which describes around 13,000 international and foreign national organizations in 180 countries outside the U.S. in government, public administration, legal, social welfare, public affairs, and health/medical.

For more details on choosing work abroad. Six books, the first two by Caryl and Ronald Krannich, are almost essential for starting your international job search. In *The Complete Guide to International Jobs & Careers* (Impact Publications, $13.95, 1992, 320 pages; available from Planning/Communications' catalog at the end of this book), the Krannichs present the most effective approaches for entering the international job market and describe, in excruciating detail, each of the different sectors of the international job market including the non–profit sector. The book is divided into three parts: understanding and action; effective job search skills and strategies; and finding your best work setting, which examines job opportunities with non–profit organizations and volunteer opportunities,

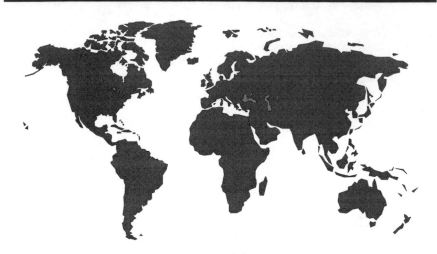

associations, foundations, educational organizations, government, international organizations, contractors, consultants, and business and travel industry.

Moving beyond this introduction, the Krannichs get down to the nitty gritty in **The Almanac of International Jobs & Careers** (Impact Publications, $19.95, 1994, 348 pages; available from Planning/Communications' catalog at the end of this book), where they provide the names, addresses, and phone numbers of over 1,000 key international employers such as international organizations, education and teaching, colleges and universities, non-profit corporations and foundations, private contractors and consultants, government, and businesses. The book goes into detail on work permit requirements, job listings, and relocation resources.

Also extremely valuable is the **Guide to Careers in World Affairs** by the editors of the Foreign Policy Association (Impact Publications, $14.95, 1993, 422 pages; available from Planning/Communications' catalog beginning on page 311). Most of this book is devoted to describing non–profit and private sector international employers. For each potential employer, you'll learn about the types of positions they fill and how to apply.

Very often a volunteer position or internship can lead to a permanent job. If you're interested in internships outside the U.S., you should see Will Cantrell's and Francine Modderno's book, **International Internships and Volunteer Programs: International Options for Students and Professionals** (WorldWise Books, $18.95, 233 pages, 1992; impossible to find in bookstores, this book is available from Planning/Communication's catalog at the end of this book). The first chapter focuses on international organizations that offer internships and the U.S. government. The next chapter focuses on academic programs tied directly to a college credit–granting program. The third chapter is devoted to independent internships and traineeships not tied to an academic program, both in the U.S. and abroad.

Chapter four reports on volunteer opportunities with non–profit organizations. Although most are unpaid, a few do entail some remuneration for you. The final chapter reports on several foreign work opportunities that are not strictly internships or volunteer positions. For each potential employer, the book tells you the types of internships offered, requirements, application procedures, and whom to contact. Internships covered include those in the U.S. and assignments abroad.

Work permits

Restrictive work permit, visa, or immigration policies may interfere with your plans to work outside the U.S. of A. Most nations require workers from abroad to acquire a resident visa that includes a work permit. Usually, a foreigner must apply for the visa and work permit before entering the country, although a few nations allow you to apply after being in the country and obtaining a job. But generally, you've got to have an employment contract, visa, and work permit before arriving in the country.

Work permits are temporary and must be periodically renewed. The permit and visa may restrict the number of times you can enter and leave the country. Some countries invalidate the work permit if you leave the country even once. You may also be restricted as to how much local currency you can take out of the country. You must pay local taxes and special resident visa fees.

Your best bet is to always learn about the local restrictions on foreign nationals before seeking a job in a particular country. Foreign embassies and consulates in the U.S. are good sources for information on work permits and visas. These are listed in some of the directories identified at the beginning of this chapter and in *The Almanac of International Jobs & Careers* discussed above. Try to have your employer handle all the paperwork necessary for you to obtain a visa and work permit.

Do not enter a country on a tourist visa and then seek work. You'll be able to find only menial, low–paying jobs and probably will not be eligible for any health benefits. So, be sure to arrange for your job, visa if needed, and work permit before you pack up for a foreign abode.

Job ads in print

Prices are given in U.S. dollars unless noted otherwise.

Advertisements for overseas employment frequently appear in the national publications listed in chapters 2 through 30. Look in the Index of this book under "Foreign jobs" to identify sources in these chapters. Be sure to also check the classified and business sections of the Sunday *New York*

Times (229 W. 43rd St., New York, NY 10036; phone: 212/556–1234) and the *Washington Post* (1150 15th St. NW, Washington, DC 20071; phone: 202/334–6000) where overseas jobs are often advertised.

International Employment Opportunities (Route 2, Box 305, Stanardsville, VA 22973; phone: 8804/985–6444) biweekly, $29/two–month subscription, $49/four months, $69/six months, $129/annual subscription, $7.50/single issue. You'll find announcements for around 500 jobs in the U.S. and abroad with non–profit entities and international institutions (as well as with the U.S. federal government and with private corporations) in foreign affairs, international trade and finance, international development and assistance, foreign languages, international program administration, international education and exchange programs.

International Employment Gazette (Global Resources Organization, Ltd., 1525 Wade Hampton Blvd., Greenville, SC 29609; phone: 800/882–9188, phones: 800/882–9188, 803/235–4444) semiweekly, $95/annual subscription (U.S.), $135/elsewhere; $55/six–month subscription (U.S.), $65/elsewhere; $35/three–month subscription (U.S.), $45/foreign. Among this magazine's 400 advertisements for positions overseas are a fair number that are with non–profits.

Community Jobs (ACCESS: Networking in the Public Interest, 50 Beacon St., Boston, MA 02108; phone: 617/720–5627) monthly, individuals: $29/three–month subscription, $39/six–month subscription. Also available at bookstores. Among the 200 to 350 non–profit job vacancies and internships in every issue are 30 to 50 positions outside the U.S., primarily in "Third World" countries. You'll usually find positions in agriculture (including economics, marketing, and production) public health, mental health, water or sanitation, and for physicians

International Jobs Bulletin (Southern Illinois University, Career Services, Woody Hall, Carbondale, IL 62901; phone: 618/453–2391) biweekly, monthly, $25/20 issues, $15/ten issues, $1.50/single issue. Write for free sample issue. The typical issue contains over 75 ads for jobs overseas for accountants, physicians, computer, economists, engineers, translators, teachers, physical therapists, horticulturists, etc.

International Employment Hotline (P.O. Box 3030, Oakton, VA 22124; phone: 403/620–1972) monthly, $36/annual subscription, $25/six–month subscription. Lists job descriptions (and to whom to apply) by country of assignment. Most ads for jobs with non–profit groups. Each issue is eight pages with two articles as well as job announcements. From 30 to 100 job descriptions are in a single issue, but usually towards the lower end of that range.

International Affairs Career Bulletin (Jeffries & Associates, 17200 Hughes Rd., Poolesville, MD 20837; phone: 301/972–8034) monthly, $95/annual subscription. Includes job listings for positions outside the U.S. with development agencies, academia, and non–profit organizations. Also includes listings for internships and fellowships.

United Nations Job News (Thomas F. Burola & Associates, Suite 7R, 6477 Telephone Rd., Ventura, CA 93003; phone: 805/647–7256, fax: 805/654–1708) bimonthly, $110/annual subscription, $55/six–month subscription, $39/three–month subscription. This newsletter compiles 50 to 100 job ads from other periodicals as well as current vacancy notices it receives for international positions with the United Nations and other international organizations.

TESOL Placement Bulletin (Teachers of English to Speakers of Other Languages, Inc., 1600 Cameron St., Suite 300, Alexandria, VA 22314–2751; phone: 703/836–0774) bimonthly, $20/members only (U.S., Mexico, and Canada), $30/elsewhere (air mail); annual dues range from $38 to $69 depending on category; contact TESOL for membership application; free if you subscribe to the *TESOL Placement Service* described below under "Job Services." Each issue features 60 or so ads for positions to teach English in the U.S. and abroad, and for curriculum developers and materials writers.

Career Network (National Council for International Health, Suite 600, 1701 K St., NW, Washington, DC 20006; phone: 202/833–5900) $120/non-members, $60/members ($75 membership rate), annual. Anywhere from 30 to 40 positions in internationalhealth care.

New Scientist (IPC Magazines, Ltd., Freepost 1061, Hawwards Heath, England RH16 3ZA) weekly, £110/United Kingdom annual subscription, $130 (U.S. dollars)/annual subscription via air mail to the U.S., $170 (Canadian dollars)/annual subscription via air mail to Canada. Over 100 science positions in England are listed throughout, including government jobs. The publisher failed to respond to our request to verify our information about this periodical. If you reach them, please use the "Reader Feedback Form" on page 298 to tell us what changes we should make to this entry.

Sound Opportunities (Nonprofit Community Network, 2708 Elliott Ave., Seattle, WA 98121; phone: 206/441–8280) biweekly, $13/four–month subscription. Includes ads for two or three jobs or internships with non–profits outside the U.S. under "International Listings."

International Internships and Volunteer Programs: International Options for Students and Professionals (WorldWise Books, $18.95, 233 pages, 1992; impossible to find in bookstores, this book is available from Planning/Communication's catalog at the end of this book). The bulk of this book focuses on internships with non–profit groups throughout the world.

For each potential employer, the book tells you the types of internships offered, requirements, application procedures, and whom to contact. Internships covered are both U.S. based and assignments abroad.

Internships and Careers in International Affairs (United Nations Association of the United States of America, 485 Fifth Ave., New York, NY 10017; phone: 212/697–3232) $10/prepaid, published in September of odd–numbered years. Lists overseas and domestic internships with U.S. government agencies, the United Nations, non–profits, and private organizations involved in international affairs. Explains the qualifications employers seek and names resources to find employment in international affairs here and abroad.

Job services

Talent Bank (TransCentury Corporation (1901 N. Fort Meyer Drive, Suite 1017, Arlington, VA 22209; phone: 703/351–5500) free. Obtain their "Professional Skills Registration Form." Submit a completed form with your resume. This service chooses consultants usually for short–term international development jobs abroad. Occasionally, someone from another international development corporation will request resumes which TransCentury forwards to the corporation. Resumes are kept on file indefinitely. Typical positions filled include accountants, agriculturists, administrators, medical personnel, teachers, refugee affairs, engineers, project managers, forestry, and environment.

International Placement Network (Global Resources Organization, Ltd., 1525 Wade Hampton Blvd., Greenville, SC 29609; phone: 800/882–9188) $45/U.S., $50/elsewhere. Request an application form. Two to three weeks after submitting your completed form and check, you get a printout of foreign positions that fit your occupational interests and geographical preferences. Printouts come with four jobs per page. The typical printout runs 15 to 40 pages.

International Career Databank (Jeffries & Associates, 17200 Hughes Rd., Poolesville, MD 20837; phone: 301/972–8034) updated monthly, $275/first year subscription plus $5/shipping, $125/each subsequent year. This database which works only on IBM–compatible computers with Microsoft Windows enables you to search its monthly listings for job openings, internships, and fellowships outside the U.S. in the non–profit sector (as well as government and the private sector), including international development positions, jobs in academia, jobs in Africa for Africans, and jobs in Latin America for Latin Americans. The database also contains general information on working overseas, how to form your own business, and self–employment.

TESOL Placement Service (Teachers of English to Speakers of Other Languages, Inc., 1600 Cameron St., Suite 300, Alexandria, VA 22314–2751; phone: 703/836–0774) $20/annual member only registration fee (U.S., Canada, and Mexico), $30/elsewhere (air mail); annual dues range from $38 to $69 depending on category; contact TESOL for membership application. Complete the "Candidate's Registration Form" which enables you to specify your worldwide geographical preferences and your qualifications. When a match is made, the prospective employer contacts you for an interview. Teaching positions are with units of higher education, public schools, government agencies, and international schools in both the public and private sectors.

Directories

Guide to Careers in World Affairs (Foreign Policy Association; available from Planning/Communication's catalog at the end of this book) $14.95, 422 pages, 1993. Furnishing an overview of alternative careers in international affairs, this book addresses careers and identifies potential employers including non–profit associations throughout the world. Includes internships with non–profits.

Directory of International Careers (Jeffries & Associates, 17200 Hughes Rd., Poolesville, MD 20837; phone: 301/972–8034) $75 plus $5/shipping, 600 pages, published each March. In addition to the printed directory, you get MS–DOS floppy disks with names, addresses, and phone numbers of organizations engaged in international employment in ASCII format which can be used with virtually any word processor to send mail–merged letters. In addition to describing how to approach virtually any type of international employment, this directory is filled with addresses and phone numbers for non–profits that place employees in jobs overseas, international organizations, groups and government agencies that hire environmental positions worldwide, translating and linguistics, general consulting, the U.S. foreign service (and its examination requirements), and information on grants, fellowships, and internships. You'll also learn how to form your own business and engage in international publishing.

Directory of Only International Recruiters (Thomas F. Burola & Associates, Suite 7R, 6477 Telephone Rd., Ventura, CA 93003; phone: 805/647–7256, fax: 805/654–1708) $65. We haven't been able to obtain a copy of this directory, but it supposedly gives you just what its title proffers. This is a useful source for identifying potential recruiters to work for as well as to find recruiters to help you find a job overseas.

Directory of Consulting Firms to USAID that Hire Professionals (Thomas F. Burola & Associates, Suite 7R, 6477 Telephone Rd., Ventura, CA 93003; phone: 805/647–7256, fax: 805/654–1708) $85. We haven't been able to obtain a copy of this directory, but it presumably gives you just what its title describes.

Career Opportunities in International Development in Washington D.C. (Overseas Development Network, 333 Valencia St., Suite 330, San Francisco, CA 94103; phones: 415/451–4202, 415/431–9205) $10, annual. Lists association members and non–profit organizations by phone number and organizational background.

Encyclopedia of Women's Associations Worldwide (Gale Research, Inc., 835 Penobscot Bldg., Detroit, MI 48226–4094; phone: 800/877–4253) $80, 850 pages, 1993. Describes 6,000 organizations throughout the world concerned with women and women's issues. Each entry includes contact person, address, phone, fax, and, usually, a description. This is a good, almost affordable source for identifying non–profit organizations in this specialty.

Directory of U.S. International Health Organizations (National Council for International Health, 1701 K Street, Suite 600, Washington, DC 20006; phone: 202/833–5900) $60/nonmembers, $30/members plus $3/shipping, 1992. A comprehensive listing of organizations working in the international health field. Information includes organization size, type, budget, area of specialty, contact person, address, and phone number.

World Guide to Scientific Associations and Learned Societies (K.G. Saur; available from Reed Reference Publishing, P.O. Box 31, New Providence, NJ 07974; phone: 800/521–8110) $275 plus seven percent shipping and handling, 940 pages, 1990. Includes 18,000 international, national, and regional associations from 150 countries in every area of science, culture, and technology. Also included are 12,000 association periodicals and bulletins; index of official association abbreviations; and a subject index of activities organized by country.

Yearbook of International Organizations 1993/94 (K.G. Saur; available from Reed Reference Publishing, P.O. Box 31, New Providence, NJ 07974; phone: 800/521–8110) $325/volume one, $325/volume two, $325/volume three, $875/complete set, add seven percent shipping and handling for all orders. Includes over 28,000 organizations active in over 200 countries. *Volume one: Organization Descriptions and Index* includes 28,000 entries covering everything from inter–governmental and national bodies to conferences and religious orders and fraternities. *Volume two: International*

Organization Participation is designed for use by national and international agencies, embassies, ministries, universities and law libraries. *Volume three: Global Action Networks* gives an overview of the range and network of activities of the international organizations themselves organized alphabetically by subject and by region. Groups international and regional bodies under 4,300 categories of common ideas,  aims, and activities. This is also available on CD–ROM. Call 800/323–3288 for price and details.

Grants for Foreign & International Programs (The Foundation Center, 79 Fifth Ave., New York, NY 10003–3076; phones: 800/424–9836, within New York State call 212/620–4230) $65 plus $4.50/shipping, October 1993. Describes recent foundation grants of at least $10,000 given to institutions and organizations outside the U.S. and to domestic recipients for international activities, development and relief, peace and security, arms control, policy research, human rights, conferences, and research. This directory is useful for identifying foundations and grant recipients for which you may wish to work.

Canadian Almanac and Directory 1993 (Gale Research, Inc., 835 Penobscot Bldg., Detroit, MI 48226; phone: 800/877–4253) $145, 1,300 pages, 1992. Includes descriptions of professional associations based in Canada.

Canadian Environmental Directory 1992 (Gale Research, Inc., 835 Penobscot Bldg., Detroit, MI 48226; phone: 800/877–4253) $175, 760 pages, 1992. Includes associations active in environmental activities in Canada.

Directory of British Associations (Gale Research, Inc., 835 Penobscot Bldg., Detroit, MI 48226; phone: 800/877–4253) $250, 560 pages, 1993. Use this directory to find associations that include government workers so you can learn if they operate any job services or have advice on finding government jobs. It lists, by subject area, over 6,500 national, local, and regional associations based in England, Wales, Scotland, and Ireland.

Trade Associations and Professional Bodies of the United Kingdom (Gale Research, Inc., 835 Penobscot Bldg., Detroit, MI 48226; phone: 800/877–4253) $145, published in odd–numbered years. Its 575 pages give details on over 4,000 associations and professional bodies in the United Kingdom. You can use this to identify associations of government employees to learn if they operate any job services or have advice for finding government work.

Local Government Yearbook: The Handbook of Local Authority Management (TPL, P.O. Box 9596, Newmarket, Auckland, New Zealand; phone: 011–64–09/529–3000, fax: 529–3001) $30 NZ (includes shipping), 184 pages, published each March. In addition to information about governmental entities in New Zealand, this directory also provides information about libraries, galleries, and museums. Each entry includes names, addresses, and phone numbers. The 50 or so professional institutes and associations it describes are potential sources of career information for anybody considering moving to New Zealand.

General information on overseas work

Work, Study, Travel Abroad: The Whole World Handbook (available through Planning/Communications' catalog at the end of this book) $13.95, issued in spring of even–numbered years, 474 pages. Organized by continent and country, this book describes hundreds of employment, volunteer, study, and travel programs throughout the world. You'll learn about scholarships, exchange programs, and government grants that enable you to work abroad. Includes essays about each country, about teaching abroad, health and safety guidelines, and recommended books and films. Written by the Council on International Educational Exchange.

Looking for Employment in Foreign Countries (World Trade Academy Press, Inc., Suite 509, 50 E. 42nd St., New York, NY 10017; phone: 212/697–4999) $16.50/paperback plus $3.50/postage, 144 pages, 1990. Profiles employment situations in 43 foreign countries. Sample resumes and cover letters.

How to Get the Jobs You Want Overseas by Arthur Liebers (Pilot Books, 103 Cooper St., Babylon, NY 11702; phone: 516/422–2225) $4.95, 1990. Includes a chapter on overseas jobs with international organizations and non–profits.

Evaluating an Overseas Job Opportunity by John Williams (Pilot Books, 103 Cooper St., Babylon, NY 11702; phone: 516/422–2225) $5.95, 1993. This book examines employer/employee contracts, family issues, financial factors, living overseas, taxation, and returning home.

Resumes for Employment in the U.S. and Overseas (World Trade Academy Press, Inc., Suite 509, 50 E. 42nd St., New York, NY 10017; phone: 212/697–4999) $16.50 plus $3.50/postage, 145 pages, 1990. Presents special techniques to use when applying for foreign jobs including requirements for work permits in foreign countries.

Chapter 17

Legal services

Legal services

The ***Professional's Private Sector Job Finder*** and the ***Government Job Finder*** both contain much more extensive sets of entries for attorneys and related professions.

Job ads in print

Clearinghouse Review (National Clearinghouse for Legal Services, 205 W. Monroe, 2nd Floor, Chicago, IL 60606; phones: 800/621–3256, 312/263–3830) monthly, $75/annual subscription (U.S.), $95/foreign. About 25 ads for attorneys and paralegals, largely with non–profits, and faculty appear under "Job Market."

Job Market Preview (National Clearinghouse for Legal Services, 205 W. Monroe, 2nd Floor, Chicago, IL 60606; phones: 800/621–3256, 312/263–3830) monthly, $35/annual subscription. About 30 job ads fill this newsletter, often the same jobs that appear in *Clearinghouse Review*.

National and Federal Legal Employment Report (Federal Reports, Inc., Suite 408, 1010 Vermont Ave., NW, Washington, DC 20005; phone: 202/393–3311) monthly, subscription rates for individuals: $34/three–month, $58/six–month, $104/annual subscription; rates for institutions: $45, $80, $140, respectively. The typical issue contains descriptions of 500 to 600 attorney and law–related positions primarily in the federal government, state

147

and local government, private employers in government–related fields, including legal aid offices, and with non–profits. Includes legal positions in the Washington DC area, throughout the U.S., and abroad.

Lawyers Job Bulletin Board (Federal Bar Association, Publications Department, Suite 408, 1815 H St., N.W., Washington, DC 20006; phone: 202/638–0252) monthly, $30/nonmember annual subscription, $20/nonmember students, $20/members. Typical issue features 25 job openings primarily with the federal government, although about 10 percent of the ads are for positions with District of Columbia area courts, private firms, and non–profits.

Legal Times (1730 M St., NW, Washington, DC 20036; phone: 202/457–0686) weekly, $175/annual subscription. The classifieds section contains job vacancies largely in the DC area, but also nationally, for attorneys, paralegals, legal assistants, and legal secretaries.

The NLADA Cornerstone (National Legal Aid and Defender Association, 8th Floor, 1625 K St., NW, Washington, DC 20006; phone: 202/452–0620) quarterly, $20/nonmember subscription, free/members. "Job Listings" usually includes 15 to 20 job announcements.

ABA Journal (American Bar Association, ATTEN: Order Fulfillment, 750 N. Lake Shore Dr., Chicago, IL 60611; phone: 312/988–5555) monthly, free/members, $66/annual nonmember subscription. In the "Legal Mart" you'll find a section labeled "The Fine Print" which contains ads for about five or so teaching or administrative positions at law schools.

ALA Management Connections Bulletin (Association of Legal Administrators, Suite 325, 175 E. Hawthron Pkwy., Vernon Hills, IL 60061–1428; phone: 708/816–1212) weekly, $150/nonmember six–month subscription, $100/members. This is the print version of the *ALA Management Connection* job hotline described below under "Job services." In it you will find job ads for law office managers with non–profits and public interest groups, although the vast majority of positions advertised are with private firms. You can place a "Position Wanted" ad of your own for $75/nonmembers, $50/members. This ad will be recorded on *ALA Management Connections* and appear in the *ALA Management Connections Bulletin*. Contact the Association of Legal Administrators for details.

Summer Legal Employment Guide (Federal Reports, Inc., Suite 408, 1010 Vermont Ave., NW, Washington, DC 20005; phone: 202/393–3311) $16 plus $2 shipping, 36 pages, published annually. Describes federal summer legal intern and clerk ship programs for law students. Since these internships go quickly, contact Federal Reports about a copy by mid–autumn of the year before you want a summer internship.

Job services

Opportunities in Public Interest Law (ACCESS: Networking in the Public Interest, 50 Beacon St., Boston, MA 02108; phone: 617/720–5627) biannually (February and October), $42.90/February edition, $42.90/October edition. Hundreds of jobs are listed for positions in non–profit and government public interest law. Subscribers can also receive an annual *Public Interest Law Employer Directory* listed below under "Directories." $113.70/both editions including directory (individuals), $175/both editions including directory (institutions).

CU Career Connection (University of Colorado, Campus Box 133, Boulder, CO 80309–0133; phone: 303/492–4127) $30/two–month fee entitles you to a "passcode" which unlocks this job hotline. You need a touch–tone phone to call and request the field in which you are interested in hearing job openings. The hotline is turned off Monday through Friday, 2 to 4 p.m. for daily updating.

ALA Management Connections (Association of Legal Administrators, Suite 325, 175 E. Hawthron Pkwy., Vernon Hills, IL 60061–1428; phone: 708/816–1212) free, updated weekly. To hear job descriptions for law office managers with law departments of public interest and non–profit agencies (as well as mostly private sector positions), call 708/810–4333 anytime. You'll need a touch–tone phone. Press "3" after the message starts so you can hear the instructions. You can place a "Position Wanted" ad of your own for $75/nonmembers, $50/members. This ad will be recorded on *ALA Manage-*

ment Connections and appear in the *ALA Management Connections Bulletin* described above under "Job ads in print." Contact the Association for Legal Administrators for details.

Directories

Directory of Legal Aid and Defender Offices in the U.S. and Territories (National Legal Aid and Defender Association, 8th Floor, 1625 K St., NW, Washington, DC 20006; phone: 202/452–0620) $30/nonmember, $15/member, published biannually.

Public Interest Law Employer Directory (ACCESS: Networking in the Public Interest, 50 Beacon St., Boston, MA 02108; phone: 617/720–5627) $27.90, annual.

Funding for Law: Legal Education, Research and Study (Oryx Press, Suite 700, 4041 N. Central, Phoenix, AZ 85012–3397; phones: 800/279–6799, 602/265–2651) $45, 184 pages, 1991. Provides details on 497 programs including funding amounts, requirements, and application procedures for law school fellowships and internships, and grants for legal research: full program descriptions, contact names (with address and phone number), deadlines, and any special restrictions.

Salary surveys

Compensation of Legal & Related Jobs (non–law firms) (Abbott, Langer & Associates, 548 First St., Crete, IL 60417; phone: 708/672–4200) $525/entire set; Vol. 1: Supervisory and Managerial Attorneys, $210; Vol. 2: Non–supervisory attorneys, $210; Vol. 3: Legal Administrators/Paralegal Assistants/Legal Secretaries, $210; annual. Findings are presented by job type, geographic area, experience, education, size of firm, and more. Includes non–profit organizations.

Legal Salary Survey (David J. White & Associates, 809 Ridge Rd., Wilmette, IL 60091; phone: 800/962–4947) $190, last issued in 1993. Covers attorney positions.

Chapter 18

Media

Media

See the **Professional's Private Sector Job Finder** for a much
more extensive collection of job sources for media careers,
some of which include positions in the non–profit sector.

Job ads in print

AEJMC News (Association for Education in Journalism and Mass Communication, University of South Carolina, 1621 College St., Columbia, SC 29208–
0251; phone: 803/777–2005) every other month beginning with January,
$10/annual subscription (U.S.), $15/foreign (surface mail), $20/foreign (airmail).
The "Placement Service" carries 20 to 90 ads for college/university faculty
positions in journalism and mass communication.

College Broadcaster Magazine (National Association of College Broadcasters, 71 George St., Box 1824, Providence, RI 02912–1824; phone: 401/863–
2225) quarterly, $20/nonmember annual subscription, free/members. Fifty
jobs and 20 internships in all areas of the media industry appear in the
"Classifieds."

Entertainment Employment Journal (Suite 815, 7095 Hollywood Blvd.,
Hollywood, CA 90028; phone: 213/969–8500) semiweekly, $95/annual
subscription (U.S.), $101/annual subscription (Canada), $60/six–month subscription (U.S.), $35/three–month subscription (U.S.). From 25 to 50 jobs in
all aspects of the media and entertainment industries fill these pages.

Spectra (Speech Communication Association, 5105 Backlick Rd., Suite E, Annandale, VA 22003; phone: 703/750–0533) 11 issues/year, $36/annual nonmember subscription, free/members. The "Classifieds" carry ads for about 15 university faculty positions in journalism, communications, and broadcasting.

Religious Broadcasting (National Religious Broadcasters, 299 Webro Rd., Parsippany, NJ 07054; phone: 201/428–5400) 11 issues/year, $24/annual nonmember subscription (U.S.), $29/Canada, $60/foreign, free/members. Five to ten positions for everything in radio and television are described under "Classified." Also includes positions sought. See *Job Registry Program* described below under "Job Services."

The Professional Communicator (Women in Communications, Inc., 2101 Wilson Blvd., Suite 417, Arlington, VA 22201; phone: 703/528–4200) $18.50/annual nonmember subscription, free/members. The "Classifieds" list from five to ten positions for communications professionals in print and broadcast journalism, public relations, advertising, marketing, and education.

PR Marcom Jobs West – Southern California (Rachel P.R. Services, 513 Wilshire Blvd., Suite 238, Santa Monica, CA 90401; phones: 310/326–2661 inside California; 800/874-8577 elsewhere in the U.S.) biweekly, $35/three–month subscription (first class mail), $45/three–month subscription (sent to you via fax). About 50 job announcements, virtually all for positions in Southern California, fill this newsletter.

PR Marcom Jobs West – Northern California (Rachel P.R. Services, 298 Fourth Avenue, Suite 344, San Francisco, CA 94118; phones: 415/666–0481 inside California; 800/874–8577 elsewhere in the U.S.) biweekly, $35/three–month subscription (first class mail), $45/three–month subscription (sent to you via fax). About 50 job announcements, virtually all for positions in Northern California and the Pacific Northwest, fill this newsletter.

PR Marcom Jobs East (Rachel P.R. Services, 208 E. 51st St., Suite 1600, New York, NY 10022; phone: 212/962–9100) biweekly, $35/three–month subscription (first class mail), $45/three–month subscription (sent to you via fax). About 50 job openings for positions in New York, New Jersey, Boston, Washington DC, and surrounding states, fill this newsletter.

PR Marcom Jobs Mid-America (Rachel P.R. Services, 513 Wilshire Blvd., Suite 238, Santa Monica, CA 90401; phones: 310/326–2661 inside California; 800/874–8577 elsewhere in the U.S.) biweekly, $35/three–month subscription (first class mail), $45/three–month subscription (sent to you via fax). About 50 job openings for positions in the Midwest, Southeast, South, and Rocky Mountain regions, fill this newsletter.

Publishers' Auxiliary (National Newspaper Association, 1627 K St., NW, Suite 400, Washington, DC 20006; phone: 202/466–7200) biweekly, $55/annual nonmember subscription, free/members. Under "Help Wanted" you'll find about half a dozen positions for editors, writers, sales, circulation, financial, newspaper management, and university faculty. Includes "situations wanted."

The Quill (Society of Professional Journalists, P.O. Box 77, Greencastle, IN 46135; phone: 317/653–3333) nine issues/year, $27/annual nonmember subscription, free/members. The "Classifieds" section has four or five positions in all aspects of the print and broadcast media, including faculty.

Job Referral Newsletter (Association for Educational Communications and Technology, 1025 Vermont Ave., NW, Suite 820, Washington, DC 20005; phone: 202/347–7834) monthly, free/members only. This newsletter is filled with 12 to 15 academic positions in library science. AECT also suggests that you submit your resume since jobs may come in after the newsletter's deadline and staff will try to match candidates to these jobs. AECT will notify you of a match and suggest you apply for the position.

The New Careers Directory: Internships and Professional Opportunities in Technology and Social Change (Student Pugwash USA, 1638 R St., NW, Suite 32, Washington, DC 20009; phone: 202/328–6555) $18, $10/students; add $3 shipping, last printed in 1993. Offers full details on where and how to apply for internships and entry–level jobs with socially responsible organizations.

Job Services

Jobphone (Editorial Freelance Association, P.O. Box 2050, Madison Square Station, New York, NY 10159; phone: 212/677–3357). Anybody can call the "Jobphone," 212/929–5411, to hear a recording that briefly describes about 40 freelance writing, editing, proofreading, and translating opportunities. Listings are updated weekly. Only EFA members who subscribe to this service can call another phone number to get details (such as pay and whom to contact) on the listed jobs. Members can subscribe to "Jobphone" for $20/year. Write for membership rates (they're a little too complicated to explain here).

Jobs for Journalists (Society of Professional Journalists, P.O. Box 77, Greencastle, IN 46135; phone: 317/653–3333) available only to members, $25/six–month fee. The job seeker submits 10 copies of his resume as well as the service's completed resume form. When the service matches a registrant with a job vacancy, it sends the resume to the employer and a post card to the job seeker so she can contact the employer herself if she wishes. This service covers all aspects of the print and broadcast media.

Job Registry Program (National Religious Broadcasters, 299 Webro Rd., Parsippany, NJ 07054; phone: 201/428–5400) $45/six–months. You submit your check and a six line classified ad which is printed in *Religious Broadcasting* magazine and *NRB Membership Newsletter*, and your resume (two–page maximum). Resumes are kept on file for 6 months. Upon request, all active resumes are sent to employers seeking personnel. Prospective employers are responsible for contacting you for an interview.

Directories

Publication Grants for Writers & Publishers (Oryx Press, Suite 700, 4041 N. Central, Phoenix, AZ 85012–3397; phones: 800/279–6799, 602/265–2651) $29.95, 112 pages, 1991. Pretty much of a "how to" book, this volume describes the best funding sources and includes a bibliography of directories, grantsmanship books, periodicals, electronic resources, and sponsored publications.

The Source (Rachel P.R. Services, 513 Wilshire Blvd., Suite 238, Santa Monica, CA 90401; phones: 310/326–2661 inside California; 800/874–8577 elsewhere in the U.S.) $45, published annually with quarterly updates included; 30 pages. Says it provides details on 1000+ job sources in public relations, journalism, advertising, and marketing: job banks, trade publications, job hotlines, free–lance cooperatives, executive recruiters, employment agencies, and associations.

Station Handbook Manual Radio Edition (National Association of College Broadcasters, 71 George St., Box 1824, Providence, RI 02912–1824; phone: 401/863–2225) $20/nonmembers, free/members. Lists employers and companies by address and phone. Also available on diskette for $10.

Station Handbook Manual T.V. Edition (National Association of College Broadcasters, 71 George St., Box 1824, Providence, RI 02912–1824; phone: 401/863–2225) $20/nonmembers, free/members. Lists employers and companies by address and phone. Also available on diskette for $10.

Executive Recruiter Labels (Rachel P.R. Services, 513 Wilshire Blvd., Suite 238, Santa Monica, CA 90401; phones: 310/326–2661 inside California; 800/874–8577 elsewhere in the U.S.) $20/set. Says it provides a set of ready-made mailing labels that put you in contact with 50+ key executive recruiters who make placements on the East and West coasts and specialize in placing advertising, PR, and marketing professionals earning $35K+.

Directory of Religious Broadcasting (National Religious Broadcasters, 299 Webro Rd., Parsippany, NJ 07054; phone: 201/428–5400) $49.95/nonmembers, $39.95/members, issued each January. Includes 4,300 stations, producers, and other key personnel.

WICI National Job Hotline (Women in Communications, Inc., 2101 Wilson Blvd., Suite 417, Arlington, VA 22201; phone: 703/528–4200) free, available only to members. WICI maintains a toll–free number members can call to hear a listing of openings. For detailed information on positions, they call the WICI office for complete job specifications. Fields covered include print and broadcast journalism, public relations, advertising, marketing, and education.

Grants for Film, Media & Communications (The Foundation Center, 79 Fifth Ave., New York, NY 10003–3076; phones: 800/424–9836, within New York State call 212/620–4230) $65 plus $4.50/shipping, October 1993. Describes recent foundation grants of at least $10,000 given for film, video, documentaries, radio, television, printing, publishing, and censorship issues. This directory is useful for identifying foundations and grant recipients for which you may wish to work.

Salary surveys

WICI Job & Salary Survey Results (Women in Communications, Inc., 2101 Wilson Blvd., Suite 417, Arlington, VA 22201; phone: 703/528–4200) published in the April/May issue of *The Professional Communicator*, $4/single issue. Includes salary levels in print and broadcast media, corporate, non–profit, advertising and public relations, government, education, and free–lance.

AEJMC Salary Survey (Association for Education in Journalism and Mass Communication, University of South Carolina, 1621 College St., Columbia, SC 29208–0251; phone: 803/777–2005) $15, annual. Salary and demographic survey of journalism/communication faculty.

Marketing

Job ads in print

Marketing News (American Marketing Association, 250 S. Wacker Dr., Suite 200, Chicago, IL 60606–5819; phone: 312/648–0536) biweekly, $60/annual nonmember subscription, $30/members. The "Marketplace" features 25 jobs in marketing and marketing research including university faculty.

Job service

American Marketing Association Academic Placement Service (American Marketing Association, 250 S. Wacker Dr., Suite 200, Chicago, IL 60606–5819; phone: 312/648–0536) $35/11–month fee. The job seeker completes an "applicant's" form. Every two months, resumes are circulated to universities that subscribe to this service. Schools are responsible for contacting potential employees for an interview. Every two months a set of open positions is sent to registrants who are free to contact the universities directly.

Directories

The Christian Media Directory (James Lloyd, P.O. Box 3, Ashland, OR 97520; phone: 503/488–1405) $35 plus $1.75/shipping, prepaid only. Lists over 7,000 producers, publishers, recording labels, studios, all–Christian music and radio stations, film and video companies, television stations, and more–all with a Christian slant.

WICI Membership and Resource Directory (Women in Communications, Inc., 2101 Wilson Blvd., Suite 417, Arlington, VA 22201; phone: 703/528–4200) $49.95/nonmembers, free/members, annual. Members are in all aspects of media and communications including print and broadcast journalism, public relations, advertising, and marketing. Directory includes a yellow pages resource section where members and nonmembers place a 50–word listing of their business product or service. $100/members, $175/nonmembers.

Chapter 19

Museums and libraries

Also see entries later in this chapter under "Libraries."

Job ads in print

AVISO (American Association of Museums, 1225 Eye St., NW, Suite 200, Washington, DC 20005; phone: 202/289–9122) $33/annual nonmember subscription (U.S.), $48/foreign, free/members. "Placement" contains 90 ads for curators, registrars, directors, development officers, internships, and all other museum positions.

ASTC Newsletter (Association of Science/Technology Centers, 1025 Vermont Ave, Suite 500, NW, Washington, DC 20005; phone: 202/783–7200) bimonthly, $30/annual nonmember subscription (U.S.), $40/foreign, free/members. Four positions with museums and teaching positions are under "Positions Available."

American Visions (Vision Foundation, P.O. Box 37049, Washington, DC 20078–4741; phones: 800/998–0864, 202/462–1779) bimonthly, $18/annual subscription (U.S.), $30/foreign. The "Queries and Announcements" section features two or three librarian and museum curator positions, generally dealing with African–American culture, history, or art.

157

Sky & Telescope (Sky Publishing Corp., P.O. Box 9111, Belmont, MA 02178; phone: 617/864–7360) monthly, $27/annual subscription (U.S.), $36.38/Canada, $42/elsewhere. About three ads for astronomers, planetarium directors, and opticians appear under "Star–Gazers Exchange" and in display ads.

Job service

Dial–a–Job and *Dial–an–Internship* (National Association of Interpretation, P.O. Box 1892, Ft. Collins, CO 80522; 303/491–6434) Call 303/491–7410 24 hours a day for a recording of full–time, seasonal, and temporary jobs in environmental education, interpretation, and related fields including historians and museum personnel. The tape runs from 10 to 30 minutes. Updated weekly. For internships, call 303/491–6784 24 hours a day. The tape runs from 5 to 20 minutes. Updated weekly.

Directories

Sky & Telescope's Astronomy Resource Guide (Sky Publishing Corp., P.O. Box 9111, Belmont, MA 02178; phone: 617/864–7360) September issue of *Sky & Telescope*, $2.95/U.S., $3.50/Canada. Lists U.S. and Canadian planetariums, museums, and observatories plus astronomy dealers and manufacturers.

The Official Museum Directory 1994 (National Register Publishing Company; available from Reed Reference Publishing, P.O. Box 31, New Providence, NJ 07974; phone: 800/521–8110) $185, $134/members of the American Association of Museums, plus 7 percent shipping and handling, November 1993 edition. Provides details on over 7,000 U.S. museums, art associations, art museums and galleries, arts and crafts museums, folk art museums, children and junior museums, college and university museums, company museums, general museums, planetariums, zoos, aquariums, arboretums, and 60 other types of institutions.

Museums of the World (K.G. Saur; available from Reed Reference Publishing, P.O. Box 31, New Providence, NJ 07974; phone: 800/521–8110) $325 plus 7 percent shipping and handling, 704 pages, 1992 edition. Includes 24,000 museums worldwide organized by country and city within individual nations with addresses, phone numbers, description of holdings, facilities, museum directors, and more.

American Art Directory, 1993–94 (R.R. Bowker; available through Reed Reference Publishing, P.O. Box 31, New Providence, NJ 07974; phone: 800/521–8110) $186 plus 7 percent shipping and handling, published in

March of odd–numbered years, 820 pages. Offers details on more than 7,000 art organizations, museums, libraries, schools, and galleries through-out the U.S. and Canada.

Libraries

*For a much more extensive listing of job sources for public libraries, see the **Government Job Finder.***

Job ads in print

American Libraries (American Library Association, 50 E. Huron St., Chi-cago, IL 60611; phones: 800/545–2433 (outside Illinois), 800/545–2444 (Illinois only), 800/545–2455 (Canada only), 312/280–4211) 11 issues/year, $50/annual subscription for libraries, subscription included in membership package. Jobs listed under "Career Leads." Typical issues features 75 to 100 job ads.

Job notices can be obtained three weeks prior to publication in *American Libraries* in **Career Leads Express** which is a copy of the uncorrected galleys of job notices that will appear in the next issue of *American Libraries*. *Career Leads Express* is available to nonmembers and members alike for $1/issue, prepaid only. With your check, send a self–addressed stamped (two ounces postage) #10 envelope to AL Leads Express, 50 E. Huron, Chicago, IL 60611. Typical issue includes 75 or more positions.

Library Journal (Cahners Publishing Company, P.O. Box 1977, Marion, OH 43305–1077; phones: 800/677–6694, 614/382–3322) 20 issues/year, $79/an-nual subscription (U.S.), $99/Canada, $138/elsewhere (air mail). Jobs listed under "Classified Advertising." Fifty to 70 ads for librarian positions grace the pages of a typical issue.

College & Research Libraries Journal (Association of College and Research Libraries, 50 E. Huron St., Chicago, IL 60611; phones: 800/545–2433, 312/944–6795) monthly, $25/annual nonmember subscription (U.S.), $30/Can-ada, $35/elsewhere, free/members. Fifteen pages or 50 job ads for academic librarians appear in a typical issue.

Library Hotline (P.O. Box 713, Brewster, NY 10509; phone: 800/722–2346) 50 issues/year, $74/annual subscription. Thirty percent of the 25 to 30 vacancies listed for librarians are with government agencies, universities, schools, and other non–profit entities.

School Library Journal (Cahners Publishing, 44 Cook St., Denver, CO 80206; phone: 303/388–4511) monthly, $67/annual subscription (U.S.), $91/Canada, $110/elsewhere. The "Classifieds" feature about 15 ads for librarians, system managers, and upper–level administrative personnel.

History News Dispatch (American Association for State and Local History, 172 Second Ave., North, Suite 202, Nashville, TN 37201; phone: 615/255–2971) monthly, $30/members only. About 20 to 35 ads for librarians, archivists, historians, and educators appear under "The Marketplace."

Job Referral Newsletter (Association for Educational Communications and Technology, 1025 Vermont Ave., NW, Suite 820, Washington, DC 20005; phone: 202/347–7834) monthly, free/members only. This newsletter is filled with 12 to 15 academic positions in library science. AECT also suggests that you submit your resume since jobs may come in after the newsletter's deadline and staff will try to match candidates to these jobs. AECT will notify you of a match and suggest you apply for the position.

Wilson Library Bulletin (The H. H. Wilson Company, 950 University Ave., Bronx, NY 10452; phones: 800/367–6770 ext. 2245, 718/588–2245) ten issues/year, $52/annual subscription. Typically, about two ads for librarians, information brokers, or library consultants appear under "Library Services Directory."

Journal of Academic Librarianship (Mountainside Publishing Co., 321 S. Main St., Suite 300, Ann Arbor, MI 48107; phone: 313/662–3925) bi-monthly, $29/annual subscription (individuals), $65/institutions. Two or three ads for university librarians appear under "Classified Ads."

Institutional Library Mail Jobline (c/o Gloria Spooner, Library Consultant, State Library of Louisiana, P.O. Box 131, Baton Rouge, LA 70821–0131; phone: 504/342–4931) monthly, free. Send self–addressed stamped envelope for copy. Lists institutional library positions in U.S. and its territories.

Jobline (American Society for Information Science, 8720 Georgia Ave., Suite 501, Silver Spring, MD 20910–3602; phone: 301/495–0900) monthly, available to nonmembers upon request, free/members.

New England Library Jobline (GSLIS, New England Library Jobline, Simmons College, 300 The Fenway, Boston, MA 02115). Call 617/738–3148 to hear a 24–hour tape recording of library and information science positions requiring an MLS degree. Updated each Wednesday.

Rural Libraries Jobline (Center for the Study of Rural Librarianship, Department of Library Science, Clarion University of Pennsylvania, Clarion, PA 16214; phone: 814/226–2383) monthly, $1/issue.

Specialist (Special Libraries Association, 1700 18th St., NW, Washington, DC 20009; 202/234–4700) monthly, $60/annual subscription (U.S.), $65/foreign. From five to ten jobs are listed under "Positions Open."

Canadian Association of Special Libraries and Information Services, *Ottawa Chapter Jobline* (Job Bank Coordinator, CASLIS, 266 Sherwood Drive, Ottawa, ONTARIO, K1Y3W4 Canada) Call 613/728–9982 for a recording of job openings.

Job services

SpeciaLine Employment Clearinghouse Job Hotline (Special Libraries Association, 1700 18th St., NW, Washington, DC 20009; 202/234–4700). Call 202/234–3632 for a 24–hour tape recording of jobs with special libraries.

American Library Association Job Hotline (American Library Association, 50 E. I luron St., Chicago, IL 60611; phones: 800/545–2433 (outside Illinois), 800/545–2444 (Illinois only), 800/545–2455 (Canada only), 312/280–4211). If you want to work for the ALA, call 312/280–2464 to hear a recording of job openings at the ALA. 24- hours, seven days a week.

ASTC JobBank (Association of Science/Technology Centers, 1025 Vermont Ave., Suite 500, NW, Washington, DC 20005; phone: 202/783–7200) free, monthly. Send your resume and a job summary of no more than six lines stating education, experience, skills, and type of job seeking. This will include you in ASTC's Job Bank publication which is sent out to over 600 individuals and organizations in the science museum, natural history, and science center fields.

Career Hotline/Job Database Service (American Association of Law Librar- ies, Suite 940, 53 W. Jackson, Chicago, IL 60604; phone: 312/939–4764). Call the 24–hour Career Hotline, 312/939–7877, for a recording of brief job descriptions of law librarian positions and where to apply. This is the index to the AALL's *Job Database Service* which is updated weekly by Friday noon. AALL members can request a free printout of all job listings by calling 312/939–4764 or faxing a request to 312/431–1097. Nonmembers can obtain a printout for $5 (send to: AALL, Dept. 77–602, Chicago, IL 60678– 6021). There are typically 10 to 25 jobs listed at any one time.

Directories

Who's Who in Special Libraries (Special Libraries Association, 1700 18th St., NW, Washington, DC 20009; 202/234–4700) $60/nonmembers, free/mem- bers, published annually in the autumn. Includes alphabetical and geo- graphical lists of special libraries.

Directory of Special Libraries and Information Centers (Gale Research, Inc., 835 Penobscot Bldg., Detroit, MI 48226; phone: 800/233–4253)

$380, in two parts, 1991. Provides comprehensive information on 18,600 information centers, archives, and special and research libraries in the U.S., Canada, and elsewhere. Includes subject index.

Libraries, Information Centers and Databases in Science and Technology (K.G. Saur; available from Reed Reference Publishing, P.O. Box 31, New Providence, NJ 07974; phone: 800/521–8110) $225 plus 7 percent shipping and handling, 696 pages, 1988 edition. Includes over 11,000 libraries, online databases, and documentation centers in all areas of pure and applied sciences. Independent specialized national libraries, technical college libraries, university and college libraries, and institute and seminar libraries are listed by country.

Subject Directory of Special Libraries (Gale Research, Inc., 835 Penobscot Bldg., Detroit, MI 48226; phone: 800/233–4253) $675/three volumes, 1990. These volumes contain the same material as the *Directory of Special Libraries and Information Centers,* but rearranged into 14 subject areas in three volumes, available individually: Business, Government, and Law Libraries, $250; Computers, Engineering, and Science Libraries, $250; Health Sciences Libraries, $250.

New Special Libraries (Gale Research, Inc., 835 Penobscot Bldg., Detroit, MI 48226; phone: 800/233–4253) $335; 1990. Furnishes comprehensive information on special libraries in the U.S., Canada, and elsewhere.

National Guide to Funding for Libraries and Information Services (The Foundation Center, 79 Fifth Ave., New York, NY 10003–3076; phones: 800/424–9836, 212/620–4230) $85, May 1993. Furnishes essential data on over 400 foundations and corporate direct giving programs. Each entry includes application information, types of support, and recent grants.

Grants for Libraries & Information Services (The Foundation Center, 79 Fifth Ave., New York, NY 10003–3076; phones: 800/424–9836, within New York State call 212/620–4230) $65 plus $4.50/shipping, October 1993. Describes recent foundation grants of at least $10,000 given for public, academic, research, special, and school libraries for archives and information centers, consumer information, and philanthropy information centers. This directory is useful for identifying foundations and grant recipients for which you may wish to work.

Salary survey

ALISE Library and Information Science Education Statistical Report (Association for Library and Information Science Education, 4101 Lake Boone Trail, Suite 201, Raleigh, NC 27607; phone: 919/787–5181) $34/nonmember (U.S.), $34/foreign, $24/members, published each May. Includes a salary survey of teachers in member schools.

Chapter **20**

Organizing

Also see the entries in the "Housing, planning, development" chapter.

Job ads in print

Community Jobs (ACCESS: Networking in the Public Interest, 50 Beacon St., Boston, MA 02108; phone: 617/720–5627) monthly, individuals: $29/three–month subscription, $39/six–month subscription (U.S.). Also available at bookstores. Each issue lists about 250 to 350 positions in the non–profit world, including a good number of organizing jobs. This is probably the single best source of job vacancies for organizers. Regional biweekly editions for New York, New Jersey, and the District of Columbia are available free upon request with subscriptions to *Community Jobs*; see the individual states in Chapter 31.

In These Times (2040 N. Milwaukee Ave., Chicago, IL 60647; phone: 312/772–0100) 26 issues/year, annual subscription: $34.95/individuals (U.S.), $59/institutions, $61.95/Canada, $75.95/elsewhere, $2/single issue. Jobs listed under "Classifieds." Publishes ads for five to ten organizing jobs per issue.

The Nation (72 Fifth Ave., New York, NY 10011; phone: 212/242–8400) weekly, $22/six–month subscription, $48/annual subscription (U.S.), $87/Canada, $149/elsewhere. Jobs listed under "Classified–Positions Available." Four or five organizing positions per issue.

The Village Voice (P.O. Box 8044, Syracuse, NY 13217; phone: 800/825–0061) weekly, $28.95/six–month subscription, $47.95/annual (U.S.), $79.20/foreign. Jobs listed under "Classifieds–Help Wanted." Includes ads for organizing positions from across the country, not just New York.

Democratic Left (Democratic Socialists of America, Suite 500, 15 Dutch St., New York, NY 10038; phone: 212/962–0390) bimonthly, $8/individuals, $15/institutions; $1.50/single copy. Jobs listed under "Classifieds." Few ads for organizing jobs.

Non–Violent Activist (War Resisters League, 339 Lafayette St., New York, NY 10012; phone: 212/228–0450) six issues/year, $15/annual subscription, $30/foreign. "Activist News–Job Openings" has just one or two vacancies an issue, sometimes none. Includes lobbyist positions.

Directories

Alternative Press Index (Alternative Press Center, P.O. Box 33109, Baltimore, MD 21218; phone: 410/243–2471) annual subscription: $35/individuals and movement groups, $175/institutions. Many of the "alternative" or "progressive" periodicals identified in this index carry ads or announcements for organizing positions. Contact for details.

Directory of U.S. Labor Organizations (Bureau of National Affairs, BNA Books, P.O. Box·6035, Rockville, MD 20850; phones: 800/372–1033) $35 plus $3/shipping, 110 pages, 1992. Give name, address, phone, and fax number for officers and key staffers of the nation's labor unions and labor publications. Includes state federations and local offices.

American Directory of Organized Labor (Gale Research, Inc., 835 Penobscot Bldg., Detroit. MI 48226–4094; phone: 800/877–4253) $275, 1,638 pages, 1992. Details over 225 national unions as well as almost 40,000 independent, regional, state, and local unions, including the growing sector of government and education unions. Great source to identify potential employers and learn more about them.

Trade Unions of the World (Gale Research, Inc., 835 Penobscot Bldg., Detroit. MI 48226–4094; phone: 800/877–4253) $139, 588 pages, 1992. Get information on labor unions operating throughout the world.

Chapter 21

Parks and recreation

*Also see listings in the "Environment" and "Forestry and horticulture"
chapters. You'll find many more job sources for both of these
fields described in the Government Job Finder.*

Camps and camping

*For a much greater selection of job sources, see the
Professional's Private Sector Job Finder.*

Job ads in print

Camping Magazine (American Camping Association, 5000 State Road 67
North, Martinsville, IN 46151; phones: 800/428–2267, 317/342–8456)
bimonthly, $18.95/annual nonmember subscription (U.S.), $25/Canada,
$31.50/elsewhere, free/members. About 25 job vacancies for camp direc-
tors, counselors, activity specialists, instructors, lifeguards, and nurses appear under "Classifieds–Help Wanted" plus ads for camp planners and ads
for camps for sale or lease. Also "Positions Wanted."

Directory

Guide to Summer Camps and Summer Schools (Porter Sargent Publishers, Inc., 11 Beacon St., Suite 1400, Boston, MA 02108; phone: 617/523–1670) $22.55/paperback, $27.98/cloth edition, 492 pages, last edition 1990–91. Reports on over 1,100 camps and summer schools as well as specialized programs for children with learning, physical, or mental disabilities.

Parks and recreation

Job ads in print

Workamper News (201 Hiram Rd., Heber Springs, AR 72543; phone: 800/446–5627) bimonthly, Call for price. Lists over 300 different employers who are actively seeking employees for public parks and campgrounds as well as commercially–operated parks, resorts, campgrounds with positions available at all levels, from housekeeping and grounds maintenance to upper management.

Park and Recreation Opportunities Job Bulletin (National Recreation and Park Association, 2775 South Quincy St., Suite 300, Arlington, VA 22206; phone: 703/820–4940) 22 issues/year, individual copies available to non-members and members for $5 prepaid; annual subscription available only to members: $30. Typical issue includes 40 to 60 jobs by geographic area in the U.S. and foreign positions.

Opportunities (Natural Science for Youth Foundation, 130 Azalea Dr., Roswell, GA 30075; phones: 800/992–6793, 404/594–9367) bimonthly, $35/annual subscription, $10/single issue, included in membership package. "Positions available " lists details on 45 to 70 jobs for naturalists, curators, raptor rehabilitators, and administrative positions, largely at nature centers.

Athletics Employment Weekly (RDST Enterprises, Route 2, Box 140, Carthage, IL 62321; phone: 217/357–3615) weekly, $40/six–month subscription, $65/annual subscription. A typical issue features 75 to 100 coaching, training, and administrative positions in athletics, for two to four year colleges nationwide. Also includes academic advisors and counselors.

NCAA News (National Collegiate Athletic Association, P.O. Box 1906, Mission, KS 66201; phone: 913/384–3220) $26, weekly. About 100 jobs appear under "The Market" for athletics directors, assistant/associate athletics directors, coaches, trainers, recreation positions, and athletics administrators.

Job service

NRPA/SCHOLE Network (National Recreation and Park Association, 2775 South Quincy St., Suite 300, Arlington, VA 22206; phone: 703/820–4940) $75/annual subscription for nonmember individuals, $225/nonmember agencies, $50/member individuals, $150/member agencies. This computer information and communications network includes NRPA's *Park and Recreation Opportunities Job Bulletin.* Updated biweekly.

Directories

NCAA Directory (National Collegiate Athletic Association, P.O. Box 1906, Mission, KS 66201; phone: 913/384–3220) $6, released every October. Includes key personnel at 1,000 NCAA member schools.

Special Recreation Inc., [for people with disabilities] (362 Koser Ave., Iowa City, IA 52246–3038; phone: 319/337–7578) $49.95/nonmembers, 1992 edition. Lists organizations that deal with recreation for people who have disabilities.

Golf Course Builders Association of America Directory (GCBAA, 920 Airport Rd., Suite 210, Chapel Hill, NC 27514; phone: 919/942–8922) $5, annual. Provides details on member companies involved in building golf courses.

Directory of Natural Science Centers (Natural Science for Youth Foundation, 130 Azalea Dr., Roswell, GA 30075; phones: 800/992–6793, 404/594–9367) $78.50/nonmembers, $58.50/members, 600 pages, 1990, next edition expected in 1994. This hefty volume furnishes details on over 1,350 nature centers.

Summer Jobs '94 (Peterson's Guides; available from Planning/Communications' catalog at the end of this book) $15.95, 424 pages, annual. Describes over 20,000 summer job openings in the United States and Canada with environmental programs, resorts, camps, amusement parks, expeditions, theaters, national parks, and government. Each detailed employer description includes salary and benefits, employer background, profile of employees, and whom to contact to apply.

Grants for Recreation, Sports & Athletics (The Foundation Center, 79 Fifth Ave., New York, NY 10003–3076; phones: 800/424–9836, within New York State call 212/620–4230) $65 plus $4.50/shipping, October 1993. Describes recent foundation grants of at least $10,000 given to clubs, leagues, camps, parks, scouting, social service agencies, and community organizations for recreation, athletics, and physical fitness. This directory is useful for identifying foundations and grant recipients for which you may wish to work.

Chapter 22

Philanthropy

Also see the "Grants and foundations" chapter.

Job ads in print

The Chronicle of Philanthropy (1255 23rd St., NW, Washington, DC 20037; phones: 800/347–6969, 202/466–1200) 24 issues/year, $67.50/annual subscription, $36/six–month subscription. The "Professional Opportunities" section runs ads for 60 to 90 job openings in all aspects of the non–profit world, from fundraisers to CEOs. Includes lots of fundraiser and director of development positions.

Corporate Giving Watch (Taft Group, 12300 Twinbrook Pkwy., Suite 520, Rockville, MD 20852–9830; phone: 800/877–8238) monthly, $139/annual subscription. Learn about new corporate grant programs, changes in giving priorities, and changes in corporate program officers. Eight pages are devoted to new and updated corporate profiles. This newsletter is also available by computer modem from NewsNet (phones: 800/345–1301, 215/527–8030).

AHP News (Association for Healthcare Philanthropy, 313 Park Ave., Suite 400, Falls Church, VA 22046; phone: 703/532–6243) eight issues/year, $50/annual nonmember subscription, free/members. Six to ten vacancies for health care or hospital fundraisers appear under "Positions Available."

OUR BUILDING FUND COULD USE A BIT OF A BOOST...

Directories

AHP Membership Directory and Buyers Guide (Association for Healthcare Philanthropy, 313 Park Ave., Suite 400, Falls Church, VA 22046; phone: 703/532–6243) $125/nonmembers, $25/members, issued each January.

Charitable Organizations of the U.S. (Gale Research, Inc., 835 Penobscot Bldg., Detroit, MI 48226–4094; phone: 800/877–4253) $139.50, 565 pages, 1992. Describes over 800 groups that actively solicit the American public for funds. This is a good source for not only identifying non–profits for which to work, but also to learn which ones need professionals with fundraising skills.

Salary survey

USA Salary & Benefits Report (Association for Healthcare Philanthropy Foundation, 313 Park Ave., Suite 400, Falls Church, VA 22046; phone: 703/532–6243) contact for price, annual. Reports on salaries by position and bedsize, type of institution, gender, as well as on age, size of staff, insurance, retirement benefits, perquisites, and vacation time.

Chapter 23

Records management and archives

*Also see the chapter on "Museums and libraries." See the **Government
Job Finder** for a more extensive set of job sources.*

Job ads in print

Archival Outlook (Society of American Archivists, Suite 504, 600 S. Federal,
Chicago, IL 60605; phone: 312/922–0140) published in alternating months
with ***SAA Employment Bulletin***, free/members only. Jobs listed under
"Employment Opportunities." About 20 job ads per issue.

SAA Employment Bulletin (Society of American Archivists, Suite 504, 600
S. Federal, Chicago, IL 60605; phone: 312/922–0140) published in alternating months with ***Archival Outlook***, available to members for $24/year;
nonmembers can purchase individual issues for $6 each. Lists only jobs.
About 20 jobs ads per issue.

AIC Newsletter (American Institute for Conservation of Historic and Artistic
Works,, Suite 340, 1400 16th St., NW, Washington, DC 20036; phone:
202/232–6636) bimonthly, free/members only. Jobs listed under "Positions
Available." Around 20 job ads per issue, largely for conservators.

Journal of the American Health Information Management Association (AHIMA, 919 N. Michigan Ave., Suite 1400, Chicago, IL 60611–1683; phone: 312/787–2672, ext. 253) monthly, $72/nonmember annual subscription, free/members. Around 10 to 15 classified ads for medical record administrators, technicians, coders, and reviewers are in the typical issue.

OAH Newsletter (Organization of American Historians, 112 N. Bryan St., Bloomington, IN 47408; phone: 812/855–7311) quarterly, free/members only. About 12 positions for government, public, and U.S. historians; archivists; and university faculty appear under "Professional Opportunities." OAH also runs a job registry at its annual national meeting.

Directory

AIC Directory (American Institute for Conservation of Historic and Artistic Works,, Suite 340, 1400 16th St., NW, Washington, DC 20036; phone: 202/232–6636) $53/nonmembers, free/members, published each August. Members listed alphabetically, geographically, and by specialty.

Chapter 24

Religion

Religion

Also see the "Social services" chapter.

Job ads in print

Christianity Today (P.O. Box 11618, Des Moines, IA 50340; phone: 800/999–1704) 15 issues/year, $24.95/annual subscription (U.S.), $32.95/foreign. "The Marketplace–Employment" features 23 ads for ministers, caseworkers, missionaries, professors, editors, lawyers, and broadcasters.

National Catholic Reporter (P.O. Box 419281, Kansas City, MO 64141; phones: 800/444–8910, 816/531–0538) weekly, semiweekly during the summer months, 44 issues/year, $32.95/annual subscription. Over 40 positions in religion (teachers, director of lay ministries, directors of religious activities and chaplain services, counselors, musicians, etc.) appear under "NCR Classifieds." Included employment wanted ads.

Catholic Digest (P.O. Box 51549, Boulder, CO 80322; phone: 800/678–2836) monthly, $15.97/annual subscription. The "Vocation Guide" includes 25 display ads from different religious orders.

Pastoral Music (National Association of Pastoral Musicians, 225 Sheridan St., NW, Washington, DC 20011; phone: 202/723–5800) bimonthly, $24/annual nonmember subscription, free/members. "Hotline" runs about 20 ads for church and synagogue musicians, ministers, and directors of music and liturgy.

Mr. Boffo reprinted by permission of Tribune Media Services. Copyright 1992. All rights reserved.

Pastoral Music Notebook (National Association of Pastoral Musicians, 225 Sheridan St., NW, Washington, DC 20011; phone: 202/723–5800) bimonthly, free/members only; $48/annual dues. "Hotline" runs about 20 ads for church and synagogue musicians, ministers, and directors of music and liturgy.

Higher Education Report (Association of Jesuit Colleges and Universities, 1 Dupont Circle, Suite 405, Washington, DC 20036; phone: 202/862–9893) ten issues/year, $17.50/annual subscription (U.S. and Canada). Five to 10 ads for faculty are listed under "Classifieds."

Religious Broadcasting (National Religious Broadcasters, 299 Webro Rd., Parsippany, NJ 07054; phone: 201/428–5400) 11 issues/year, $24/annual nonmember subscription (U.S.), $29/Canada, $60/foreign, free/members. Five to ten positions for everything in radio and television are described under "Classified." Also includes positions sought. See *Job Registry Program described below under "Job Services."*

Jewish Monthly (B'nai B'rith International, 1640 Rhode Island Ave., NW, Washington, DC 20036; phone: 202/857–6645) eight issues/year, $12/nonmember annual subscription, free/members, $2/single issue. One or two jobs for rabbis and camp counselors appear in the "Classifieds."

The Christian Reader (P.O. Box 1913, Marion, OH 43305; phone: 800/347–6969) bimonthly, $14.95/annual subscription (U.S.), $19.95/Canada. "Classifieds–Employment" runs two or three ads for positions with Christian publishers.

Job services

Job Registry Program (National Religious Broadcasters, 299 Webro Rd., Parsippany, NJ 07054; phone: 201/428–5400) $45/six–months. You submit your check and a six line classified ad which is printed in Religious Broadcasting magazine and NRB Membership Newsletter, and your resume (two–page maximum). Resumes are kept on file for 6 months. Upon request, all active resumes are sent to employers seeking personnel. Prospective employers are responsible for contacting you for an interview.

Job Hotline (National Association of Pastoral Musicians, 225 Sheridan St., NW, Washington, DC 20011; phone: 202/723–5800) monthly, $25/non-members, $15/members. These are the same 20 vacancies for church and synagogue musicians, ministers, and directors of music and liturgy that appear in Pastoral Music Notebook and Pastoral Music described above under "Job ads in print." However, NPM members can access them before publication by calling this live job hotline.

Presbyterian Association of Musicians Referral Service (100 Witherspoon, Louisville, KY 40202–1396; phone: 502/569–5288) $10/members only, annual. Churches that wish to hire musicians submit a job description which is then mailed to subscribing members. Listings are mailed on the first Monday of every month.

Christian Placement Service (Intercristo, 19303 Fremont Avenue N, Seattle, WA 98133; phones: 800/426–1342, 800/251–7740) $41.50/three–month subscription, $16/renewal subscription. You must fill out a personal profile application form which includes selecting up to four occupations, three geographic preferences, compensation, denomination, experience, education, skills, and more. This will put you into an extensive database connected to ministries all over the world from which you will be matched with jobs available and be sent four printouts that match your qualifications and interests. There are literally thousands of jobs available which are updated frequently. If you are interested in integrating your faith with your employment this is the service to join.

National Association of Temple Administrators Placement Service (NATA, 310 E. 70th St., Suite 6K, New York, NY 10021; phone: 212/861–5728) $100/year nonmember registration fee, free/members. Positions filled are with reform Jewish congregations. You submit a copy of your resume to the service. When the service receives a job description from a congregation for an administrator, it sends a notice to all registrants. You contact the service and ask it to send your resume to the congregation which is then responsible for contacting you for the next step in the hiring process. About 25 to 30 jobs a year are filled through this service.

North American Association of Synagogue Executives Placement Service (NASA, c/o United Synagogue of Conservative Judaism, 155 Fifth Ave., New York, NY 10010; phone: 212/533–7800, ext. 2250) free/members only. You submit your own resume and the service's completed form. Figuring out how this service works is even more difficult than reading the Torah without vowels. If you are a member, or wish to join one of NAASE's assemblies, you should inquire directly. Jobs are with conservative synagogues.

Lost your way? Chances are you didn't read Chapter One which tells you how to get the most out of the Non-Profits' Job Finder. So, please go back to the beginning and learn how to find all the job sources for your occupation.

Directories

National Directory of Churches, Synagogues, and Other Houses of Worship (Gale Research, Inc., 835 Penobscot Bldg., Detroit, MI 48226; phone: 800/877–4253) $300/four volume set, 600 pages total, 1993. With a volume for each of four geographic regions, this tome describes over 350,000 houses of worship in the U.S. You'll find each congregation's name, address, phone, size, denomination, date established, and leader's name.

Directory of Religious Organizations in the United States (Gale Research, Inc., 835 Penobscot Bldg., Detroit, MI 48226; phone: 800/877–4253) $125, 1993. Details about 2,500 nondenominational, interdenominational, and inter–faith organizations that provide services, information, or support for religious bodies: churches, denominations, sects, and cults. You'll learn the name and phone number of each organization's chief executive officer, its goals and activities, and its products, including publications, audio and video tapes, and radio and television programs. This is a good source to identify potential employers in the "affiliated" religion industry.

The Official Catholic Directory 1993 (National Register Publishing Company; available from Reed Reference Publishing, P.O. Box 31, New Providence, NJ 07974; phone: 800/521–8110) $169, $199/with midyear supplement, plus 7 percent shipping and handling, call for special clergy rate, 1,886 pages. Lists 60,000 leaders in the Roman Catholic Church in the U.S.A. including: parish clergy, chancery officials, colleges and universities, novitiates and provincialities, seminaries, and foreign missions.

Directory of Religious Broadcasting (National Religious Broadcasters, 299 Webro Rd., Parsippany, NJ 07054; phone: 201/428–5400) $49.95/nonmembers, $39.95/members, issued each January. Includes 4,300 stations, producers, and other key personnel.

The Christian Media Directory (James Lloyd, P.O. Box 3, Ashland, OR 97520; phone: 503/488–1405) $35 plus $1.75/shipping, prepaid only. Lists over 7,000 producers, publishers, recording labels, studios, all–Christian music and radio stations, film and video companies, television stations, and more.

National Guide to Funding in Religion (The Foundation Center, 79 Fifth Ave., New York, NY 10003–3076; phones: 800/424–9836, 212/620–4230) $135 plus $4.50/shipping, June 1993. Presents details on 3,000 foundations and corporate direct giving programs that have a history of funding churches, missionary societies, religious welfare, and religious education programs.

Fund Raiser's Guide to Religious Philanthropy (Taft Group, 12300 Twinbrook Pkwy., Suite 520, Rockville, MD 20852–9830; phone: 800/877–8238) $140, 375 pages, annual. About 420 of the most important funding sources of religious and religiously–affiliated organizations are detailed.

Grants for Religion, Religious Welfare & Religious Education (The Foundation Center, 79 Fifth Ave., New York, NY 10003–3076; phones: 800/424–9836, within New York State call 212/620–4230) $65 plus $4.50/shipping, October 1993. Describes recent foundation grants of at least $10,000 given to synagogues, churches, missionary societies, religious orders, and associations and organizations concerned with religious welfare and education. This directory is useful for identifying foundations and grant recipients for which you may wish to work.

Salary survey

Presbyterian Association of Musicians Referral Service (100 Witherspoon, Louisville, KY 40202–1396; phone: 502/569–5288) $2, last published June 1993. Published every two or three years. Salary guidelines, sample contracts, and code of ethics included.

Chapter 25

Research

Also see the "Foundations and grants" chapter as well as Chapter 31 on "State–by–state job and grant sources."

Job ads in print

Professional Staff Position Openings (National Research Council, Personnel Office, ATTEN: Professional Vacancy Listing, 2101 Constitution Ave., NW, Washington, DC 20418; phone: 202/334–2000) weekly, free. Send a self–addressed #10 business envelope with two ounces postage stamped on it for each issue you'd like to receive. About 40 vacancies are described in each issue. Half of the positions are for research in a wide variety of agencies including social science, science or engineering, agriculture, environment, life sciences, medicine, mathematics, transportation.

SRA News (Society of Research Administrators, 500 N. Michigan Ave., Suite 1400, Chicago, IL 60611; phone: 312/661–1700) bimonthly, free/members only. The "Classifieds" carry two or three ads for administrator positions for all types of research projects and programs. Ads do not appear in every issue.

NCURA Newsletter (National Council of University Research Administrators, 1 Dupont Cr., NW, Suite 420, Washington, DC 20036; phone: 202/466–3894) bimonthly, free/members only. About one to four ads for research administrators appear throughout the newsletter.

ACA Newsletter (American Crystallographic Association, P.O. Box 96, Ellicott Station, Buffalo, NY 14205–0095; phone: 716/856–9600, ext. 321) quarterly, available only to members, included in dues. "Positions Available" features about ten job ads for chemistry and physics positions in research laboratories and universities.

Job service

Professional Resume File (National Research Council Personnel Office, ATTEN: Professional Resume File, 2101 Constitution Ave., NW, Washington, DC 20418; phone: 202/334–2000) free. Send a copy of your resume and request that it be placed in this file. Supervisors at the National Research Council, Institute of Medicine, National Academy of Sciences, and National Academy of Engineering frequently review these resumes to fill open positions.

Directories

Directory of Research Grants, 1993 (Oryx Press, Suite 700, 4041 N. Central, Phoenix, AZ 85012–3397; phones: 800/279–6799, 602/265–2651) $125, 1,216 pages, 1993. Describes over 6,000 sources of research funding in dozens of disciplines and subject areas.

Research Centers Directory (Gale Research, Inc., 835 Penobscot Bldg., Detroit, MI 48226–4094; phone: 800/877–4253) $435, 2,500 pages in two volumes, July 1993. Provides details on 12,800 non–profit research units in all fields including university research parks and technology transfer centers. Entries are grouped into 17 chapters covering five broad categories: life sciences; physical sciences and engineering, private and public policy, social and cultural studies, and multidisciplinary and coordinating centers.

New Research Centers Supplement (Gale Research, Inc., 835 Penobscot Bldg., Detroit, MI 48226–4094; phone: 800/877–4253) $280, 185 pages, October 1993. Furnishes the same information cited under the *Research Centers Directory* immediately above, but for new research centers only.

International Research Centers Directory 1993–94 (Gale Research, Inc., 835 Penobscot Bldg., Detroit, MI 48226; phone: 800/877–4253) $395, 1,481 pages, 1993. Get details on 7,200 research centers throughout the world, including non–profit and university centers.

NCURA Membership Directory (National Council of University Research Administrators, 1 Dupont Circle, NW, Suite 420, Washington, DC 20036; phone: 202/466–3894) free/members only, published every April.

SRA Membership Directory (Society of Research Administrators, 500 N. Michigan Ave., Suite 1400, Chicago, IL 60611; phone: 312/661–1700) free/members only, issued each January.

The Air, Waste, and Environmental Management Research Faculty Profile
(Air & Waste Management Association, P.O. Box 2861, Pittsburgh, PA
15230) $79.95/nonmembers book format, $64/members, $495/nonmem-
ber data file, $415/members. Information on 1,200 researchers, repre-
senting over 350 colleges and universities. Catagorized by name and address,
title, phone and fax, general and specific research interests, waste treat-
ment/control sub–specialties, funding sources, courtroom/litigation experience, staff size and qualifications, collaboration interest with industry, and
commercial readiness. Data file information is MAC and PC compatible and
can be used with many data management systems.

Salary survey

Compensation in Research & Development (Abbott, Langer & Associates,
548 First St., Crete, IL 60417; phone: 708/672–4200) $550/entire set, 648
pages; Part I: Directors/Managers/Supervisors, $225; Part II: Engineers/Sci-
entists/Technologists, $225; Part III: Technicians, $225. Sponsored by the
Society of Research Administration, the entire set covers 17 job categories.

Chapter 26

Safety

*If criminal justice is your thing, see the **Government Job Finder** for a much more extensive list of job sources.*

Job ads in print

NELS—National Employment Listing Service (Criminal Justice Center, Sam Houston State University, Huntsville, TX 77341–2296; phone: 409/294–1692, 1690) monthly, individuals: $30/annual subscription, $37.50/foreign, $17.50/six–month subscription; institutions and agencies: $65/annual subscription (U.S.), $85/foreign; Texas residents must include 8.25 percent sales tax; tax–exempt institutions must include proof of tax exempt status. Each issue describes 100 to 200+ positions in four categories: Academics and research (criminal justice); Law enforcement and security (police officers, document examiners, print examiners, criminologists, public service aides, jailers); Community services and corrections (correctional trainees, psychologists, social workers, physicians, speech pathologists, communications, clerical, counselors, probation officers); and Institutional corrections (correctional officers, psychologists, nurses, chaplains, cooks, therapists, pharmacists, trades and laborers).

The Criminologist (American Society of Criminology, 1314 Kinnear Rd., Suite 212, Columbus, OH, 43212; phone: 614/292–9207) bimonthly, $7.50/annual nonmember subscription (U.S.), $10/foreign, free/members. Ten to 12 jobs for probation officers, police, and faculty are listed under "Positions Announcements."

Law Enforcement News (John Jay College of Criminal Justice, Suite 438, 899 Tenth Ave., New York, NY 10019; phone: 212/237–8442) bimonthly, $18/annual subscription (U.S.) $28/foreign countries. Jobs listed under "Jobs."

Employment Bulletin (American Sociological Association, 1722 N St., NW, Washington, DC 20036; phone: 202/833–3410) monthly, $23/nonmember annual subscription, $8/members. This newsletter features about 70 positions in academic, applied, and fellowship settings. Most positions are in sociology, but also related areas such as anthropology and criminology.

Directories

American Society of Criminology Membership Directory (American Society of Criminology, 1314 Kinnear Rd., Suite 212, Columbus, OH, 43212; phone: 614/292–9207) free/members only, published in even–numbered years.

Anderson's 1991 Directory of Criminal Justice Education (Anderson Publishing Company, P.O. Box 1576, Cincinnati, OH 45201; phone: 800/582–7295) $59.95. Features information on all levels of criminal justice education, including 1,100 colleges and universities. Includes department chairs (address and phone), faculty characteristics, enrollment, and course offerings.

Crime, Law Enforcement & Abuse Prevention (The Foundation Center, 79 Fifth Ave., New York, NY 10003–3076; phones: 800/424–9836, within New York State call 212/620–4230) $65 plus $4.50/shipping, October 1993. Describes recent foundation grants of at least $10,000 for crime prevention, rehabilitation services for offenders, courts and the administration of justice, law enforcement agencies, and protection against and prevention of neglect, abuse, or exploitation. This directory is useful for identifying foundations and grant recipients for which you may wish to work.

Chapter 27

Science

*Also see the "Museums and libraries" and "Research" chapters in this book. For a much more extensive listing of science and engineering job sources, see the **Professional's Private Sector Job Finder.** The job sources presented in this chapter focus on academic and research laboratory employment.*

Science in general

Job ads in print

Science (American Association of the Advancement of Science, 1333 H St., NW, Washington, DC 20005; phone: 202/326–6539) 51 issues/year, $87/annual subscription (U.S.), call for foreign rates. "Personnel Placement" overflows with around 200 advertisements for scientists of all types, although most ads seem to be for biologists and scientists in academia.

Nature (P.O. Box 1733, Riverton, NJ 08077–9733; phone: 800/524–0384) weekly, $135/annual subscription. Job ads for over 300 scientists of all sorts appear in "Classified."

AAS Job Register (American Astronomical Society, 1630 Connecticut Ave., NW, Suite 200, Washington, DC 20009; phone: 202/328–2010) monthly, free/members only. The entire issue is packed to the gills with ads for 20 or more astronomy positions, with universities or laboratories.

AWIS Magazine (Association for Women in Science, 1522 K St., NW, Suite 820, Washington, DC 20005; phone: 202/408–0742) bimonthly, $55/annual nonmember subscription, included in member dues. From 10 to 25 ads for life, physical, social, and mathematical sciences and engineering appear under "Help Wanted–Employment Advertisements."

GSA Today (Geological Society of America, P.O. Box 9140, Boulder, CO 80301; phones: 800/472–1988, 303/447–2020) monthly, $40/annual nonmember subscription, free/members. Four or five openings in the earth sciences appear under "Classifieds–Positions Open."

New· Scientist (IPC Magazines, Ltd., Freepost 1061, Hawwards Heath, England RH16 3ZA) weekly, £110/United Kingdom annual subscription, $130 (U.S. dollars)/annual subscription via air mail to the U.S., $170 (Canadian dollars)/annual subscription via air mail to Canada. Over 100 science positions in England are listed throughout, including government jobs. The publisher failed to respond to our request to update information from the 1992 edition of this book. If you reach the publisher, please use the *Reader Feedback Form* near the end of this book to tell us the updated subscription and address information.

ACA Newsletter (American Crystallographic Association, P.O. Box 96, Ellicott Station, Buffalo, NY 14205–0095; phone: 716/856–9600, ext. 321) quarterly, available only to members, included in dues. "Positions Available" features about ten job ads for chemistry and physics positions in research laboratories and universities.

The New Careers Directory: Internships in Technology and Social Change (Student Pugwash USA, 1638 R St., NW, Suite 32, Washington, DC 20009; phone: 202/328–6555) $18, $10/students; add $3 shipping, 1993. Offers full details on where and how to apply for internships and entry–level jobs in science and society.

Job service

Employment Matching Service (Geological Society of America, P.O. Box 9140, Boulder, CO 80301; phones: 800/472–1988, 303/447–2020) $60/annual nonmember fee, $30/members. Registrants complete a form and include a two–page resume. Employers receive printouts of these forms throughout the year and are responsible for contacting applicants directly.

Directories

AAS Membership Directory (American Astronomical Society, 1630 Connecticut Ave., NW, Suite 200, Washington, DC 20009; phone: 202/328–2010) $20/nonmembers (you must write to AAS and state why you want the directory), free/members, issued each January.

GSA Membership Directory (Geological Society of America, P.O. Box 9140, Boulder, CO 80301; phones: 800/472–1988, 303/447–2020) available only to members, $16, usually issued each May, last published June 1993.

Geotimes (American Geological Institute, 4220 King St., Alexandria, VA 22302; phone: 703/379–2480) $3.50, October issue only. Contains a directory of members of the world's geoscience community.

Directory of the American Association of Physics Teachers (AAPT, 5112 Berwyn Rd., 2nd Floor, College Park, MD 20740; phone: 801/345–4200) free/members only, last issued in 1989.

Grants for Science & Technology Programs (The Foundation Center, 79 Fifth Ave., New York, NY 10003–3076; phones: 800/424–9836, within New York State call 212/620–4230) $65 plus $4.50/shipping, October 1993. Describes recent foundation grants of at least $10,000 for education and research in computer science and technology; scientific societies, associations and institutes; science museums; planetariums; and libraries. This directory is useful for identifying foundations and grant recipients for which you may wish to work.

Salary survey

Careers in Biotechnology (Industrial Biotechnology Association, 1625 K St., NW, Washington, DC 20006; phone: 202/857–0244) contact for price, most recently published in 1990. In addition to explaining this emerging field in some detail, this directory describes the training needed, sources of additional information, relevant associations, sample job ads and job descriptions, a guide to recruiters for biotechnology jobs, and results of a salary survey. Specialties included in biotechnology are chemists, chemical engineers, physicists, engineers, biologists, and geneticists.

Biological sciences

Job ads in print

ASM News (American Society for Microbiology, 1325 Massachusetts Ave., NW, Washington, DC 20005; phone: 202/737–3600) monthly, $25/annual nonmember subscription, free/members. You'll find between 22 to 50 job opportunities for biologists, molecular biologists, and microbiologists under "Employment."

Journal of National Technical Association (Black Collegiate Services, 1240 N. Broad Ave., New Orleans, LA 70125; phone: 504/821–5694) bimonthly, $30/annual subscription. 30 to 40 jobs ads appear throughout the magazine for engineer, science, and technology positions.

The FASEB Journal (Federation of American Societies for Experimental Biology, 9650 Rockville Pike, Bethesda, MD 20814–3998; phone: 301/530–7020) monthly, $95/annual subscription (U.S.), $115/Canada and Mexico, $143/foreign. About 20 ads for life science positions, mostly at the doctoral level, appear under "Employment Opportunities." An equal number of "Position Desired" ads also appear.

ASC Bulletin (American Society of Cytology, 1015 Chestnut St., Suite 1518, Philadelphia, PA 19107; phone: 215/922–3880) bimonthly, free, available only to members. Around 5 to 10 positions for cyto–technologists are in the "Classifieds."

The Physiologist (American Physiological Society, 9650 Rockville Pike, Bethesda, MD 20814; phone: 301/530–7180) bimonthly, $25/nonmember annual subscription (U.S.), $35/foreign, free/members. "Positions Available" carries ads for five or six university teaching and research positions.

Bio/Technology (Nature Publishing Company, P.O. Box 1721, Riverton, NJ 08077–7321; phone: 800/524–0328) monthly, $29.50/annual subscription (U.S., Canada). Around 20 job ads are under "Classified."

ESA Newsletter (Entomological Society of America, 9301 Annapolis Rd., Suite 300, Lanham, MD 20706–3115; phone: 301/731–4535) monthly, $15/nonmember annual subscription, $8/members, $2/single copies. "Opportunities" lists ten to 15 jobs for entomologists, biologists, geneticists, and toxicologists.

SOT Newsletter (Society of Toxicology, 1101 14th St., NW, Suite 1100, Washington, DC 20005; phone: 202/371–1393) five issues/year, free, available only to members. "Placement Service" typically has about eight job ads for toxicologists.

American Journal of Botany (Botanical Society of America, 1735 Neil Ave., Columbus, OH 43210–1293; phone: 614/292–3519) monthly, $155/annual subscription (U.S.), $165/Canada, $180/elsewhere. Four to eight ads for botanists and biologists appear under "Positions Available." Four times a year, *Plant Science Bulletin* is included free. It also includes job ads.

BioScience (American Institute of Biological Sciences, 703 11th St., NW, Washington, DC 20001–4521; phone: 202/628–1500) 11 issues/year, $49.50/annual subscription. "Professional Opportunities" features about three ads for biologists.

SIM News (Society for Industrial Microbiology, PO Box 329, Annandale, VA 22203; phone: 703/941–5373) bimonthly, free/members, $6/per copy nonmembers. One or two ads for microbiologists are in "Placement."

Genetic Engineering News (1651 Third Ave., New York, NY 10128; phone: 212/289–2300) twenty–one issues/year, $190/annual subscription. Only one or two ads for biochemists, bioengineers, and biologists appear under "Classified."

Job services

FASEB Placement Service (Federation of American Societies for Experimental Biology, 9650 Rockville Pike, Bethesda, MD 20814–3998; phone: 301/530–7020) $20/annual registration fee. If you register before January 22, you'll be included in the annual Candidates, a bound collection of current registrations published and distributed each February to about 300 potential employers. All registrants are entitled to place a "Position Desired" ad in one issue of the *FASEB Journal* (described earlier under "Job Openings"). You can place additional "Position Desired" ads for $15 each. Employers may also see your registration "resume" form when they review registrants at the FASEB office. FASEB staff refer about 1,400 registrants each year to employers with whom they match position qualifications. For an additional $20 you can receive a copy of Positions, published each March, in which vacancies are listed. You can also use the interview scheduling services, but you must report in person at the Placement Service at the appropriate meeting to initiate this last service.

SOT Placement Service (Society of Toxicology, 1101 14th St., NW, Suite 1100, Washington, DC 20005; phone: 202/371–1393) $10/full–associate member, free/post–doctoral member, free/full–time student member, $25/full–associate eligible nonmember, $20/post–doctoral nonmember, $15/full–time student nonmember. Complete this services narrative resume form and computer form to be a part of SOT's annual meeting placement service. This is a service that matches job seekers to employers through networking by attending their annual meeting. At the meeting, job listings are posted in a separate room and contact between candidates and employers are made through a message board and interviews. Although it may be helpful for a candidate to attend the meeting to make personal contact with employers it is not necessary. Even if you are not registered for the meeting, jobs posted at the meeting may be obtained by calling SOT. Meetings held annually, usually towards the beginning of the year. 1994 meeting is held March 13–17th. Call for registration cut–off date. You are able to register late but fee triples if you do.

American Society for Microbiology Placement Service (ASM, 1325 Massachusetts Ave., NW, Washington, DC 20005; phone: 202/737–3600) $100/nonmember annual fee, $40/members. You fill out their registry form. When there is a match, your form is sent to the employer who is responsible for contacting you.

SIM Placement Service (Society for Industrial Microbiology, c/o Jim Kowowski, Abbot Laboratories, D47P Building AP9A, Abbot Park, IL 60064–3500; phone: 708/937–7967) free. You submit your own resume. When a job match is made, you are notified and are responsible for contacting the potential employer. Positions include microbiologists, quality assurance, fermentation, bioremediation, process control, and research.

BioTron (American Institute of Biological Sciences, 703 11th St., NW, Washington, DC 20001–4521; phone: 202/628–1500) free. Using your computer modem, call 202/628–2427 anytime to access job vacancies. The communications configuration is 300, 1200, or 2400 baud, 8 data bits, 1 stop bit, no parity, full duplex, Xon/Xoff active, carriage return (ASCII 13) at end of lines. Received text may be stopped and started by pressing Control–S/Q.

Questionnaire on Employment Status of Women in Physiology (American Physiological Society, 9650 Rockville Pike, Bethesda, MD 20814; phone: 301/530–7171) free/female members only. You complete the resume questionnaire which is kept on file indefinitely. When a university department chair is hiring faculty, she can request copies of these questionnaires as part of the faculty search.

Directories

FASEB Directory of Members (Federation of American Societies for Experimental Biology, 9650 Rockville Pike, Bethesda, MD 20814; phone: 301/530–7000) $50/nonmembers, free/members of American Physiological Society, American Society for Biochemistry and Molecular Biology, American Society for Pharmacology and Experimental Therapeutics, American Association of Pathologists, American Institute of Nutrition, American Association of Immunologists, and American Society for Cell Biology; over 450 pages, annual.

Society of Toxicology Membership Directory (SOT, 1101 14th St., NW, Suite 1100, Washington, DC 20005; phone: 202/371–1393) free/members only, issued each June.

SIM Membership Directory (Society for Industrial Microbiology, PO Box 329, Annandale, VA 22203; phone: 703/941–5373) free, available only to members, issued in odd–numbered years.

Membership Directory (Genetics Society of America, 9650 Rockville Pike, Bethesda, MD 20814; phone: 301/571–1825) free/members only, issued in the spring of even–numbered years. Includes members of GSA, American Society of Human Genetics, and the American Board of Medical Genetics.

Botanical Society of America Directory (BSA, 1735 Neil Ave., Columbus, OH 43210–1293; phone: 614/292–3519) $10/nonmembers, free/members, published in the spring of even–numbered years.

Salary survey

Salaries of Scientists, Engineers, and Technicians (Commission on Professionals in Science and Technology, 1500 Massachusetts Ave., NW, Suite 831, Washington, DC 20005; phone: 202/223–6995) $75/nonmembers, $50/members, issued every two years, last published August 1993. Reports the results of about 50 salary surveys.

Chemistry

Also see listings under "Engineers" in this chapter.

Job ads in print

Chemical & Engineering News (American Chemical Society, 1155 16th St., NW, Washington, DC 20036; phones: 800/227–5558, 202/872–4363) weekly, call for rates. "Classifieds" contain around 25 to 30 private sector positions as another 25 to 30 positions in academia.

Chemical Engineering (McGraw–Hill, P.O. Box 507, Hightstown, NJ 08520; phone: 800/257–9402) monthly, $29.50/annual subscription (U.S.), $35.50/Canada. You'll find 15 to 20 vacancies for chemical, process, mechanical, and environmental engineers under "Employment Opportunities."

CHEMJOBS USA (American Chemical Society, 1155 16th St., NW, Washington, DC 20036; phones: 800/227–5558, 202/872–4363; press code 3) weekly, contact for nonmember and member rates. This bulletin includes abstracts of job ads for chemists from several major U.S. publications. It is also accessible by computer modem via ACS/NET for a small fee. Contact ACS for details.

Clinical Chemistry News (American Association for Clinical Chemistry, 2101 L St., NW, Suite 202, Washington, DC 20037; phones: 800/892–1400, 202/857–0717) monthly, $30/annual nonmember subscription,

free/members. About six positions for clinical chemists and clinical laboratory personnel are printed under "Classified." "Positions Wanted" ads also
appear.

Analytical Chemistry (American Chemical Society, 1155 16th St., NW,
Washington, DC 20036; phones: 800/227–5558, 202/872–4363) semimonthly, call for rates. Ads for private sector and academia are included.

CHEMTECH (American Chemical Society, 1155 16th St., NW, Washington,
DC 20036; phones: 800/227–5558, 202/872–4363) monthly, call for rates.
Includes job ads.

Job services

Year–Round Professional Data Bank (American Chemical Society, 1155
16th St., NW, Washington, DC 20036; phones: 800/227–5558, 202/872–
4363, press code 3) free/members only. Complete the "Professional Information Summary Form" which is then entered into ACS's Professional Data
Bank. When a job match is made, your entry is sent to the employer who
is responsible for contacting you. Each month all registrants' forms are sent
to participating employers.

Confidential Employment Listing Service (American Chemical Society,
1155 16th St., NW, Washington, DC 20036; phone: 800/227–5558, press
code 3) available only to members, fee charged. This is a part of the ACS's
Year–Round Professional Data Bank. You provide a list of employers who
should *not* receive your qualifications. The information sent to employers
does not include your name or other personal information. Interested
employers contact ACS which then contacts you. If you are interested, you
contact the employer.

American Association for Clinical Chemistry Employment Service (AACC,
2101 L St., NW, Suite 202, Washington, DC 20037; phones: 800/892–
1400, 202/857–0717) $45/annual nonmember fee, $25/members; add $25
for AACC to type your form for you. You complete the AACC Candidate
Registration Form which is then placed in the AACC's *Resume Book* which
is distributed to over 100 employers at the annual national meeting and
throughout the year. Interested employers contact you directly. Interviewing
is available at the annual meeting held at the end of July. In addition,
registrants receive the AACC *Jobs Packet* which gives details on up to 250
job openings for clinical laboratory professionals at all levels. Throughout
the year, until April, you will be sent new position postings as AACC receives
them.

Salary survey

Salaries (American Chemical Society, 1155 16th St., NW, Washington, DC 20036; phones: 800/227–5558, 202/872–4363) annual, call for rate. Results of salary survey of ACS members.

Engineers

Also see entries under "Chemistry" and "Physics" in this chapter.

Job ads in print

Prism (American Society for Engineering Education, 11 Dupont Cr., Suite 200, Washington, DC 20036; phone: 202/986–8500) ten issues/year, $75/annual nonmember subscription, free/members. Around 30 to 75 vacancies in private industry and academia are published under "Classified."

Minority Engineer (Equal Opportunity Publications, 150 Motor Parkway, Suite 420, Hauppauge, NY 11788–5145; phone: 516/273–0066) three issues/year, $17/annual subscription, free/minority engineering professionals and minority. college students within two years of graduation (must complete detailed form). Around 40 vacancies for engineers are scattered throughout.

Woman Engineer (Equal Opportunity Publications, 150 Motor Parkway, Suite 420, Hauppauge, NY 11788–5145; phone: 516/273–0066) three issues/year, $17/annual subscription. Over 20 display ads throughout this magazine feature positions in all areas of engineering.

U.S. Woman Engineer (Society of Women Engineers, 120 Wall Street, New York, NY 10005; phone: 212/509–9577) bimonthly, $20/nonmember annual subscription, free/members. Five to 25 ads for all types of engineers appear under "Classified/Recruitment Advertising."

NSBE Magazine (National Society of Black Engineers, 1454 Duke St., PO Box 25588, Alexandria, VA 22313–5588; phone: 703/549–2207) five issues/year; $10/nonmember annual subscription, included in membership package. 40 engineering positions are advertised in every issue including college and university teaching positions.

Nuclear News (American Nuclear Society, 555 N. Kensington Ave., La Grange Park, IL 60525; phone: 708/352–6611) 15 issues/year, $194/annual subscription (U.S.), $194/Canada, $226/elsewhere) "Employment" runs about 40 job vacancy announcements for nuclear engineers, quality assurance engineers, and mechanical engineers.

Chemical Engineering Progress (American Institute of Chemical Engineers, 345 E. 47th St., New York, NY 10017; phone: 212/705–7663) monthly, $75/annual nonmember subscription (U.S.), $125/foreign, free/members. Between 70 and 90 job ads for chemical engineers grace the "Classified Advertising." In even–numbered years, the June issue contains the *AIChE Salary Survey Report*, described below under "Salary surveys."

InTech (Instrument Society of America, 67 Alexander Dr., Research Triangle Park, NC 27709; phone: 800/334–6391) monthly, free, available only to members. "Special Classifieds" include 20 to 30 job ads for engineers.

Microwaves and RF (Penton Publications, 1100 Superior Ave., Cleveland, OH 44114; phone: 216/696–7000) 13 issues/year, $60/annual subscription, free to qualified professionals. Three to ten display ads for engineers, primarily in microwave technology and instrumentation (some management) appear throughout.

ASME News (American Society of Mechanical Engineers, 22 Law Drive, Fairfield, NJ 07007; phones: 800/843–2763, 212/705–7722) monthly, free, available only to members. Around two positions for mechanical engineers appear in "Opportunities."

The Environmental Engineer (American Academy of Environmental Engineers, Suite 100, 130 Holiday Ct., Annapolis, MD 21401; phone: 410/266–3311) quarterly, $20/annual subscription (U.S. and Canada), $30/elsewhere. Typical issue features two to four display ads for jobs.

Cost Engineering (American Association of Cost Engineers International, P.O. Box 1557, Morgantown, WV 26507–1557; phone: 304/296–8444) monthly, $42/nonmember annual subscription, free/members. Scattered throughout are four to eight ads for cost engineers, control managers, and cost estimators and controllers.

Job services

Resume Referral Service (Instrument Society of America, 67 Alexander Dr., Research Triangle Park, NC 27709; phone: 800/334–6391) free/members only. The resume service form you complete is kept on file for three months. When a match is achieved, you are contacted. Positions included are engineers and technicians.

Job Referral Service (American Institute of Chemical Engineers, 345 E. 47th St., New York, NY 10017; phone: 212/705–7525) one–time registration fee: $70/nonmembers, $35/employed members, $25/unemployed members. Request the "Position Desired Form," complete it and submit it with your payment. To avoid tipping off your current employer that you are looking for another job, you can check a box on the form so your name will not be released to your present employer. The information on your form will be placed in the *Job Referral Service's* database and kept there for as long as you wish. When you are matched to a job, you'll be asked to send your resume to the contact person at the prospective employer's office. The service will also notify the prospective employer of your job match.

Placement Service (American Nuclear Society, 555 N. Kensington Ave., La Grange Park, IL 60525; phone: 708/352–6611) $35/nonmembers, $25/members. Fill out this service's form and your resume will be on file for six months. When a match is made, this service notifies you. You are responsible for contacting the potential employer.

American Association of Cost Engineers International Resume Service (AACE, P.O. Box 1557, Morgantown, WV 26507–1557; phone: 304/296–8444) free/members only. A member submits his resume which is kept in the database for six months. When a match is made, the resume is given to the potential employer who is responsible for contacting the job candidate.

Directories

National Association of Minority Engineering Program Administrators Membership Directory (NAMEPA, 500 N. Michigan Ave., Suite 1400, Chicago, IL 60611; phone: 312/661–1700) free/members only, published each January.

ASCE Membership Directory (American Society of Civil Engineers, 345 E. 47th St., New York, NY 10017; phone: 212/705–7288 or 7276) $100/nonmembers, $25/members.

Directory of Engineering Societies and Related Organizations (American Association of Engineering Societies, 1111 19th St., NW, Suite 608, Washington, DC 20036–3690; phones: 800/658–8897, 202/296–2237) $185/nonmembers, $115/members, 327 pages, last published in 1993. Provides information on over 950 organizations in the U.S. and overseas.

Directory of Engineering Societies and Related Organizations, 1994 Supplement (American Association of Engineering Societies, 1111 19th St., NW, Suite 608, Washington, DC 20036–3690; phones: 800/658–8897, 202/296–2237) $85/nonmembers, $48/members. Adds over 200 organizations to the 1993 edition. If purchasing both the 1993 edition and the supplement, the total cost is $200/nonmembers, $125/members.

The Biotechnology Directory (Stockton Press, 257 Park Avenue South, New York, NY 10010; phones: 800/221–2123 [outside New York state], 212/673–4400 [from within New York state]) $235 plus $5/shipping, 1993. Includes the often hard–to–find government departments engaged in biotechnology as well as over 10,000 companies, research centers, and academic institutions involved in the field.

Directory of Engineering Graduate Studies and Research (American Society for Engineering Education, 11 Dupont Circle, Suite 200, Washington, DC 20036; phone: 202/986–8500) $69.95/nonmembers, $34.95/members and students, plus $3 shipping, annual, issued each September. Lists schools by type of program, dean's names, address, phone number, accredited or not, and specific types of engineering.

Directory of Undergraduate Programs in Engineering and Engineering Technology (American Society for Engineering Education, 11 Dupont Circle, Suite 200, Washington, DC 20036; phone: 202/986–8500) $49.95/nonmembers, $24.95/members and students, plus $3 shipping, annual. Lists school information by type of program and specific types of engineering.

Salary surveys

Annual Salary Survey by Engineering Manpower Consortium (American Society of Mechanical Engineers, 22 Law Drive, Fairfield, NJ 07007; phones: 800/843–2763, 212/705–7782) annual, free/members only.

AIChE Salary Survey Report (American Institute of Chemical Engineers, 345 E. 47th St., New York, NY 10017; phone: 212/705–7523) $40/nonmembers, $20/members, 11 pages, published in June of even–numbered years. Included in the June issue of *Chemical Engineering Progress* described above under "Job ads in print."

Salaries of Engineers in Education (American Association of Engineering Societies, 1111 19th St., NW, Suite 608, Washington, DC 20036–5703; phones: 800/658–8897, 202/296–2237) $115/nonmembers, $70/members, 100 pages, published every July. Details the median, quartile, decile, and mean salaries of engineers in educational institutions, quantified by academic rank, length of contract, and years of experience.

American Association of Cost Engineers International Salary Survey (AACE, P.O. Box 1557, Morgantown, WV 26507–1557; phone: 304/296–8444) appears in the September or October issue of *Cost Engineering*, described above under "Job ads in print."

Mathematics

Job ads in print

AMSTAT News (American Statistical Association, 1429 Duke St., Alexandria, VA 22314–3402; phone: 703/684–1221) monthly, free/members only. The number of job ads for statisticians, biostatisticians, and educators that are printed in "Professional Opportunities" typically varies between 30 and 100.

Employment Information in the Mathematical Sciences (American Mathematical Society, PO Box 6248, Providence, RI 02904; phones: 800/321–4267, 401/455–4000) bimonthly, $93/annual subscription. Dozens upon dozens of job vacancies for mathematics–related positions for Ph.D. level mathematicians in universities, and a small number of positions in industry and government.

SIAM News (Society for Industrial and Applied Mathematics, 3600 University City Science Center, Philadelphia, PA 19104–2688; phone: 215/382–9800) eight issues/year, $18/annual nonmember subscription, free/members. Fifty to 60 job ads, primarily for mathematics and engineering professors, appear under "Professional Opportunities."

Directory

Directory of Members (American Statistical Association, 1429 Duke St., Alexandria, VA 22314–3402; phone: 703/684–1221) $125/nonmembers, $25/members, published in May of 1991 and every three years thereafter. Includes members of the ASA, Biometric Society (Eastern and Western North American Regions), Institute of Mathematical Statistics, and Statistical Society of Canada.

Physics

Also see entries under "Engineers" in this chapter.

Job ads in print

Physics Today (American Institute of Physics, 500 Sunnyside Blvd., Wood-bury, NY 11797–2999; phone: 516/576–2200) monthly, $130/annual non-member subscription (U.S.), $145/Canada and Mexico, $160/elsewhere, free/members, $20/per copy nonmember, $15/per copy member. Around 115 job openings for physicists, university and college professors, lecturers, physicians, engineers, and chemists appear under "Information Exchange."

Directory

Listing of Members (American Physical Society, American Institute of Physics, 500 Sunnyside Blvd., Woodbury, NY 11797; phone: 516/399–5810) contact for nonmember price, free/members. This is an issue of the *Bulletin of the American Physical Society*. This directory of member physicists is published in December of odd–numbered years.

Salary survey

Salary Report (American Institute of Physics, Education and Employment Division, 335 E. 45th St., New York, NY 10017; phone: 212/661–9404) free; most recent survey published in 1990.

Utilities

*For a much more extensive listing of job sources, see both the **Government Job Finder** and the **Professional's Private Sector Job Finder.***

Job ads in print

Public Utilities Fortnightly (Public Utilities Reports, Inc., Suite 200, 2111 Wilson Blvd., Arlington, VA 22201; phone: 703/243–7000) bimonthly; $97/annual subscription. Few job ads.

APGA Newsletter (American Public Gas Association, 11094–D Lee High-way, Suite 102, Fairfax, VA 22033; phone: 703/352–3890) biweekly, free/members only. Jobs listed under "Position Available." Few job ads; job ads not in every issue.

Chapter 28

Social sciences

*Also see the "Housing, planning, and development"
chapter and the "Education" chapter.*

Job ads in print

Anthropology Newsletter (American Anthropological Association, 4350 N. Fairfax Dr., Suite 640, Arlington, VA 22203; phone: 703/528–1902) nine issues/year, $55/annual nonmember subscription, free/members. "Placement" runs around 50 ads for faculty and research positions.

Bulletin of the SAA (Society for American Archaeology, The Railway Express Building, 900 2nd Street, NE, Suite 12, Washington, DC 20006; phone: 202/789–8200) five issues/year, $15/annual nonmember subscription, included in dues. About six ads for archaeologists and anthropologists are listed under "Positions Open."

History News Dispatch (American Association for State and Local History, 530 Church St., Suite 600, Nashville, TN 37219–2325; phone: 615/255–2971) monthly, $30/members only. About 20 to 35 ads for historians, archivists, and educators appear under "The Marketplace." Includes positions with historical societies, historic sites, libraries, archives, and museums.

Personnel Service Newsletter (American Political Science Association, 1527 New Hampshire Ave., NW, Washington, DC 20036; phone: 202/483–2512) monthly, $32/members only. Each issue has 25 or more job vacancies in political science. Most positions are for faculty and researchers.

Employment Bulletin (American Sociological Association, 1722 N St., NW, Washington, DC 20036; phone: 202/833–3410) monthly, $23/nonmember annual subscription, $8/members. This newsletter features about 70 positions in academic, applied, and fellowship settings. Most positions are in sociology, but also related areas such as anthropology and criminology.

The Rural Sociologist (Rural Sociological Society, c/o Patrik Jobes, Treasurer, Department of Sociology, Wilson Hall, Montana State University, Bozeman, MT 59717) quarterly, $18/annual nonmember subscription, free/members. "Announcements" carries two or three positions for faculty and researchers. "Grants and Fellowships" includes announcements for four or five opportunities.

Job services

Placement Service (American Anthropological Association, 4350 N. Fairfax Dr., Suite 640, Arlington, VA 22203; phone: 703/528–1902) $110/nonmember annual fee, $35/members. There are three aspects to this service. First, you will receive a small newsletter with all the job ads that will appear three weeks later in the *Anthropology Newsletter* described above under "Job ads in print." Second, you are requested to complete a short resume form which is sent to prospective employers prior to the AAA's annual convention in late autumn. Interested employers will contact you to arrange an interview at the annual meeting. Third, you are sent a list of job openings from employers who will be interviewing at the annual meeting. You may contact them to arrange an interview there.

Dial–a–Job and *Dial–an–Internship* (National Association for Interpretation, P.O. Box 1892, Ft. Collins, CO 80522; 303/491–6434) Call 303/491–7410 24 hours a day for a recording of full–time, seasonal, and temporary jobs in environmental education, interpretation, and related fields including historians, archaeologists, museum personnel, and publication designers. The tape runs from 10 to 30 minutes. Updated weekly. For internships, call 303/491–6784 24 hours a day. The tape runs from 5 to 20 minutes. Updated weekly.

Directories

AAA Guide (American Anthropological Association, 4350 N. Fairfax Dr., Suite 640, Arlington, VA 22203; phone: 703/528–1902) $50/nonmembers, $35/members, issued each September. Lists 11,000 members plus university anthropology departments.

Directory of Historical Organizations in the United States and Canada (American Association for State and Local History, 530 Church St., Suite 600, Nashville, TN 37219–2325; phone: 615/255–2971) $79.95/nonmembers, $71.95/members, 1990. Includes history–related organizations with brief descriptions of staff. Also includes product and service vendors.

Directory of Members (American Society for Eighteenth–Century Studies, Computer Center 108, Utah State University, Logan, UT 84322–3730; phone: 801/750–4065 [till March 1994], 801/797–0128 [after March 1994]) $12.50/nonmembers, free/members, approximately 200 pages, issued in odd–numbered years.

Grants for Social and Political Science Programs (The Foundation Center, 79 Fifth Ave., New York, NY 10003–3076; phones: 800/424–9836, within New York State call 212/620–4230) $65 plus $4.50/shipping, October 1993. Describes recent foundation grants of at least $10,000 for research and education in political science, sociology, anthropology, psychology, economics, behavioral science, population studies, international studies, ethnic studies, women's studies, urban and rural studies, poverty studies, and law. This directory is useful for identifying foundations and grant recipients for which you may wish to work.

Salary survey

APSA Survey of Political Science Departments (American Political Science Association, 1527 New Hampshire Ave., NW, Washington, DC 20036; phone: 202/483–2512) $20, annual. Last published April 1993. Gives salary information and enrollment trends of four–year institutions offering political science.

Chapter 29

Social services

*Also see the job sources described in this book's "Health care" chapter, the **Government Job Finder's** "Social services" and "Mental health" sections, and in the **Professional's Private Sector Job Finder's** "Social services" and "Health care" chapters.*

Job ads in print

NASW News (National Association of Social Workers, 750 First St., Suite 700, NE, Washington, DC 20002; phone: 800/638–8799) 10 issues/year, $25/nonmember subscription, included in membership package. Jobs listed under "The Classifieds." The typical issue is filled to the brim with over 200 job ads in the arenas of social work, human services, mental health, public health, and social services.

in COMMON BULLETIN–Career Opportunities Working with Deaf People (Parkhill Press, P.O. Box 60, New Market, MD 21774; phone: 301/865–1701) biweekly, $25/three–month subscription, $40/six months, $60/annual subscription. Each issue features 100 to 120 positions in human services, sign language interpreting, social work, counseling, psychology, school administration, teaching, and other areas of working with people who are deaf or hard of hearing.

Social Service Jobs (Employment Listings for Social Services, 10 Angelica Dr., Framingham, MA 01701; phone: 508/626–8644) biweekly, $42/six issues, $62/twelve issues, $118/annual subscription. Typical issue features 140+ positions listed by geographic region.

Professional Opportunities Bulletin (Association Jewish Family and Children's Services, 3086 Highway 27, Suite 11, Kendall Park, NJ 08824; phones: 800/634–0909, 980/821–0909) bimonthly, free. Each issue is filled with over 15 vacancies for social workers, family and childrens' services, family and children therapists, and group home staff. Includes senior management and direct client contact positions.

Management Opportunities (Family Service America, Inc., 11700 W. Lake Park Dr., Milwaukee, WI 53224; phone: 414/359–1040) monthly, $25/six–month subscription, free/members. Each issue has six to 12 job ads for management positions in social work including executive directors. This organization also has services that consist of a resume critique ($25/nonmembers, free/members) and CEO candidate consultation ($100/nonmembers, free/members). Call for further details.

Job Exchange (Association for Education and Rehabilitation of the Blind, 206 N. Washington St., Suite 320, Alexandria, VA 22314; phone: 703/836–6060) monthly, available only to members: first six months free, $10/year thereafter. From 40 to 60 vacancies for administrators and practitioners (orientation and mobility specialists, teachers of persons with visual impairments, etc.) grace a typical issue.

Newsounds (Alexander Graham Bell Association, 3417 Volta Place, NW, Washington, DC 20007; phone: 202/337–5220) ten issues/year, $42/annual nonmember subscription, free/members. The "Classified" section carries ads for about ten positions for audiologists, teachers of persons with hearing impairments, interpreters, and administrators.

American Annals of the Deaf (Kendall School, Outreach Services KDES–PAS–6, 800 Florida Ave., NE, Washington, DC 20002; phone: 202/651–5342) five issues/year, $50/annual subscription. One or two ads for teachers of children with hearing impairments appear as classifieds or display ads.

Occupational Therapist Weekly (164 Rollins Ave., Suite 301, Rockville, MD 20852; phone: 301/881–2490) weekly, free to qualified professionals. About 225 positions fill the pages of this newsletter.

Guidepost (American Rehabilitation Counseling Association, 5999 Stevenson Ave., Alexandria, VA 22304–3300; phone: 703/823–9800, ext. 244) 12 issues/year, $30/annual subscription. "Employment Classifieds" describe around 35 vacancies for psychologists and counselors in private practice, agencies, and universities.

Hospital and Community Psychiatry (American Psychiatric Association, 1400 K St., NW, Washington, DC 20005; phone: 202/682–6228) monthly, $40/annual subscription (U.S.), $60/foreign. About 75 jobs are listed under "Classified Advertising."

Special Recreation Digest (Special Recreation, Inc., 362 Koser Ave., Iowa City, IA 52246–3038; phone: 319/337–7578) quarterly, $39.95/annual subscription. Fifteen activity or recreation positions such as therapists, coordinators, and administrators appear under "Recreation."

The U.S. Journal of Drug and Alcohol Dependence (Enterprise Center, 3201 SW 15th St., Deerfield Beach, FL 33442; phones: 800/851–9100, 305/360–9233) monthly, $49/annual subscription (U.S.); inquire for foreign rates. Jobs listed under "Classifieds." Seven to 15 job ads per issue.

The Counselor (National Association of Alcoholism and Drug Abuse Counselors, 3717 Columbia Pike, Suite 300, Arlington, VA 22204; phone: 703/920–4644) bimonthly, $36/nonmember annual subscription, included in membership package. Jobs listed under "Employment Classifieds." Typical issue features over 10 job ads, usually for upper level counselors with medical facilities.

Professional Report (National Rehabilitation Counseling Association, 1910 Association Drive, Suite 206, Reston, VA 22091; phone: 703/620–4404) bimonthly, available to members only. Jobs listed under "Job Openings." Some issues have no jobs listed. Few job ads.

AAMR News & Notes (American Association on Mental Retardation, 1719 Kalorama Rd., NW, Washington, DC 20009; phones: 800/424–3688, 202/387–1968) six issues/year, $35/nonmember annual subscription (U.S.), $50/elsewhere, included in dues. Jobs listed under "Classifieds." Five to 20 ads appear in the typical issue.

Mental Retardation (American Association on Mental Retardation, 1719 Kalorama Rd., NW, Washington, DC 20009; phones: 800/424–3688, 202/387–1968) bimonthly, $75/nonmember annual subscription (U.S.), $81/Canada, $90/elsewhere. Jobs listed under "The Exchange." Five to ten ads an issue.

TASH Newsletter (The Association for Persons with Severe Handicaps, 11201 Greenwood Ave. North, Seattle, WA 98133; phones: 206/361–8870, **TDD**: 206/361–0113) monthly, free/members only. About ten jobs are advertised under "Positions Open."

The Family Therapy Networker (8528 Bradford Rd., Silver Spring, MD 20901; phone: 301/589–6536) bimonthly, $20/annual subscription. One or two ads for clinical social workers and in mental health are under "Classified—Employment."

Family Therapy News (American Association for Marriage and Family Therapy, 1100 17th St., NW, Washington, DC 20036; phone: 202/452–0109) bimonthly, $25/annual subscription (U.S.), $35/foreign. "Classified Ads" has about 25 openings for marriage and family therapists including practitioners, researchers, pastoral counselors, faculty, and practices for sale.

Job Training and Placement Report (Joe Jones Publishing, 121 N. Main St., Iola, WI 54945; phone: 715/445–5000) monthly, $106/annual subscription (U.S.), $126/foreign. 25 to 30 positions for professionals who train and place people with disabilities appear under "Position Openings." The number of job vacancies described in this relatively new section is increasing each month.

Medical Rehabilitation Review (National Association of Rehabilitation Facilities, P.O. Box 17675, Washington, DC 20041; phone: 703/648–9300) biweekly, available only as part of membership package. Jobs listed under "Employment Exchange." About ten job ads per issue.

Vocational/Developmental Rehabilitation Review (National Association of Rehabilitation Facilities, P.O. Box 17675, Washington, DC 20041; phone: 703/648–9300) biweekly, free/members only. About five to ten jobs are listed under "Employment Exchange."

Rehabilitation Management Review (National Association of Rehabilitation Facilities, P.O. Box 17675, Washington, DC 20041; phone: 703/648–9300) monthly, free/members only. Jobs listed under "Employment Exchange." About five to ten job ads per issue.

Journal of Rehabilitation (National Rehabilitation Association, 633 S. Washington St., Alexandria, VA 22314; phone: 703/836–0850) quarterly, $40/annual subscription (U.S.), $50/Canada, $60/elsewhere, free/members. About ten openings are touted under "Classified."

NRA Newsletter (National Rehabilitation Association, 633 S. Washington St., Alexandria, VA 22314; phone: 703/836–0850) eight issues/year, free/members only. Two to eight job openings are advertised under "Classified."

Contemporary Long–Term Care (Bill Communications, P.O. Box 3599, Akron, OH 44309; phone: 216/867–4401) monthly, $32/annual subscription (U.S.), $75/Canada, $60/elsewhere. The "Classifieds" runs ads for around 30 positions for administrators, managers, marketing, sales representatives, and nursing directors.

Personnel Bulletin (Evangelical Lutheran Church in America, 8765 W. Higgins Rd., Chicago, IL 60631; phone: 312/380–2690) monthly, $5/annual subscription. The entire issue is filled with about 25 job vacancies for administrators for nursing homes and hospitals, counselors, professors, and the whole gamut of social services. Employers are all affiliated with the Lutheran Church.

Long–Term Care Administrator (American College of Health Care Administrators, 325 S. Patrick St., Alexandria, VA 22314; phone: 703/739–7913) monthly, $45/annual nonmember subscription, free/members. Two to five openings for long–term care administrators at nursing homes and hospices are advertised under "Professional Referral Service."

Journal of Long–Term Care Administration (American College of Health Care Administrators, 325 S. Patrick St., Alexandria, VA 22314; phone: 703/739–7913) quarterly, $70/annual nonmember subscription, free/members. A display ad for nursing home administrators, directors of nursing, and medical directors makes it into an issue occasionally.

AAHA Provider News (American Association of Homes for the Aging, 901 E Street, Suite 500, NW, Washington, DC 20004; phone: 202/783–2242) monthly, free/members only. "Job Mart" carries about ten ads for administrative positions for residential facilities for senior citizens plus five or six "Positions Wanted."

Aging Today (American Society on Aging, 833 Market St., Suite 511, San Francisco, CA 94103; phone: 415/882–2910) bimonthly, $25/annual nonmember subscription, free/members, $80/annual dues. Two to four display ads for positions in caring for older people are in a typical issue.

Job services

CU Career Connection (University of Colorado, Campus Box 133, Boulder, CO 80309–0133; phone: 303/492–4127) $30/two–month fee entitles you to a "passcode" which unlocks this job hotline. You need a touch–tone phone to call and request the field in which you are interested in hearing job openings. The hotline is turned off Monday through Friday, 2 to 4 p.m. for daily updating.

Career Connection (Association for Humanistic Education and Development, c/o American Counseling Association, 5999 Stevenson Ave., Alexandria, VA 22304; phones: 800/545–2223, 703/823–9800) free/members only; $100/annual dues. Job seeker submits resume which is matched to available jobs. Employer contacts job hunter. Available positions are largely academic and counselors.

Career Guidance and Placement Service (Special Recreation, Inc., John Nesbitt, 362 Koser Ave., Iowa City, IA 52246–3038; phone: 219/337–7578) free. Call the SRI career advisement hotline for career planning and tracking suggestions, recommendations, and referrals. This informal service requests that you be familiar with the book *What Color is Your Parachute?* by Richard Bolles before calling. (Available for your convenience through Planning Communications; See catalog at the end of the book). After calling, you may submit your resume and this service will match you with appropriate activity or recreation coordinator, specialist, or therapy positions.

The Job Bank (Occupational Therapist Weekly, 164 Rollins Ave., Suite 301, Rockville, MD 20852; phone: 301/881–2490). This is an on–line databank that computers can access to learn about 650 jobs in occupational therapy. Contact for details.

Job Bank (National Association of Activity Professionals, 1225 I St., NW, Suite 300, Washington, DC 20005; phone: 202/289–0722) free. Your resume is kept on file for a year. When a match is made, a copy is sent to the employer who is responsible for contacting you. Jobs include activity directors and their assistants, largely at nursing homes.

Directories

National Directory of Private Social Agencies (Croner Publications, 34 Jericho Turnpike, Jericho, NY 11753; phones: 800/441–4033, 516/333–9085) $79.90, includes monthly updates. Lists more than 15,000 private social agencies: phone and hotline numbers, contact person, services provided, population served, locations where services provided, and more.

Fund Raiser's Guide to Human Service Funding (Taft Group, 12300 Twinbrook Pkwy., Suite 520, Rockville, MD 20852–9830; phone: 800/877–8238) $103, 736 pages, annual. Over 1,000 funders of human service agencies are detailed in 24 different categories of human services. Included in each entry are the funder's human service priorities, grant types, types of recipients, names of officers and directors, application procedures, and a list of recent grants.

National Guide to Funding for Children, Youth, and Families (The Foundation Center, 79 Fifth Ave., New York, NY 10003–3076; phones: 800/424–9836, 212/620–4230) $135, 1993. Each of the 3,000 entries includes application information and a list of recent grants for child development, disadvantaged youth, family planning, homelessness, and many other concerns.

National Guide to Funding for Women and Girls (The Foundation Center, 79 Fifth Ave., New York, NY 10003–3076; phones: 800/424–9836, 212/620–4230) $95, 1993. Each of the 800+ entries includes application information and a list of recent grants awarded for shelters for abused women, girls' clubs, health clinics, employment centers, and many other concerns.

Handicapped Funding Directory (Research Grant Guides, P.O. Box 1214, Loxahatchee, FL 33470) $45.50 plus $4/shipping, prepaid, last published summer 1993. Describes over 1,200 foundations, corporations, government agencies, and associations–in 21 areas of service–that offer grants to organizations for programs and services to people who have disabilities.

National Guide to Funding in Aging (The Foundation Center, 79 Fifth Ave., New York, NY 10003–3076; phones: 800/424–9836, 212/620–4230) $80, 1992. Describes federal and state programs and private foundations that support aging projects. Each of the 761 entries includes application information and a list of recent grants.

Directory of Member Agencies (Family Service America, 11700 W. Lake Park Dr., Milwaukee, WI 53224; phone: 414/359–1040) free/members only, issued each February. Presented by state, these are social service agencies that tend to employ social workers.

National Staff Development and Training Association Directory (810 First St., NE, Suite 500, Washington, DC 20002; phone: 202/682–0100) $70/nonmembers, $65/members. In depth directory of public welfare program and agencies by state. Published each August.

Directory of Experiential Therapy and Adventure Based Counseling Programs (Association for Experiential Education, 2885 Aurora Ave., Suite 28, Boulder, CO 80303–2252; phone: 303/440–8844) $15/nonmembers, $12.50/members, add $3.50/shipping. This is a state–by–state listing of adventure and experiential alternative programs for people with special needs which use adventure programming as part of their therapeutic process.

National Black Child Development Institute Membership Directory (NBCDI, 1463 Rhode Island Ave., NW, Washington, DC 20005; phone: 202/387–1281) $60/nonmembers, $30/members, published every January and July. Members are engaged in child welfare and health education.

Drug, Alcohol, and Other Addictions: A Directory of Treatment Centers and Prevention Programs Nationwide (Oryx Press, Suite 700, 4041 N. Central, Phoenix, AZ 85012; phone: 800/279–6799) $195, 1993, 656 pages. Describes programs, most of which are in the non–profit sector.

Directory of Member Agencies (Child Welfare League, 440 First St., NW, Suite 310, Washington, DC 20001; phone: 202/638–2952) $14/nonmembers, free/members, semiannually.

Directory of Victim Assistance Programs (National Organization for Victim Assistance, 1757 Park Rd., NW, Washington, DC 20010–2101; phone: 202/232–6682) $34.85/nonmembers, $29.85/members, last published fall 1993. Listings of 8,000 victim assistance programs in the U.S. Contact for directories or lists of international programs.

Experience Based Training and Development: International and Domestic Programs (Association for Experiential Education, 2885 Aurora Ave., Suite 28, Boulder, CO 80303–2252; phone: 303/440–8844) $15/nonmembers, $12.50/members, add $3.50/shipping. Descriptions of training and development programs in the U.S. and abroad.

National Organization for Human Service Education Membership Directory (NOHSE, c/o Douglas Whyte, Community College of Philadelphia, 1700 Spring Garden St., Philadelphia, PA 19130–3991; phone: 215/751–8522) free/members only, issued every two years, latest edition Spring 1994.

National Association of Area Agencies on Aging Membership Directory (National Association of Area Agencies on Aging, 1112 16th St., NW, Suite 100, Washington, DC 20036; phone: 202/296–8130) $40/nonmembers, $30/members, annual. Lists state and area agencies on aging as well as providers of services to elderly persons.

Register of Marriage and Family Therapy Providers (American Association for Marriage and Family Therapy, 1100 17th St., NW, Washington, DC 20036; phone: 202/452–0109) $50/nonmembers, $35/members, issued in June of even–numbered years.

College and Career Programs for Deaf Students (Gallaudet Research Institute, 800 Florida Ave., NE, Washington, DC 20002; phone: 202/651–5575) $15.45, annual. Describes programs at colleges that provide services for deaf and hard of hearing persons.

Directory of Services for Blind and Visually Impaired Persons in the United States and Canada (American Foundation for the Blind, 15 W. 16th St., New York, NY 10011; phone: 212/620–2155) $75/print edition plus $5.50 shipping, 550 pages, $100/electronic edition, plus $6.50 shipping. Lists details on over 3,000 local, state, regional, and national services including medical and research organizations, schools, and clinics.

Directory of Residential Centers for Adults with Mental Illnesses (Oryx Press, Suite 700, 4041 N. Central, Phoenix, AZ 85012–3397; phones: 800/279–6799, 602/265–2651) $68.50, 328 pages, 1990. Describes the services and programs at over 900 group homes (community residences), supervised apartment programs, crisis shelters, other community–based facilities, inpatient hospitals, and outpatient/day treatment centers.

Directory of Residential Centers for Adults with Developmental Disabilities (Oryx Press, Suite 700, 4041 N. Central, Phoenix, AZ 85012–3397; phones: 800/279–6799, 602/265–2651) $78.50, 408 pages, 1989. Lists over 1,400 community residence arrangements.

REMEMBER...

BE SURE TO ALSO CHECK THE INDEX FOR JOB SOURCES THAT APPEAR IN THE NON—PROFITS' JOB FINDER WHERE YOU WOULD NOT INTUITIVELY EXPECT THEM TO BE LOCATED.

Substance Abuse Residential Treatment Centers for Teens (Oryx Press, Suite 700, 4041 N. Central, Phoenix, AZ 85012–3397; phones: 800/279–6799, 602/265–2651) $55, 304 pages, 1990.

Women's Recovery Programs: A Directory of Residential Addiction Treatment Centers (Oryx Press, Suite 700, 4041 N. Central, Phoenix, AZ 85012–3397; phones: 800/279–6799, 602/265–2651) $55, 360 pages, 1990. Profiles over 1,200 centers across the nation that specialize in the treatment of alcoholism, chemical dependence, sexual addiction and abuse, eating disorders, codependency, and other behavioral disorders.

NARF Membership Directory (National Association of Rehabilitation Facilities, P.O. Box 17675, Washington, DC 20041; phone: 703/648–9300) $100/nonmembers, $35/members. Latest edition September 1994.

Senior Citizen Services (Gale Research, Inc., 835 Penobscot Bldg., Detroit, MI 48226; phone: 800/877–4253) $90/set of four volumes: Northeast, Southeast, Midwest, West; $29.95/each individual volume, 1993. Features extensive details on 16,000 private and local government agencies and organizations that furnish services for America's older citizens

including adult day care, case management, respite care, and home delivered meals. A good source for identifying potential employers and learning about them.

The National Housing Directory for People with Disabilities (Gale Research, Inc., 835 Penobscot Bldg., Detroit, MI 48226; phone: 800/877–4253) $180, 1993. You'll find descriptions of 6,500 referral agencies, 3,700 large institutional and intensive care facilities, 7,500 group homes, and 3,200 independent living centers and facilities in addition to information on 900 state and federal agencies involved in providing or regulating housing for individuals who have disabilities. This is a fine source for anybody seeking to identify potential employers or learn about their programs prior to a job interview.

Directory of Nursing Homes (Oryx Press, Suite 700, 4041 N. Central, Phoenix, AZ 85012; phone: 800/279–6799) $225, last published in 1991, may still be available in libraries, 1,512 pages. Rather extensive directory with details on nursing homes, nursing home chains, and corporate headquarters.

National Directory of Adult Day Care Centers (Health Resources Publishing, 3100 Highway 138, Wall Township, NJ 07719; phone: 908/681–1133) $149 plus $6/shipping, published every spring.

Grants for Social Services (The Foundation Center, 79 Fifth Ave., New York, NY 10003–3076; phones: 800/424–9836, within New York State call 212/620–4230) $65 plus $4.50/shipping, October 1993. Describes recent foundation grants of at least $10,000 to human service organizations for children's and youth services, family services, personal social services, emergency assistance, residential or custodial care, and services to promote the independence of specific population groups such as people who have developmental disabilities or persons who are homeless. This directory is useful for identifying foundations and grant recipients for which you may wish to work.

Grants for Aging (The Foundation Center, 79 Fifth Ave., New York, NY 10003–3076; phones: 800/424–9836, within New York State call 212/620–4230) $65 plus $4.50/shipping, October 1993. Describes recent foundation grants of at least $10,000 for advocacy and legal rights, housing, education and community services, employment, health and medical care, recreation, arts and culture, volunteer services, and social research. This directory is useful for identifying foundations and grant recipients for which you may wish to work.

Grants for Alcohol & Drug Abuse (The Foundation Center, 79 Fifth Ave., New York, NY 10003–3076; phones: 800/424–9836, within New York State call 212/620–4230) $65 plus $4.50/shipping, October 1993. Describes recent foundation grants of at least $10,000 for counseling, education, treatment, medical research, residential care, halfway houses, and programs on alcohol and drug abuse prevention. This directory is useful for identifying foundations and grant recipients for which you may wish to work.

Grants for Children & Youth (The Foundation Center, 79 Fifth Ave., New York, NY 10003–3076; phones: 800/424–9836, within New York State call 212/620–4230) $65 plus $4.50/shipping, October 1993. Describes recent foundation grants of at least $10,000 to support neonatal care, child welfare, adoption, foster care, services for abused children, research on child development, pregnancy counseling and adolescent pregnancy prevention, prevention and rehabilitation of juvenile delinquency, and youth centers and clubs. This directory is useful for identifying foundations and grant recipients for which you may wish to work.

Grants for Physically & Mentally Disabled (The Foundation Center, 79 Fifth Ave., New York, NY 10003–3076; phones: 800/424–9836, within New York State call 212/620–4230) $65 plus $4.50/shipping, October 1993. Describes recent foundation grants of at least $10,000 to schools, hospitals, and primary care facilities for research, medical and dental care, employment and vocational training, education, diagnosis and evaluation, recreation and rehabilitation, and legal aid. This directory is useful for identifying foundations and grant recipients for which you may wish to work.

Salary survey

Residential Services and Developmental Disabilities in the United States (American Association on Mental Retardation, 1719 Kalorama Rd., NW, Washington, DC 20009; phones: 800/424–3688, 202/387–1968) $44.95 plus $4/shipping, 1992. Reports on wages and benefits of direct care workers based on a study of over 1,000 public and private residential facilities by state.

Chapter **30**

Transportation

Traffic engineering and parking

*For much more extensive listings of job sources in this field,
see the **Government Job Finder** and the **Professional's
Private Sector Job Finder.***

Job ads in print

The Parking Professional (Institutional and Municipal Parking Congress,
901 Kenmore Ave., Fredericksburg, VA 22401; phone: 703/371–7535)
monthly, $60/annual subscription (U.S. and Canada), $72/elsewhere. One
or two ads for parking administrators or directors appear in a typical issue.

The Professional Register (Institutional and Municipal Parking Congress,
901 Kenmore Ave., Fredericksburg, VA 22401; phone: 703/371–7535)
contact IMPC for details. At the time of this writing, procedures and the fee
schedule had not been established.

METRO Magazine (Bobit Publishing Co., 2512 Artesia Blvd., Redondo
Beach, CA 90278; phone: 310/376–8788) bimonthly, $25/annual subscription
(U.S.), $30/Canada, $38/elsewhere. Jobs listed under "Classified Ads."
Few job ads.

Chapter 31

State-by-state job and grant sources

Obviously most job sources — namely your local classifieds — are not national in scope. In addition to the local classifieds, there are many sources of job openings that are local, regional, or statewide in coverage. This chapter explains what those job sources are and introduces you to the free job recruitment service that every state operates, but of which few habitually–employed workers avail themselves.

Because many foundations award grants only within the state in which they are located, this chapter also reports on directories of foundations for each state so you can locate potential funding sources. In addition, you can use these directories to identify potential employers.

State–by–state job sources

State Operated Job Services. Perhaps the most underutilized "free lunch" ever offered to job seekers is the Job Service every state government operates. Although the quality of their services varies, each Job Service office provides employment services that include career counseling and a job–matching service of some type.

Popularly known as the "unemployment office," a state Job Service office can put you in contact with job vacancies in the non–profit sector that range from low–paid and entry–level jobs to top–level positions.

Each Job Service office maintains a frequently updated list of available job vacancies from throughout the state. You are able to read these on a microfiche machine, and in some states, on a computer. You can usually obtain a full job description from the Job Service office for those positions that interest you.

The entries in this chapter note if a state's Job Service offices also operate a job–matching service.

You should be able to find the address and phone number for a nearby Job Service office in your local telephone directory. In case you can't, this chapter offers information that enables you to locate each state's employ-ment services, including Job Service offices. You should write directly, or call, for more information from the state(s) of your choice. Please note that while most states call these "Job Services," some assign a different moniker like "Employment Security Department." So before you go to the govern-ment section of your local phone directory to find the Job Service office nearest you, be sure to see the entry in this chapter for that state to learn what it calls its Job Service offices.

In addition, practically all state–operated Job Service offices or centers participate in the Interstate Job Bank Service developed by the U.S. Depart-ment of Labor's Employment and Training Administration. Jobs in other states are on microfiche which can be read at your local Job Service office, and in over 20 percent of the Job Service offices, are accessible on comput-ers, including computer terminals you can use yourself. Over 7 million non–agricultural job openings are listed during a typical year. These vacan-cies are typically two weeks old before they get on the list. Many are what are called "constant hires" which means that there are almost always job vacancies for that position. Keep in mind that many employers take more than two weeks to fill positions, particularly higher–level ones.

If you want additional information on any of the out–of–state jobs listed, ask the Job Service office to call the Interstate Job Bank on its toll–free number to get this additional information on the positions.

We're told that 30 percent of those who search for a job at a Job Service office find a job through it. There is research that shows that more than half of those people who find a job through a Job Service office stay on the job less than a month. Any number of factors may explain this finding. It is very likely that this job loss rate occurs because so few habitually–employed people use the "unemployment office." A disproportionately large percent-age of people who use the service may be people who always have difficulty holding a job. But at least they have the good sense to use this free service which is more successful at placing people in appropriate jobs than most private employment agencies (as distinguished from recruiting or executive search firms which usually are more successful at placing job candidates).

The job matching services furnished by Job Service offices really amount to a free employment service for professionals, technical, labor, trades, and office support workers. However, habitually–employed individuals rarely take advantage of these services. Perhaps they are turned off by the generic moniker for these offices: the "unemployment office." Don't let preconceptions steer you away from a state's Job Service offices no matter how high in the non–profit sector hierarchy you wish to work. They are often an effective source of non–profit job openings.

Regional and local jobs periodicals. There are some regional jobs periodicals that cover several states that are excellent sources of local jobs. Several of these that are very specialized were described in earlier chapters of this book. This chapter identifies a few that are broader in scope.

Where we could identify them, we've included local or state periodicals that include announcements of job vacancies in the non–profit sector. This is a particularly difficult set of periodicals to identify. If you know of any we missed, please use the *Reader's Feedback Form* on page 298 to tell us about them so we can add them to the next *Update Sheet* and to the next edition of the *Non–Profits' Job Finder.*

Chapter newsletters of speciality organizations. The newsletters produced by the state or local chapters of many professional and trade associations frequently carry job advertisements. Usually, these newsletters are available only to chapter members. Some chapters, however, allow nonmembers to subscribe or join only the chapter. Because officers of state chapters change so frequently, you should contact the national headquarters of the appropriate organization to obtain the address of any chapter president you wish to contact. We are not so foolhardy as to try to list these in one book. Many of these local association chapters are listed in the *JobBank* books and *How to Get a Job in "X"* city books described in this chapter.

Job services operated by chapters of associations. Similarly, state or metropolitan chapters of some professional and trade associations operate job–matching services or job hotlines. These services are usually available only to chapter members. Some chapters, however, allow nonmembers to register for a job service or join only the chapter. Because officers of state chapters change so frequently, you should contact the national headquarters of the appropriate organization to obtain the address of any chapter president you wish to contact. Many of these local association chapters are listed in the *JobBank* books and *How to Get a Job in "X"* city books described in this chapter.

You might also want to see the latest edition of **National Trade and Professional Associations of the United States** (Columbia Books, Suite 300, 1212 New York Ave., NW, Washington, DC 20005; phone: 202/898–

Photocopying strictly prohibited

0662; $55) which provides details on over 6,450 trade and professional associations. This is a good and affordable source for finding state and local professional organizations that might provide local job services. You can also use this directory to identify state and local non–profit organizations for which you might wish to work.

You may also want to see if your library has a copy of the *Encyclopedia of Associations: Regional, State, and Local Organizations, 1992–1993* (Gale Research, Inc., 835 Penobscot Bldg., Detroit, MI 48226; phone: 800/877–4253; $469/five–volume set, $99 for each regional volume individually, 3,716 pages total, 1992) which describes over 50,000 non–profit organizations with national, regional, state, city, or local scope and interest, including professional associations for just about every specialty within the non–profit sector. It's also available on CD–ROM and online via DIALOG as File 114 (DIALOG Information Services, 3460 Hillview Ave., Palo Alto, CA 94304; phones: 800/334–2564). This is a good source for finding state and local professional organizations that might provide local job services. You can also use this directory to identify state and local non–profit organizations for which you might wish to work.

Local newspapers. As mentioned earlier, the classified section of local newspapers is sometimes a decent source for job vacancies in the local non–profit sector. The job sources in the *Non–Profits' Job Finder* get you to the job vacancies that are not advertised in the local classifieds. If you are seeking a new job in your local area, you would be prudent to use both the local classifieds and the job sources described in this book to find job vacancies. If you are considering jobs outside your local area, the local classifieds rarely help. However, the sources described in the preceding chapters, and the sources enumerated in this chapter, will be most useful.

State associations of non–profit organizations. In response to suggestions sent by readers of the first two editions of this book, we've added state associations of non–profit organizations to this chapter. We've been able to identify associations of non–profit organizations for more than half the states and include all job publications and services they operate, as well as any relevant directories they publish. Even if an association doesn't offer any direct job sources, it may still serve an an informal clearinghouse for job opportunities. You can't lose by contacting the association in the states where you're seeking work and asking if they can give you any hints for finding a job with a non--profit in that state.

State–by–state sources of grants

Foundations and grants. To help you locate grant funds, as well as foundations within your state for which you might wish to work, this chapter describes directories of foundations for most of the 50 states. We included only fairly recent directories for which we could verify publication information and their contents. We generally left out directories that are now out–of–print. As always, most foundations do not award grants to individuals. However, we do note when a directory includes some foundations that issue grants to individuals.

We also were forced to exclude several foundation directories published by Logos Associates because they never responded to our phone calls or written requests for information about them. However, if you want to contact them for information, you may have better luck. Maybe they will send you a catalog if you can get reach them. You can try to reach Logos Associates at 247 Lisbon, NH 03585; phone: 603/838–6209. Good luck and caveat emptor. If you do get a catalog from them, could you please send a copy to us. See the *Reader Feedback Form* on page 298 for instructions.

Job and grant sources: State–by–state

Alabama

To locate **Job Service Offices**, contact the Employment Services Division (Department of Industrial Relations, 649 Monroe St., Montgomery, AL 36131; director's phone: 205/242–8003).

Foundations and grants

Alabama Foundation Directory (Birmingham Public Library, Government Documents Department, 2100 Park Pl., Birmingham, AL 35203; phone: 205/226–3600) $10/prepaid only, 53 pages, 1990, tentative plans for a new edition in 1994. Reports on over 240 foundations: areas of interest, officers.

A Guide to Funders in Central Appalachia and the Tennessee Valley (Appalachia Community Fund, Suite 206, 517 Union Ave., Knoxville, TN 37902; phone: 615/523–5783) $58, over 300 pages, January 1994. Among the 399 funders reported on are those that give grants in northern Alabama. Includes everything you need to seek funding: contact name, types of grants, grant application process, average grant size, plus how to write a grant proposal, funders from outside the region that make grants in the region, religious funding sources, and Japanese corporations with grantmaking programs.

Alaska

Membership List (Association of Nonprofit Corporations, c/o Jeanine Triplett, President, P.O. Box 100956, Anchorage, AK 99510; phone: 907/279–2511) $25, published each November. You'll get the addresses and phone numbers for the 350 non–profits that belong to this organization.

Find **Job Service Offices** by contacting the Alaska Employment Service (Department of Labor, Suite 208, 111 W. Eighth St., P.O. Box 25509, Juneau, AK 99802–5509; phone: 907/465–4531).

Job hotlines. Several of the Alaska Employment Service offices offer a daily recorded job hotline message which include the following information about non–profits as well as private sector and government job openings:

> **Anchorage** (907/269–4740), professional, technical, and clerical positions: requirements, salary for new and hard–to–fill positions
> **Dillingham** (907/842–5575): titles of all job openings
> **Eagle River** (907/694–6999): titles of rush and hard–to–fill jobs
> **Fairbanks** (907/451–2875): titles and salary of all job openings, descriptions of some jobs
> **Homer** (907/235–7200): titles of all job vacancies
> **Juneau** (907/790–4571): titles of new job openings
> **Kenai** (907/283–4606): qualifications of all job openings, no salary information
> **Kodiak** (907/486–6838): titles and salary of all job openings, descriptions of some positions
> **MatSu** (907/376–8860): titles and salary of new job openings, titles only for previously listed positions
> **Seward** (907/224–5274): titles of all job vacancies

Foundations and grants

Pacific Northwest Grantmakers Forum Member Directory (Pacific Northwest Grantmakers Forum, Suite 214, 1305 Fourth Ave, Seattle, WA 98101; phone: 206/624–9899) 106 pages, published in March of even–numbered years, the 1992 edition cost $20 plus $1.30/shipping and $1.64 sales tax for

Washington state residents; check with the Forum for the price of subsequent editions. Among the 75 or so grantmakers described in this directory
are a handful from Alaska. Included in each listing are contact name's
address and phone, application procedures, range of grant amounts awarded,
and types of projects funded.

Arizona

Rocky Mountain Employment Newsletter (Intermountain Publishing, 311–B0 14th St., Glenwood
Springs, CO 81601–3949; phone: 303/945–8991)
18 issues/year, $21/three–month subscription to one edition, $26/any two
editions, $31/three editions, $36/four editions. Two and one–month subscriptions also available. Published in four editions: Colorado–Wyoming,
Arizona–New Mexico, Idaho–Montana, and Washington–Oregon. Combined, the four editions include over 400 job openings, some in non–profits.
The positions tend to orient toward the outdoors, with quite a few in natural
resources, environment, and wildlife.

The Phoenix JobBank (Bob Adams Publications; available from Plan-
ning/Communications' catalog at the rear of this book) $15.95, annual. Over
360 pages list 1,500 of the major non–profit and private sector employers
in the metropolitan area including whom to contact at each about job
vacancies. Also included is a list of professional employment services (always
be cautious about these; there are some charlatans out there who have
sullied this profession's reputation), the addresses of the local chapter of
many professional and trade associations, and profiles of many occupations.

To locate **Job Service Offices**, contact the Employment and Rehabilitation Services Division (Department of Economic Security, P.O. Box 6123–
010A, Phoenix, AZ 85005; director's phone: 602/542–4016).

Foundations and grants

Arizona Foundation Directory 1991–92 (Junior League of Phoenix, P.O.
Box 10377, Phoenix, AZ 85064; phone: 602/234–3388) $15, 60 pages.
Profiles more than 150 foundations which have awarded at least $500 in
grants. Descriptions include contact persons, sample grants, number of
grants and dollar amounts.

Arkansas

Arkansas Employment Security Department Job–Matching Service (Employment Security Department, 2 Capitol Mall, Little Rock, AR 72201; director's phone: 501/682–2121; available at any of the 30 local Employment Security Department offices) free. A job seeker completes the service's resume form and is then matched with jobs. The service contacts matched applicants to arrange job interviews with employers. Applications are kept active for 60 days.

For information on the location of the 30 **Job Service Offices** (known in Arkansas as local Employment Security Department offices), contact the Employment Security Department, (Room 506, ESD Building, P.O. Box 2981, Little Rock, AR 72203; phone: 501/682–2121).

California

Opportunity NOCs (The Management Center, Suite 700, 944 Market St., San Francisco, CA 94102; phone: 415/362–9735) weekly, $16/three–month subscription. From 50 to 70 positions with non–profits in the Bay Area and Sacramento are described in every issue.

California Philanthropy Report Calendar (Suite 291, 406 E. First St., Long Beach, CA 90802; phone: 714/675–7157) monthly, $68/annual subscription plus 8.75 percent sales tax for California residents. Each issue sports five to ten positions of all types with California foundations advertised under "Jobs and Professional Opportunities." We've been trying to reach them for two months, but keep getting a recording saying they are undergoing renovation. They have not responded to our letters. So, we suggest that you first send them a letter about obtaining a subscription before sending them a check.

PiES Job Alert! (Public Interest Clearinghouse, 200 McAllister St., San Francisco, CA 94102–4978; phone: 415/255–1714) semimonthly, three–month subscriptions: $30/employed nonmembers, $15/unemployed nonmembers, students, or members; annual subscription: $125/schools and institutions. Over 50 professional and support positions are described per issue for work with legal services, progressive law firms, and other kinds of law/advocacy–related public interest organizations largely in the San Francisco Bay area, but also increasingly from throughout the state and from other western states.

The Advocate (Public Interest Clearinghouse, 200 McAllister St., San Francisco, CA 94102–4978; phone: 415/255–1714) eight issues/year, $75/annual subscription, $50 if also subscribing to *PiES Job Alert!* described immediately above. Describes several dozen jobs, largely in California, of interest to law students such as internships, clerkships, and work–study positions with legal services and non–profits.

The CAN Alert (California Association of Nonprofits, P.O. Box 1478, Santa Cruz, CA 95061–1478; phone: 408/458–1955) nine issues/year, free/members only. Do not presently have job ads but expect to sometime in 1994.

CAN Membership Directory (California Association of Nonprofits, P.O. Box 1478, Santa Cruz, CA 95061–1478; phone: 408/458–1955) quarterly, will charge for the cost of shipping and reproduction only. Sends out its list of 2,000 members by request only.

Non–Profit Directory of Santa Clara County (The Nonprofit Development Center, 1762 Technology Dr., San Jose, CA 95110; phone: 408/452–8181) $65 plus $3/shipping, annual. Includes addresses, phone numbers, contact names, and board members for all non–profits in Santa Clara County.

Directory of Bay Area Public Interest Organizations (Public Interest Clearinghouse, 200 McAllister St., San Francisco, CA 94102–4978; phone: 415/255–1714) $27/nonmembers, $22/members. Features 600 organizations working for social change in the nine–county San Francisco Bay Area. Indexed by subject and county. Includes a chapter on finding paid public interest jobs in the Bay Area that tells you about over 40 local job resources including local periodicals with job ads and job services. Most recent edition published in 1991.

Public Interest, Private Practice: A Directory of Public Interest Law Firms in Northern California (Public Interest Clearinghouse, 200 McAllister St., San Francisco, CA 94102–4978; phone: 415/255–1714) $11/nonmembers, $8/members; last published in 1991, updated slightly in 1993. Lists over 200 for–profit law firms that devote a substantial portion of their legal work to the public interest.

Public Interest Employment Service Resource Center Clipboards (Public Interest Clearinghouse, 200 McAllister St., San Francisco, CA 94102–4978; phone: 415/255–1714) free for members and subscribers to the Public Interest Clearinghouse's publications, $1/nonmembers. You can drop in between 9 a.m. and 5 p.m. Monday through Friday (open to 7 p.m. on Wednesdays) to examine the five *Job Clipboards* (attorneys, paralegals, more non–attorneys, law students, and other public interest jobs) which are updated daily with new job openings. These vacancies appear later in the

next issue of the *PiES Job Alert!* described above under "California." Also available for examination are other job newsletters and resource files on potential employers.

How to Get a Job in Southern California (Surrey Books; available from Planning/Communications' catalog at the end of this book) $15.95, annual, 451 pages. This easy–to–use book tells you whom to contact for job vacancies at over 1,500 top private sector and non–profit employers in the southern half of the state. It also lists local chapters of professional and trade associations (which may publish a periodical with jobs ads or operate a local job service), local trade magazines, useful local professional publications, directories, and lists of executive search firms and of employment services. Always be careful with employment services. Too many employment services engage in practices that embarrass the legitimate members of the industry.

The Los Angeles JobBank (Bob Adams Publications; available from Planning/Communications' catalog at the end of this book), $15.95, annual, 672 pages. Includes a list of 1,500 of the major non–profit and private sector employers in the metropolitan area including whom to contact at each about job vacancies. Also included is a list of professional employment services (always be cautious about these; there are some charlatans out there who have sullied this profession's reputation), the addresses of the local chapter of many professional and trade associations, and profiles of many occupations.

The San Francisco Bay Area JobBank (Bob Adams Publications; available from Planning/Communications' catalog at the end of this book), $15.95, annual, 408 pages. Includes a list of 1,500 of the major non–profit and private sector employers in the Bay Area including whom to contact at each about job vacancies. Also included is a list of professional employment services, the addresses of the local chapter of many professional and trade associations, and profiles of many occupations.

How to Get a Job in the San Francisco Bay Area (Surrey Books; available from Planning/Communications; see the catalog at the end of this book) $15.95, annual, 496 pages. This easy–to–use book tells you whom to contact for job vacancies at over 1,800 top private sector and non–profit employers in the Bay Area. It also lists local chapters of professional and trade associations (which may publish a periodical with jobs ads or operate a local job service), local trade magazines, useful local professional publications, directories, and lists of executive search firms and of employment services. Always be careful with employment services. Too many employment services engage in practices that embarrass the legitimate members of the industry.

To locate **Job Service Offices**, contact the Employment Development Department (P.O. Box 826880, MIC 62, Sacramento, CA 94280–0001; phone: 916/653–0707).

Foundations and grants

Guide to California Foundations (Community Information Program, 462 Harbor Blvd., Belmont, CA 94002; Northern California Grant makers, 116 New Montgomery St., Suite 742, San Francisco, CA 94105; phone: 415/777–5761) $53.75, 1,000 pages, published in odd–numbered years; price includes original book, shipping, sales tax and updates issued in November 1994 (reports on changes for foundations A through K) and in November 1995 (reports on changes for foundations L through Z). Includes descriptions of 914 foundations that annually award grants totaling at least $40,000. Each entry includes a contact name, the foundation's purpose and fields of grantmaking, range of awards, giving patterns, officers and directors, and application procedures.

San Diego County Foundation Directory (San Diego Community Foundation, 101 W. Broadway, Suite 1120, San Diego, CA 92101; phone: 619/239–8815) $20, 140 pages, last published in 1993. Reports on application procedures, range of grants, type of support, contact person, and directors for over 67 foundations and 56 corporations.

Santa Clara County Foundation Directory (The Nonprofit Development Center, 1762 Technology Dr., San Jose, CA 95110; phone: 408/452–8181) $45 plus $3/shipping, 90 pages, most recent edition, August 1993. Provides contact person and phone number, application guidelines, preferred program areas, and more.

Corporate Contributions Guide to Santa Clara County (The Nonprofit Development Center, 1762 Technology Dr., San Jose, CA 95110; phone: 408/452–8181) $65 plus $3/shipping, 225 pages, annual. Provides contact person and phone number, application guidelines, preferred program areas, and more.

Colorado

CANPO Newsletter (Colorado Association of Non-profit Organizations, 1600 Sherman Street, Suite 210, Denver, CO 80203; phone: 303/832–5710) bimonthly, $40/annual subscription, $12/annual subscription for person unemployed. Three to five job ads appear under "Job Board" along with a "Situations Wanted" section.

Rocky Mountain Employment Newsletter (Intermountain Publishing, 311–B0 14th St., Glenwood Springs, CO 81601–3949; phone: 303/945–8991) 18 issues/year, $21/three–month subscription to one edition, $26/any two editions, $31/three editions, $36/four editions. Two and one–month subscriptions also available. Published in four editions: Colorado–Wyoming, Arizona–New Mexico, Idaho–Montana, and Washington–Oregon. Combined, the four editions include over 400 job openings, some in non–profits. The positions tend to orient toward the outdoors, with quite a few in natural resources, environment, and wildlife.

The Denver JobBank (Bob Adams Publications; available from Planning/Communications' catalog at the end of this book) $15.95, annual, 384 pages. Lists 1,000+ of the major non–profit and private sector employers in the metropolitan area including whom to contact at each about job vacancies. Also included is a list of professional employment services, the addresses of the local chapter of many professional and trade associations, and profiles of many occupations.

1993–95 Colorado Directory of Nonprofits (Colorado Association of Non-profit Organizations, 1600 Sherman Street, Suite 210, Denver, CO 80203; phone: 303/832–5710) $50/nonmembers, $20/members. Lists executive directors, addresses, phone numbers, budget range, geographic area served, statement of purpose, and number of employees and volunteers for 1,500 501(c)(3)s.

To locate **Job Service Offices,** contact the Department of Labor and Employment (600 Grant St., Denver, CO 80203–3528; phone: 303/837–3819).

Foundations and grants

Colorado Foundation Directory (Junior League of Denver, 6300 E. Yale Ave., Denver,, CO 80222; phone: 303/692–0270) $12, 250 pages, issued in March of even–numbered years. Offers details on over 170 foundations: purpose statement, field of interest, sample grants, etc.

Connecticut

To locate the state **Job Service Offices** (called "Job Centers" in Connecticut) in Ansonia, Bridgeport, Bristol, Danbury, Danielson, Enfield, Hamden, Hartford, Manchester, Meriden, Middletown, New Britain, New London, Norwich, Stamford, Torrington, Waterbury, and Willimantic, see the state government section (the blue pages) of the local white pages telephone directory or contact the Connecticut Department of Labor (200 Folly Brook Blvd., Wethersfield, CT 06109; phone: 203/566–5031) for a list of Job Center Offices.

Foundations and grants

Connecticut Foundation Directory (D.A.T.A., 70 Audubon St., New Haven, CT 06510; phone: 203/772–1345) $50 plus $4/postage, last issued 1990; currently out of print but may be available at local libraries. Reports on over 1,200 foundations: purpose statement, principal officer, list of selected grants.

Guide to Corporate Giving in Connecticut 1993–94 (D.A.T.A., 70 Audubon St., New Haven, CT 06510; phone: 203/772–1345) $80, 252 pages, 1993. Reports on over 850 corporate foundations: purpose statement, contact name and phone number, giving interests, cash and non–cash giving policies, matching gift information, officers and directors, grant range, and list of selected grants.

Delaware

Opportunity NOCs (The Nonprofit Management Development Center at LaSalle University, 1900 N. Olney, Philadelphia, PA 19141; phone: 215/951–1701) monthly, $10/three–month subscription, $30/annual subscription. From 10 to 20 positions with non–profits in Delaware, southern New Jersey, and Pennsylvania are described in every issue.

DANA UPDATE (Delaware Association of Nonprofit Agencies, P.O. Box 2849, Wilmington, DE 19805; phone: 302/762–9240) monthly, free/members only. From four to ten positions with non–profits are advertised under "Nonprofit Job Openings." This is a monthly mailing to DANA members which will be transformed into a newsletter sometime during 1994.

Delaware Nonprofit Directory (Delaware Association of Nonprofit Agencies, P.O. Box 2849, Wilmington, DE 19805; phone: 302/762–9240) $30/nonmembers, $20/members, 60 pages. This directory of about 1,800 non–profits in the state is custom generated off their computer for your order — so it's about as up–to–date as possible. Each description includes a contact name and the services the non–profit agency offers.

Nonprofits Wage and Benefits Survey (Delaware Association of Nonprofit Agencies, P.O. Box 2849, Wilmington, DE 19805; phone: 302/762–9240) $15/nonmembers, $10/members, 8 pages, annual. Expect this survey to grow in size beginning with the 1994 edition.

To locate **Job Service Offices**, contact the Division of Employment and Training (Delaware Department of Labor, The Hudson State Service Center, 501 Ogletown Rd., Newark, DE 19711; phone: 302/368–6825).

Foundations and grants

Delaware Foundations (United Way of Delaware, 625 Orange St., Third Floor, Wilmington, DE 19801; phone: 302/573–2400) $15 plus $1.25/shipping, 121 pages, July 1991. New edition should be out in the middle of 1994, call for new price. Describes over 300 foundations and trusts: purpose statement, officers, type of recipient, analysis of grants.

District of Columbia

Community Jobs/D.C. (ACCESS: Networking in the Public Interest, 50 Beacon St., Boston, MA 02108; phone: 617/720–5627) semimonthly, $29/three–month subscription, $39/six–month subscription, $69/annual subscription; but if you also subscribe to the national edition of *Community Jobs*, you can get *Community Jobs/D.C.* for just an additional $5/three months, $10/six months, $20/year; see the description of *Community Jobs* in Chapter 2 under "Job ads in print."). Includes advertisements for positions with a broad range of non–profits in the Washington, D.C. metropolitan area. The vast majority of these job announcements do not appear in the national edition of *Community Jobs*.

The Nonprofit Agenda (Washington Council of Agencies, 1001 Connecticut Ave., NW, Suite 925, Washington, DC 20036; phone: 202/457–0540) $40/nonmembers, free/members and nonprofit institutions. A handful of job ads appear under "Classified." They also keep on file a list of updated job announcements.

Opportunities in Public Affairs (Brubach Publishing Company, P.O. Box 15629, Chevy Chase, MD 20825) $29/two–month subscription, $49/four months, $69/six months, $129/annual, $7.95/single issue. You'll find announcements of over 200 positions with local, state, and federal government agencies; non–profits; and private companies in government affairs, public relations, broadcasting, and publishing. In addition to job announcements, this periodical also reports on unadvertised jobs its editors have uncovered. Most job openings are in the District of Columbia area. It includes a good number of positions with Congress.

The 1993 Washington Job Source (MetCom, Inc. 1708 Surrey Lane, NW, Washington, DC 20007) $14.95 plus $3/shipping. Briefly describes 2,100 federal agencies, Congressional committees and commissions, non–profits, and corporations with the name, address, and phone number of the hiring contact.

The Washington, D.C. Giving Guide (ACCESS: Networking in the Public Interest, 50 Beacon St., Boston,.MA 02108; phone: 617/720–5627) $4/prepaid, 115 pages, 1993. Lists hundreds of non–profits in the Washington, D.C. area by subject area.

Jobs in Washington, DC: 1001 Great Opportunities for College Graduates (available from Planning/Communications' catalog at the end of this book) $11.95, 217 pages, 1992. Includes over 1,000 names, addresses, and phone numbers of many non–profit organizations, associations, and international development groups located in the District as well as for federal government agencies.

How to Get a Job in Washington DC (Surrey Books; available from Planning/Communications' catalog at the end of this book) $15.95, annual, over 300 pages. This easy–to–use book tells you whom to contact for job vacancies at over 1,400 top non–profit and private sector employers in the metropolitan area. It also lists local chapters of professional and trade associations (which may publish a periodical with jobs ads or operate a local job service), local trade magazines, useful local professional publications, directories, and lists of executive search firms and of employment services.

The Metropolitan Washington DC JobBank (Bob Adams Publications; available from Planning/Communications' catalog at the end of this book) $15.95, annual, 420 pages. Lists 1,600+ of the major private sector and non–profit employers in the metropolitan area including whom to contact at each about job vacancies. Also included is a list of professional employment services, the addresses of the local chapter of many professional and trade associations, and profiles of many occupations.

1994 Internships (Peterson's Guides; available from Planning/Communications' catalog at the end of this book) $29.95. With a new edition each October, this 422–page book describes several hundred internship opportunities in and around the District of Columbia, mostly with the federal government, but also a good many in the non–profit sector.

Internships + Job Opportunities in New York City and Washington, DC (Graduate Group, 86 Norwood Rd., West Hartford, CT 06117; phones: 203/232–3100, 203/236–5570) $27.50, published annually. Describes internship and job opportunities in a wide variety of fields.

Washington 93 (Columbia Books, 1212 New York Ave., NW, Suite 330, Washington, DC 20005; phone: 202/898–0662) $75, published annually each June. Nearly 600 pages of addresses, phone numbers, and information on companies and businesses in the D.C. area. Includes chapters on national associations, labor unions, law firms, medicine and health, foundations and philanthropy, science and policy research, education, religion, cultural institutions, clubs, and community affairs.

The Capital Source: The Who's Who, What, Where in Washington (National Journal, Inc., 1730 M St., NW, Washington, DC 20036; phones: 800/424–2921, 202/862–0644) $26.45, published every April and November. This directory includes names, addresses, and phone numbers for corporations, interest groups, think tanks, labor unions, real estate, financial institutions, trade and professional organizations, law firms, political consultants, advertising and public relations firms, private clubs, and the media. All entries are also available on computer diskette. Call 202/857–1449 for information.

For information on **Job Service Offices**, contact the District's Department of Employment Services (500 C St., NW, Washington, DC 20001; phone: 202/724–7100).

Foundations and grants

Directory of Foundations of the Greater Washington Area (Foundation for the National Capital Region, 1002 Wisconsin Ave., NW, Washington, DC 20007; phone: 202/338–8993) $25 plus $3/shipping, published in late spring of even–numbered years. Includes public and private foundations as well as some corporate foundations. Each entry includes contact person, areas of interest, application guidelines, financial and grant data, and more. Also includes a list of foundations not included in the directory and a list of foundations that do not accept proposals.

Florida

Newsletter of the Florida Association of Nonprofit Organizations (7480 Fairway Drive, Suite 206, Miami Lakes, FL 33014; phone: 305/557–1764) bimonthly, free. Under "Wanted" appear six job ads for all positions in the non–profit sector.

The Florida JobBank (Bob Adams Publications; available from Planning/Communications' catalog at the end of this book) $15.95, annual, 564 pages. Lists 1,500+ of the major private sector and non–profit employers in the state including whom to contact at each about job vacancies. Also included is a list of professional employment services (always be cautious about these; there are some charlatans out there who have sullied this profession's reputation), the addresses of the local chapter of many professional and trade associations, and profiles of many occupations.

FANO Salary Survey (Florida Association of Nonprofit Organizations, 7480 Fairway Drive, Suite 206, Miami Lakes, FL 33014; phone: 305/557–1764) annual, contact for price.

To locate **Job Service Offices**, contact the Department of Labor and Employment Security (2012 Capital Cr., SE, Tallahassee, FL 32399–2154; phone: 904/488–4398).

Foundations and grants

The Complete Guide to Florida Foundations (John L. Adams & Co., 9350 S. Dixie Highway, Suite 1560, Miami, FL 33156; phone: 305/670–2203) $90, 250 pages, published each January. Details 1,500 foundations: officers, total grants, range of grants, funding priorities, and geographic preferences.

A Guide to Florida State Programs (Florida Funding Publications, 9350 S. Dixie Highway, Suite 1560, Miami, FL 33156; phone: 305/670–2203) $80, published early each autumn. Describes state–funded grant programs by state government department: contact persons and phone numbers, program description, eligibility, deadlines, fund availability, matching requirements, and more.

Georgia

How to Get a Job in Atlanta (Surrey Books; available from Planning/Communications' catalog at the end of this book) $15.95, annual, 490 pages. This easy–to–use book tells you whom to contact for job vacancies at over 1,500 top private sector and non–profit employers in the metropolitan area. It also lists local chapters of professional and trade associations (which may publish a periodical with jobs ads or operate a local job service), local trade magazines, useful local professional publications, directories, and list of executive search firms and of employment services. Always be careful with employment services. Too many employment services engage in practices that embarrass the legitimate members of the industry.

The Atlanta JobBank (Bob Adams Publications; available from Planning/Communications' catalog at the end of this book) $15.95, annual, 408 pages. Lists 1,500+ of the major private sector and non–profit employers in the metropolitan area including whom to contact at each about job vacancies. Also included is a list of professional employment services (always be cautious about these; there are some charlatans out there who have sullied this profession's reputation), the addresses of the local chapter of many professional and trade associations, and profiles of many occupations.

Job Information Service (Georgia Department of Labor, 148 International Blvd., NE, Atlanta, GA 30303). Descriptions of non–profit sector vacancies throughout the state, and nation, are available on a computerized statewide database which can be viewed at any of the department's 35 field offices throughout the state. Two **Job Service** offices are in Atlanta (North Metro, 2943 N. Druid Hills Rd., Atlanta, GA 30329; phone: 404/679–5200; and South Metro, 2636–14 Martin Luther King, Jr. Dr., Atlanta, GA 30311; phone: 404/699–6900). Contact the department for a list of all field offices of this Job Service or check the local phone book.

Foundations and grants

A Guide to Funders in Central Appalachia and the Tennessee Valley (Appalachia Community Fund, 517 Union Ave., Suite 206, Knoxville, TN 37902; phone: 615/523–5783) $58, over 300 pages, January 1994. Among the 399 funders reported on are those that give grants in northern Georgia. Includes everything you need to seek funding: contact name, types of grants, grant application process, average grant size, plus how to write a grant proposal, funders from outside the region that make grants in the region, religious funding sources, and Japanese corporations with grantmaking programs.

Hawaii

The Honolulu Advertiser (605 Kapiolani Blvd., Honolulu, HI 96813; phone: 808/525–8000) published weekly on Sunday. Write for subscription prices. This is a fair source for non–profit sector positions throughout the state.

Star–Bulletin (605 Kapiolani Blvd., Honolulu, HI 96813; phone: 808/525–8000) published Monday through Sunday. Write for subscription prices. This is a fair source for non–profit sector positions throughout the state.

For information on **Job Service Offices**, contact the Department of Labor and Industrial Relations (830 Punchbowl St., Honolulu, HI 96813; phone: 808/586–8812).

Foundations and grants

Foundation Grants in Hawaii: 1991–1993 (Hamilton Library, ATTEN: Rachelle Liang, University of Hawaii at Manoa, 2550 The Mall, Honolulu, HI 96822; phone: 808/956–2532) if you get it in person, you pay for photocopying it, contact for cost of copying and mailing it to you, 118 pages, 1993. Reports in detail on all foundations that have issued grants to recipients in Hawaii. This compilation is based on data extracted from The Foundation Center's DIALOG computer database, *Grants Index* DIALOG file 27, described in the chapter "Foundations and grants."

Directory of Charitable Trusts and Foundation's for Hawaii's Non–Profit Organizations (Helping Hands Hawaii, 680 Iwilei Rd., Suite 430, Honolulu, HI 96817; phone: 808/536–7234) $20 plus $2/shipping, 115 pages, 1992. Describes over 80 foundations and charitable trusts.

Idaho

Rocky Mountain Employment Newsletter (Intermountain Publishing, 311–B0 14th St., Glenwood Springs, CO 81601–3949; phone: 303/945–8991) 18 issues/year, $21/three–month subscription to one edition, $26/any two editions, $31/three editions, $36/four editions. Two and one–month subscriptions also available. Published in four editions: Colorado–Wyoming, Arizona–New Mexico, Idaho–Montana, and Washington–Oregon. Combined, the four editions include over 400 job openings, some with non–profits. The positions tend to orient toward the outdoors, with quite a few in natural resources, environment, and wildlife.

For the addresses and phones of **Job Service Offices**, contact the Department of Employment (317 Main St., Boise, ID 83735; phone: 208/334–6100).

Foundations and grants

Directory of Idaho Foundations (Caldwell Public Library, 1010 Dearborn St., Caldwell, ID 83605–4195; phone: 208/459–3242) $10, 95 pages, 1993. Covers 123 foundations. Includes range of grants, sample grants, application information.

Illinois

Opportunity NOCs (Council of Illinois Nonprofit Organizations, Suite A1507, 175 W. Jackson Blvd., Chicago, IL 60604; phone: 312/435–1156) semimonthly, $15/three–month subscription, $45/annual subscription. Each issue includes 10 to 20 jobs at all levels with non–profit groups in Illinois.

IANO Monthly Memo (Illinois Association of Nonprofit Organizations, Suite 3000, 8 S. Michigan Ave., Chicago, IL 60603; phone: 708/386–9385) monthly, free/members, $30/annual nonmember subscription. The "Nonprofit Job Line" column includes announcements of 10 to 30 openings with non–profit entities, particularly upper–level positions. Also included are four or five notices of available grants under "Grant Information."

Illinois Nonprofit Directory (Council of Illinois Nonprofit Organizations, Suite A1507, 175 W. Jackson Blvd., Chicago, IL 60604; phone: 312/435–1156) contact for price (probably under $35), published in April of even–numbered years. Describes over 1,700 leading non–profits in Illinois. Identifies department heads, including personnel directors.

Illinois Nonprofit Salary and Benefit Survey (Council of Illinois Nonprofit Organizations, Suite A1507, 175 W. Jackson Blvd., Chicago, IL 60604) $49 plus $4/shipping, published every spring, 220 pages. Gives information on salaries and benefits for 66 job functions and nine different responsibility levels with non–profit organizations that have annual revenues up to $10 million.

How Do We Compare? (Council of Illinois Nonprofit Organizations, Suite A1507, 175 W. Jackson Blvd., Chicago, IL 60604; phone: 312/435–1156) contact for price, November 1994. Compares salary and fringe benefits paid by non–profits to those paid by the private sector.

How to Get a Job in Chicago (Surrey Books; available from Planning/Communications; see the catalog at the end of this book) $15.95, annual, 477 pages. This easy–to–use book tells you whom to contact for job vacancies at over 1,500 top private sector and non–profit employers in the metropolitan area. It also lists local chapters of professional and trade associations (which may publish a periodical with jobs ads or operate a local job service), local trade magazines, useful local professional publications, directories, and lists of executive search firms and of employment services. Always be careful with employment services. Too many employment services engage in practices that embarrass the legitimate members of the industry.

The Greater Chicago JobBank (Bob Adams Publications; available from Planning/Communications' catalog at the end of this book) $15.95, annual, 408 pages. Lists 1,500+ of the major private sector and non–profit employers in the metropolitan area including whom to contact at each about job vacancies. Also included is a list of professional employment services (always be cautious about these; there are some charlatans out there who have sullied this profession's reputation), the addresses of the local chapter of many professional and trade associations, and profiles of many occupations.

Illinois Department of Employment Security Offices (401 S. State St., Chicago, IL 60605; 312/793–3500). Sixty–three of these **Job Service Offices** across the state offer computer–based job searches. For a list of Job Service Offices, contact one of these offices or see the state government section of your local white pages telephone directory.

Foundations and grants

Corporate Foundations in Illinois – A Directory (c/o Ellen Dick, 838 Fair Oaks, Oak Park, IL 60302; phone: 708/386–9385) $35/mail orders only, March 1992. Reports details on over 120 corporate foundations (including Japanese foundations) and gift–matching programs: contact person, fields of interest, program and geographic limitations, application deadlines, grant amounts, officers and directors, and in–kind services contact person.

Illinois Foundation Directory (Foundation Data Center, 401 Kenmar Cr., Minnetonka, MN 55305; phone: 612/542–8582) $650, $255/annual update service (gets you three updates a year), new edition published quarterly,

1994. Reports details on over 2,000 Illinois foundations: contact person, officers and directors, territory and interest areas covered, list of grant recipients and amounts.

The Directory of Illinois Foundations (Donors Forum of Chicago, Suite 430, 53 W. Jackson, Chicago, IL 60604; phone: 312/431–0264) $60 plus $4.50/shipping, 297 pages, autumn 1993. Presents details on over 400 Illinois foundations and trusts with assets of at least $100,000 and total grants of $50,000 or more each year: contact person, geographic limits, contact and application procedures, deadlines, total grants, grant range, officers, and directors. Includes selected information on another 1,900 corporate, independent, and community foundations plus detailed tables on the assets and grants of the 100 largest Illinois foundations.

Members and Forum Partners Directory (Donors Forum of Chicago, Suite 430, 53 W. Jackson, Chicago, IL 60604; phone: 312/431–0264) $25, issued each autumn, available in ASCII format (for importing into a word processor) on MS–DOS 3.5–inch or 5.25–inch disks. Offers information on over 140 Donors Forum member foundations and corporate giving programs: names and phone numbers of contact persons and professional staff, total grants, availability of grant guidelines, and principle funding areas. Includes information on over 500 non–profit organizations, donor affinity groups, and regional associations of grantmakers.

Report on Capital/Endowment Fund Campaigns in the Greater Chicago Area (Donors Forum of Chicago, Suite 430, 53 W. Jackson, Chicago, IL 60604; phone: 312/431–0264) $10, published each spring. Reports on over 75 Illinois non–profit organizations conducting capital and endowment fund campaigns.

1990 Members Giving Report (Donors Forum of Chicago, Suite 430, 53 W. Jackson, Chicago, IL 60604; phone: 312/431–0264) $30, 1990. Currently out of print, you can view this report at the Donors Forum or at some local libraries. Reports on grants received by over 50 organizations that belong to the Donors Forum. Includes profiles of foundations and corporate givers by grant category.

Indiana

Indiana Department of Employment and Training Service (IDETS) (10 N. Senate Ave., Indianapolis, IN 46204; phone: 317/232–7670) has personnel who specialize in matching applicants with government jobs through the statewide automated **Job Service** Matching System. This service is available only by an in–person visit to a IDETS office. Write for a list of offices or consult the state government section in local telephone directories. All these services are free.

Foundations and grants

Directory of Indiana Donors (Indiana Donors Alliance, Seventh floor, 22 E. Washington St., Indianapolis, IN 46204–3529; phone: 317/630–5200) $20, 242 pages, 1993. Profiles almost 800 active grantmaking foundations, trusts, and scholarship programs: contact person, range of grants, eligibility for grants, geographic and program preferences, limitations, and application information.

Iowa

To locate **Job Service Offices**, contact the Department of Employment Services (1000 E. Grand, Des Moines, IA 50319; phone: 515/281–5365).

Kansas

To find **Job Service Offices**, contact the Department of Human Resources (Pat Pritchard, 401 SW Topeka Blvd , Topeka, KS 66603; phone: 913/296–7474) for a copy of the "DHR Office Directory" which lists the 36 offices the Department of Human Resources operates.

Foundations and grants

The Directory of Kansas Foundations (Topeka Public Library Foundation Center Collection, 1515 W. 10th St., Topeka, KS 66604; phone: 913/233–2040) $30, 254 pages, published in autumn of odd–numbered years. Reports on over 300 trusts and foundations: application information, limitations, types of support and sample grants, funding priority areas, and board members.

Kentucky

To locate the state's 28 **Job Service Offices**, contact the Field Services Division (Department for Employment Services, Suite 2W, 275 E. Main St., Frankfort, KY 40621; phone: 502/564–7456) and ask for a copy of the *Professional Placement Network* (PNN) brochure. This brochure will also tell you how to participate in the *PNN's* computer job–matching service which matches your resume with job openings on file with the Department of Employment Services. This free service keeps your resume on file for one year. When you are matched with an employer, your resume is forwarded to the employer who is then responsible for contacting you for an interview. You submit a one–page typewritten resume, a six–line mini–resume summary, and complete and sign an Applicant Profile Form which you obtain from the department. Call 800/562–6397 to obtain the Applicant Profile Form and instructions, or contact your local Department of Employment Services office.

Foundations and grants

The Kentucky Foundation Directory (MR & Company, P.O. Box 9223, Cincinnati, OH 45209; phone: 513/793–6636) $50 plus 5.5 percent sales tax for Ohio residents, 120 pages, June 1992. Reports on about 250 Kentucky foundations and charitable trusts: areas of interest, officers and trustees, application procedures, sample grants, financial data.

A Guide to Funders in Central Appalachia and the Tennessee Valley (Appalachia Community Fund, 517 Union Ave., Suite 206, Knoxville, TN 37902; phone: 615/523–5783) $58, over 300 pages, January 1994. Among the 399 funders reported on are those that give grants in eastern Kentucky. Includes everything you need to seek funding: contact name, types of grants, grant application process, average grant size, plus how to write a grant proposal, funders from outside the region that make grants in the region, religious funding sources, and Japanese corporations with grantmaking programs.

Louisiana

For information on the location of **Job Service Offices**, contact the Department of Labor (1001 N. 23rd Street, Baton Rouge, LA 70804; phone: 504/342–3111).

Foundations and grants

Citizens' Handbook of Private Foundations in New Orleans, Louisiana (The Greater New Orleans Foundation, 2515 Canal St., Suite 401, New Orleans, LA 70119; phone: 504/822–4906) $10/prepaid, about 200 pages, published in May of even–numbered years. Profiles over 120 foundations: contact person, officers, managers, financial data, grant recipients, amounts awarded.

Maine

Maine Sunday Telegram and *Portland Press Herald* (P.O. Box 1460. Portland, ME 04104; phone: 207/780–9000) are the best sources of job openings for non–profit sector positions throughout the state.

To locate **Job Service Offices**, contact the Department of Labor (State House Station #54, Augusta, ME 04333; director's phone: 207/287–3431).

Foundations and grants

Corporate Philanthropy in New England: Maine (D.A.T.A., 70 Audubon St., New Haven, CT 06510; phone: 203/772–1345) $5 plus $3/shipping, 1988; currently out of print but may be available at local libraries. Reports on over 180 corporate giving programs foundations: contact person, corporate profile, general philanthropic policies, giving priorities and interests.

Directory of Maine Foundations (University of Southern Maine, Office of Sponsored Research, 246 Deering Ave., Room 628, Portland, ME 04103; phone: 207/780–4871) 60 pages, 1992. Available only at libraries; not for sale. Reports on giving activities of about 62 Maine foundations and 20 corporate giving programs: contact person, sample grants, amounts awarded. We can't report the price or size of the book because these folks would not give us the information.

Maryland

Community Jobs/D.C. (ACCESS: Networking in the Public Interest, 50 Beacon St., Boston, MA 02108; phone: 617/720–5627) semimonthly, $29/three–month subscription, $39/six–

month subscription, $69/annual subscription; but if you also subscribe to the national edition of *Community Jobs,* you can get *Community Jobs/D.C.* for just additional $5/three months, $10/six months, $20/year; see the description of *Community Jobs* in Chapter 2 under "Job ads in print."). Includes advertisements for positions with a broad range of non–profits in the Washington, D.C. metropolitan area. The vast majority of these job announcements do not appear in the national edition of *Community Jobs.*

Opportunities in Public Affairs (Brubach Publishing Company, P.O. Box 15629, Chevy Chase, MD 20825) $29/two–month subscription, $49/four months, $69/six months, $129/annual, $7.95/single issue. You'll find announcements of over 200 positions with non–profits; local, state, and federal government agencies; and private companies in government affairs, public relations, broadcasting, and publishing. In addition to job announcements, this periodical also reports on unadvertised jobs its editors have uncovered. Most job openings are in the District of Columbia metropolitan area.

The Washington, D.C. Giving Guide (ACCESS: Networking in the Public Interest, 50 Beacon St., Boston, MA 02108; phone: 617/720–5627) $4/prepaid, 115 pages, 1993. Lists hundreds of non–profits in the Washington, D.C. area by subject area.

The 1993 Washington Job Source (MetCom, Inc. 1708 Surrey Lane, NW, Washington, DC 20007) $14.95 plus $3 shipping. Gives you the name, address, and phone number of the hiring contact for 2,100 non–profits, federal agencies, Congressional committees and commissions, and corporations.

Washington 93 (Columbia Books, 1212 New York Ave., NW, Suite 330, Washington, DC 20005; phone: 202/898–0662) $75, published annually each June. Here are nearly 600 pages of addresses, phone numbers, and information on private sector businesses and companies including suburban Maryland. Included are chapters on national associations, labor unions, law firms, medicine and health, foundations and philanthropy, science and policy research, education, religion, cultural institutions, clubs, and community affairs.

Job–Matching Service (Job Training and Placement Administration, Department of Economic and Employment Development, 1100 N. Eutaw St., Baltimore, MD 21201; director's phone: 410/333–5353) free. Matches your skills to job vacancies. Available at Job Service offices throughout the state.

M 'PO Membership Directory (Maryland Association of Nonprofit Organizations, 190 W. Ostend Street, Suite 201, Baltimore, MD 21230; phone: 410/727–6367) annual, $100. Lists 350 members.

To pinpoint **Job Service Offices**, contact the Job Training and Placement Administration (Department of Economic and Employee Development, Room 700, 1100 N. Eutaw St., Baltimore, MD 21201; director's phone: 410/333–5070).

Maryland is among the first states to use ALEX, the *Automated Labor EXchange* computer service that enables job seekers to look up job vacancies in Maryland and nationwide, themselves. ALEX terminals are available at Job Service Offices and in shopping malls, libraries, and schools. Note that many of the ALEX terminals in Maryland give you access only to jobs within the state and are not part of the national hookup.

Foundations and grants

Annual Index of Foundation Reports and Appendix (Maryland Attorney General, 200 St. Paul Pl. Baltimore, MD 21202; phone: 410/576–6491) $70, issued each January. Reports on over 500 foundations that have filed with the state's Attorney General: foundation managers, contact person, application process, contributions, and more.

Massachusetts

◁ ***How to Get a Job in Boston*** (Surrey Books; available from Planning/Communications; see the catalog at the end of this book) $15.95, roughly annual, 370 pages. Among the 1,500 employers in the metropolitan area described in this book are many non–profit entities. It also lists local chapters of professional–and trade associations (which may publish a periodical with jobs ads or operate a local job service), local trade magazines, useful local professional publications, directories, and lists of executive search firms and of employment services. Always be careful with employment services. Too many employment services engage in practices that embarrass the legitimate members of the industry.

The Boston JobBank (Bob Adams Publications; available from Planning/Communications' catalog at the end of this book) $15.95, annual, 408 pages. Lists 1,500+ of the major private sector and non–profit sector employers in the metropolitan area including whom to contact at each about job vacancies. Also included is a list of professional employment services (always be cautious about these; there are some charlatans out there who have sullied this profession's reputation), the addresses of the local chapter of many professional and trade associations, and profiles of many occupations.

To locate **Job Service Offices**, contact the Department of Employment and Training (19 Staniford St., Boston, MA 02114; phone: 617/727–6529).

Foundations and grants

Massachusetts Grantmakers (Associated Grantmakers of Massachusetts, 294 Washington St., Suite 840, Boston, MA 02108; phone: 617/426–2606) $53, 223 pages, 1993. Describes over 466 foundations and corporate grant makers: contact person, whether support is given to non–profit organizations and/or individuals, program emphasis and grantmaking philosophy, geographic focus, and application procedures.

Michigan

The Detroit JobBank (Bob Adams Publications; available from Planning/Communications' catalog at the end of this book) $15.95, 1993, 360 pages. Lists 1,000+ of the major private sector and non–profit employers in the metropolitan area including whom to contact at each about job vacancies. Also included is a list of professional employment services (always be cautious with these services; there are some charlatans out there who have sullied this profession's otherwise good reputation), the addresses of the local chapter of many professional and trade associations, and profiles of many occupations.

Michigan Occupational Information System (4–Sights Network, 16625 Grand River, Detroit, MI 48227; phone: 313/272–3900) free. *This service is strictly for people who are blind or who have visual impairments.* Updated annually, this computer database includes a description of every job title in the state in both the private and public sectors. Each listing defines the nature of the job, working conditions, methods of entry, earnings, employment outlook, and more. For details on how to connect your computer into this database via modem, contact the 4–Sights Network. This directory is available *only* through computer modem.

To find **Job Service Offices**, contact the Employment Security Commission (7310 Woodward Ave., Detroit, MI 48202; phone: 313/876–5000).

Foundations and grants

The Michigan Foundation Directory (Michigan League for Human Services, 300 N. Washington Sq., Suite 401, Lansing, MI 48933; phone: 517/487–5436) $30/nonmembers plus $2/shipping, prepaid only, $25/members of Michigan

League for Human Services or Council of Michigan Foundation, 290 pages, published in even–numbered years with a free supplement sent in odd–numbered years. Covers over 1,144 foundations granting at least $25,000 yearly, 377 foundations awarding over $50,000 a year in grants, and 79 corporate giving programs: contact person, purpose and activities, geographic priorities, grant ranges, officers and trustees. Includes analysis of grantmaking patterns and a guide to proposal writing.

Minnesota

Minnesota Nonprofit Directory (Minnesota Council of Nonprofits, Suite 250, 2700 University Ave., West, St. Paul, MN 55114; phone: 612/642–1904) $40/non-members, $25/members; everyone add 6.5 percent sales tax plus $2.50/shipping, 295 pages, published in the last quarter of even–numbered years. For each of over 3,000 Minnesota non–profits, you'll get the executive director's name, number of employees, a program description, revenue sources, expenses, and assets. Indexed by activity area and geography. Mailing labels are also available.

Minnesota Nonprofit Survey: Factors in Executive Director Compensation (Minnesota Council of Nonprofits, Suite 250, 2700 University Ave., West, St. Paul, MN 55114; phone: 612/642–1904) $10/nonmembers, $5/members; everyone add 6.5 percent sales tax plus $2.50/shipping, 20 pages, published in November 1993 and every four years thereafter. Activity area, location, budget size, structure, and gender are all reported to be elements affecting the salary received by executive directors of non–profits in Minnesota.

Human Services Survey of the Twin Cities Area (Robert Fjerstad, Human Relations Consultants, 3409 Kilmer Lane, North, Minneapolis, MN 55441; phone: 612/546–3870) $50, 140 pages, published every spring. Reports on salaries for over 70 different job categories with over 100 non–profits in the Saint Paul–Minneapolis area.

Human Services Benefits Survey of the Twin Cities Area (Robert Fjerstad, Human Relations Consultants, 3409 Kilmer Lane, North, Minneapolis, MN 55441; phone: 612/546–3870) $50, 57 pages, autumn 1991 (might do a new edition in 1994 or 1995). Reports on benefits paid to employees by size of non–profit agency.

The Minneapolis–St. Paul JobBank (Bob Adams Publications; available from Planning/Communications' catalog at the end of this book) $15.95, annual, 416 pages. Lists 1,500+ of the major private sector and non–profit employers in the metropolitan area including whom to contact at each about job vacancies. Also included is a list of professional employment services, the addresses of the local chapter of many professional and trade associations, and profiles of many occupations.

For information on the location of **Job Service Offices**, contact J.S. and U.I. Operations (Department of Jobs and Training, 390 N. Robert St., St. Paul, MN 55101; phone: 612/296–3644).

Foundations and grants

Minnesota Foundation Directory (Foundation Data Center, 401 Kenmar Cr., Minnetonka, MN 55305; phone: 612/542–8582) $450, $225/annual update service (gets you three updates a year plus new information faxed to you bimonthly), new edition published quarterly, 1994. Reports details on over 700 Minnesota foundations: contact person, officers and directors, territory and interest areas covered, list of grant recipients and amounts.

Guide to Minnesota Foundations and Corporate Giving Programs (Minnesota Council on Foundations, Suite 800, 706 Second Ave. South, Minneapolis, MN 55402; phone: 612/338–1989) $38.95 (includes sales tax and shipping), 296 pages, issued in odd–numbered years. Describes over 600 grantmakers: program interests, range of grants, sample grants, officers, and directors. Also lists foundations that do not accept applications.

Minnesota Grants Directory (Minnesota Council of Nonprofits, Suite 250, 2700 University Ave., West, St. Paul, MN 55114; phone: 612/642–1904) $25 plus 6.5 percent sales tax and $2.50/shipping, 82 pages, published every June. Provides information on 250 Minnesota foundations, corporate and religious giving programs, and government grants for non–profits: contact person, deadlines, availability of funds, staff, trustees, and more.

Mississippi

Mississippi 501 News (Mississippi Center for Nonprofits, 633 North State Street, Suite 602A, Jackson, MS 39202; phone: 601/968–0061) quarterly, call for price. Presently there are no job ads but expect to have some in 1994.

Mississippi Center for Nonprofits Salary Survey (633 North State Street, Suite 602A, Jackson, MS 39202; phone: 601/968–0061) call for price, 1989. Profiles 60 non–profit organizations in Jackson.

For a list of **Job Service Offices**, contact the Mississippi State Employment Service (1520 W. Capitol St., Jackson, MS 39203; phone: 601/354–8711) for a copy of the "Directory of Employment Service Offices."

Foundations and grants

A Guide to Funders in Central Appalachia and the Tennessee Valley (Appalachia Community Fund, 517 Union Ave., Suite 206, Knoxville, TN 37902; phone: 615/523–5783) $58, over 300 pages, January 1994. Among the 399 funders reported on are those that give grants in Mississippi. Includes everything you need to seek funding: contact name, types of grants, grant application process, average grant size, plus how to write a grant proposal, funders from outside the region that make grants in the region, religious funding sources, and Japanese corporations with grantmaking programs.

Missouri

The St. Louis JobBank (Bob Adams Publications; available from Planning/Communications' catalog at the end of this book) $15.95, 1993, 360 pages. Lists 1,000+ of the major private sector and non–profit employers in the metropolitan area including whom to contact at each about job vacancies. Also included is a list of professional employment services (always be cautious about these; there are some charlatans out there who have sullied this profession's reputation), the addresses of the local chapter of many professional and trade associations, and profiles of many occupations.

Missouri Wage Surveys and *Employment Projections* (Division of Employment Security, Research and Analysis Section, 421 E. Dunklin, Box 59, Jefferson City, MO 65105; phone: 314/751–3591).

To locate **Job Service Offices**, contact the Division of Employment Security (Labor and Industrial Relations Department, 421 E. Dunklin, Box 59, Jefferson City, MO 65104; director's phone: 314/751–3215).

Foundations and grants

The Directory of Missouri Foundations (Swift Associates, 110 Orchard Ave., St. Louis, MO 63119; phone: 314/962–2940) $35 plus $3.50/shipping, 1993. Reports on over 1,000 foundations that make grants to organizations or individuals: contact person, funding priorities, grant amounts, assets, total contributions, and trustees.

The Directory of Greater Kansas City Foundations (Clearinghouse for Midcontinent Foundations, P.O. Box 22680, Kansas City, MO 64113; phone: 816/235–1176) $58, 200 pages, last published October 1993, published each fall. Features detailed profiles on over 400 foundations and trusts in the eight–county greater Kansas City metropolitan area: contact person, officers and directors, recipient information, range of grants, limitations, purpose, and more.

Montana

Rocky Mountain Employment Newsletter (Intermountain Publishing, 311–B0 14th St., Glenwood Springs, CO 81601–3949; phone: 303/945–8991) 18 issues/year, $21/three–month subscription to one edition, $26/any two editions, $31/three editions, $36/four editions. Two and one–month subscriptions also available. Published in four editions: Colorado–Wyoming, Arizona–New Mexico, Idaho–Montana, and Washington–Oregon. Combined, the four editions include over 400 job openings, some in non–profits. The positions tend to orient toward the outdoors, with quite a few in natural resources, environment, and wildlife.

To locate **Job Service Offices**, obtain a copy of the *Directory of Job Service Offices* (Job Service Division, Department of Labor and Industry, P.O. Box 1728, Helena, MT 59624; phone: 406/444–4100) free. Lists detailed information on the state's 24 Job Service Offices.

Foundations and grants

The Montana and Wyoming Foundation Directory (Eastern Montana College Library, 1500 N. 30th, Billings, MT 59101; phone: 406/657–1666) $10, last issued in 1992. Reports on 65 foundations in Montana: contact person, application procedures, areas of interest, and geographic preferences.

Nebraska

To locate **Job Service Offices**, contact the Job Service Division (Department of Labor, 550 S. 16th St., Lincoln, NE 68509; phone: 402/471–9828).

Foundations and grants

Nebraska Foundation Directory (Junior League of Omaha, 11915 Pierce Plaza, Omaha, NE 68144; phone: 402/330–0197) $15, 31 pages, last published in January 1992. Reports on over 200 foundations: officers, statement of purpose.

Nevada

To obtain a list of **Job Service Centers**, contact the Employment Security Department (500 E. Third St., Carson City, NV 89713; phone: 702/687–4630).

Foundations and grants

Nevada Foundation Directory (Las Vegas–Clark County Library District, 1401 E. Flamingo Rd., Las Vegas, NV 89119; phone: 702/733–7810) contact for price, new edition March/April 1994. Profiles foundations, state funding, and block grants in Nevada and those that fund projects in Nevada: contact person, field of interest, sample grants.

New Hampshire

Jobs with non–profits for the whole state are advertised in local newspapers and the *New Hampshire Sunday News* (100 William Loeb Dr., Manchester, NH 03109; phone. 603/668 4321), *Maine Sunday Telegram* (P.O. Box 1460, Portland, ME 04104; phone: 207/775–5811), and *Boston Globe* (135 Morrissey Blvd., Boston, MA 02125; phone: 617/929–2000).

To locate **Job Service Offices**, contact the Bureau of Employment Services (Department of Employment Security, 32 S. Main St., Concord, NH 03301; phone: 603/224–3311).

Foundations and grants

Corporate Philanthropy in New England: New Hampshire (D.A.T.A., 70 Audubon St., New Haven, CT 06510; phone: 203/772–1345) $7, last issued in 1987. Reports on over 275 corporate giving programs: contact person, giving priorities, and interests.

Directory of Charitable Funds in New Hampshire (Department of Justice, Division of Charitable Trusts, State House Annex, 25 Capitol St., Concord, NH 03301; phone: 603/271–3591) $5, 84 pages, 1991. Describes over 240 foundations: purpose statement, officers, and assets.

Northern New England Nonprofits Membership Directory (Granite State Association of Nonprofits, 125 Airport Rd., Concord, NH 03301; phone: 603/225–0900) $15, annual, last published October 1993. List of 300 members: addresses, phone numbers, mission statements, and more.

New Jersey

Opportunity NOCs (The Nonprofit Management Development Center at LaSalle University, 1900 N. Olney, Philadelphia, PA 19141; phone: 215/951–1701) monthly, $10/three–month subscription, $30/annual subscription. From 10 to 20 positions with non–profits in southern New Jersey, Delaware, and Pennsylvania are described in every issue.

Community Jobs/N.Y/N.J. (ACCESS: Networking in the Public Interest, 50 Beacon St., Boston, MA 02108; phone: 617/720–5627) semimonthly, $29/three–month subscription, $39/six–month subscription, $69/annual subscription; but if you also subscribe to the national edition of *Community Jobs*, you can get *Community Jobs/N.Y./N.J.* for an additional $5/three months, $10/six months, $20/year; see the description of *Community Jobs* in Chapter 2 under "Job ads in print."). Includes advertisements for positions with a broad range of non–profits in the New York and New Jersey metropolitan area. The vast majority of these job announcements do not appear in the national edition of *Community Jobs*.

Update (Center for Nonprofit Corporations, 15 Roszel Rd., Princeton, NJ 08540; phone: 609/951–0800) bimonthly, $50/nonmember subscription to both *Update* and *Front & Center* which is described immediately below (they cannot be purchased separately), free/members. Two or three job ads appear under "Classifieds."

Front & Center (Center for Nonprofit Corporations, 15 Roszel Rd., Princeton, NJ 08540; phone: 609/951–0800) quarterly, $50/nonmember

subscription to both *Front & Center* and *Update* which is described immediately above (they cannot be purchased separately), free/members. Two or
three job ads appear under "Classifieds."

CNC Salary Survey (Center for Nonprofit Corporations, 15 Roszel Rd.,
Princeton, NJ 08540; phone: 609/951–0800) 1993, contact for price. Lists
positions by budget, staff size, gender, geographic location, and benefits.

To locate **Job Service Offices**, obtain a copy of ***Job Service Offices***
(Division of Programs, Department of Labor, John Fitch Plaza, Trenton, NJ
08625; phone: 609/984–7481). Request this list of the 23 full–service Job
Service Offices and 16 satellite offices. Job vacancies are available on
computer.

Foundations and grants

The Mitchell Guide to Foundations, Corporations, and Their Managers:
New Jersey (The Mitchell Guide, 430 Federal City Rd., Pennington, NJ
08534; phone: 609/737–7224) contact for price of new edition, issued in
late autumn of even–numbered years; the 1992 edition is out of print but
may be available at local libraries; the 1994 edition will be published in late
1994. Provides information on 452 foundations: foundation managers,
restrictions and program priorities, sample grants.

New Jersey Notes (The Mitchell Guide, 430 Federal City Rd., Pennington,
NJ 08534; phone: 609/737–7224) bimonthly, $25/annual subscription (this
is currently available). Supplements *The Mitchell Guide to Foundations,
Corporations, and Their Managers: New Jersey* described immediately above,
with information about new foundations and grant programs, and changes
in existing foundation funding programs.

New Jersey Foundations and Other Sources (New Jersey State Library,
ATTEN: Linda Kay, CN520, Trenton, NJ 08625; phone: 609/292–6220)
$30/prepaid only (includes postage, make check payable to: "Treasurer,
State of New Jersey"), 90 pages, published each August. This directory
essentially sends you to the right place to find detailed information on over
1,800 foundations and corporate givers in the State of New Jersey. For each
entry, you'll get the foundation's or corporate giver's name, county, where
to find information on it in standard printed sources, termination or inactive
status, name changes, and whether the foundation or giver accepts grant
applications

New Mexico

Rocky Mountain Employment Newsletter (Intermountain Publishing, 311–B0 14th St., Glenwood Springs, CO 81601–3949; phone: 303/945–8991) 18 issues/year, $21/three–month subscription to one edition, $26/any two editions, $31/three editions, $36/four editions. Two and one–month subscriptions also available. Published in four editions: Arizona–New Mexico, Colorado–Wyoming, Idaho–Montana, and Washington–Oregon. Combined, the four editions include over 400 job openings, some in non–profits. The positions tend to orient toward the outdoors, with quite a few in natural resources, environment, and wildlife.

Albuquerque Journal (7777 Jefferson, NE, Albuquerque, NM 87109; phone: 505/823–4400). The Sunday edition is the best source of ads for jobs in three–fourths of the state. For the southern and southeast portions of the state, see the Sunday *El Paso Times* (300 N. Campbell, El Paso, TX 79901; phone: 915/546–6260). For jobs in the extreme southern section, beginning with Clovis and going south, the Sunday editions of the local newspapers from nearby Texas are the best sources.

To locate **Job Service Offices**, contact the Department of Labor (400 Broadway, Albuquerque, NM 87102; phone: 505/841–8609).

New York

Community Jobs/N.Y/N.J. (ACCESS: Networking in the Public Interest, 50 Beacon St., Boston, MA 02108; phone: 617/720–5627) semimonthly, $29/three–month subscription, $39/six–month subscription, $69/annual subscription; but if you also subscribe to the national edition of *Community Jobs,* you can get *Community Jobs/N.Y./N.J.* for an additional $5/three months, $10/six months, $20/year; see the description of *Community Jobs* in Chapter 2 under "Job ads in print."). Includes advertisements for positions with a broad range of non–profits in the New York and New Jersey metropolitan area. The vast majority of these job announcements do not appear in the national edition of *Community Jobs.*

Job Listing Service (The Foundation Center, 79 Fifth Ave., Eighth floor, New York, NY 10003; phone: 212/620–4230) free, walk–in service only. Positions with non–profit entities in New York and elsewhere are listed here. These job vacancies can be viewed *only* in person. They are *not* published.

NPCC'S New York City Nonprofits Mailing List (Nonprofit Coordinating Committee of New York, 121 Sixth Ave., 6th Floor, New York, NY 10013; phone: 212/925–5340) $100/per hour, $55/per hour non–profit organizations, $40 members of NPCC; minimum charge is for 30 minutes use. Contains names, addresses, and telephone numbers of approximately 14,800 non–profit organizations. Data is sorted by categories: geographic location, number of employees, tax status, site or parent organization, activities, social services, health/mental health, arts and culture, schools, auxiliary services, religion, foundation, trade association, housing, and other. Data is also available on self–adhesive mailing labels (two across, five–inch x 15/16–inch, self adhesive), lists, or on computer disk in Paradox, dBase, or ASCII text. Price is determined by the length of time it takes to put information together. All requests should be made in writing to Tim Legg at address above. Be sure to specify the geographic areas you want, size of non–profit organizations, and number of employees. If ordering the information on disk, please specify data format and disk size.

The Source Book 1992–93: Social and Health Services in the Greater New York Area (Oryx Press, Suite 700, 4041 N. Central, Phoenix, AZ 85012; phone: 800/279–6799) $52.50, 1,120 pages, 1993. Produced by the United Way of New York City and the City of New York, this directory describes hospitals, social service organizations, libraries, and about 2,000 other non–profit public and private agencies in the New York City metropolitan area.

Greater Capital Region Human Services Directory (Council of Community Services, 901A Madison Ave., Albany, NY 12208; phone: 518/489–4791) $12 plus $2/shipping, 150 pages, published every February. Includes descriptions of about 1,500 non–profit human service agencies and 600 private care providers located in Warren, Washington, Saratoga, Fulton, Montgomery, Schenectady, Albany, Schoharie, Rensselaer, Green, and Columbia counties.

How to Get a Job in New York (Surrey Books; available from Planning/Communications; see the catalog at the end of this book) $15.95, annual, 420 pages. Among the 1,800 employers in the metropolitan area described in this book are many non–profit entities. It also lists local chapters of professional and trade associations (which may publish a periodical with jobs ads or operate a local job service), local trade magazines, useful local professional publications, directories, and lists of executive search firms and of employment services.

The Metropolitan New York JobBank (Bob Adams Publications; available from Planning/Communications' catalog at the end of this book) $15.95, annual, 672 pages. The 1,500+ employers in the metropolitan area listed here include non–profit entities. Information provided includes whom to contact to apply for a job vacancy. Also included is a list of professional employment services (always be cautious with these services; there are some charlatans out there who have sullied this profession's reputation), the addresses of the local chapter of many professional and trade associations, and profiles of many private sector and non–profit occupations.

Internships + Job Opportunities in New York City and Washington, DC (Graduate Group, 86 Norwood Rd., West Hartford, CT 06117; phones: 203/232–3100, 203/236–5570) $27.50, published annually. Describes internship and job opportunities in a wide variety of fields.

To find **Job Service Offices**, dubbed "Community Service Centers" in New York, contact the Department of Labor (Room 590, State Campus Building #12, Albany, NY 12240; phone: 518/457–7030).

Foundations and grants

New York State Foundations: A Comprehensive Directory (The Foundation Center, 79 Fifth Ave., New York, NY 10003; phones: 800/424–9836, 212/620–4230) $165, 800+ pages, published in May of odd–numbered years. Reports details on over 5,200 independent, corporate, and community foundations based in New York State. Also includes information on over 300 grantmakers from outside the state that fund non–profits within New York State.

Guide to Grantmakers in the Rochester Area: 1993–1995 (Rochester Grantmakers Forum, 55 St. Paul St., Rochester, NY 14604; phone: 716/232–2380) $49.50, individuals add 8 percent sales tax, 303 pages, published in the summer of odd–numbered years. Includes over 150 sources of funding, lists of sample grants, common application and report forms, and types of support index.

The Mitchell Guide to Foundations, Corporations, and Their Managers: Central New York, including Binghamton, Corning, Elmira, Geneva, Ithaca, Oswego, Syracuse, Utica (Rowland L. Mitchell, Jr., P.O. Box 172, Scarsdale, NY 10583; phone: 914/723–7770) $40/includes shipping, 1993. Provides information on over 90 foundations: managers, sample grants, and financial data. Also reports on more than 100 corporations.

The Mitchell Guide to Foundations, Corporations, and Their Managers: Long Island, including Nassau and Suffolk Counties (Rowland L. Mitchell, Jr., P.O. Box 172, Scarsdale, NY 10583; phone: 914/723–7770) $40/includes shipping, 1993. Provides information on over 180 foundations: managers, sample grants, and financial data. Also reports on more than 130 corporations.

The Mitchell Guide to Foundations, Corporations, and Their Managers: Upper Hudson Valley, including Capital Area, Glens Falls, Newburgh, Plattsburgh, Poughkeepsie, Schenectady (Rowland L. Mitchell, Jr., P.O. Box 172, Scarsdale, NY 10583; phone: 914/723–7770) $40/includes shipping, 1993. Provides information on over 60 foundations: managers, sample grants, and financial data. Also reports on more than 40 corporations.

The Mitchell Guide to Foundations, Corporations, and Their Managers: Westchester, including Putnam, Rockland and Orange Counties (Rowland L. Mitchell, Jr., P.O. Box 172, Scarsdale, NY 10583; phone: 914/723–7770) $40/includes shipping, 1993. Provides information on over 215 foundations: managers, sample grants, and financial data. Also reports on more than 75 corporations.

The Mitchell Guide to Foundations, Corporations, and Their Managers: Western New York, including Buffalo, Jamestown, Niagara Falls, Rochester (Rowland L. Mitchell, Jr., P.O. Box 172, Scarsdale, NY 10583; phone: 914/723–7770) $40/includes shipping, 1993. Provides information on over 130 foundations: managers, sample grants, and financial data. Also reports on more than 90 corporations.

North Carolina

Philanthropy Journal of North Carolina (News and Observer Foundation, P.O. Box 191, Raleigh, NC 27602; phone: 919/829–8991) monthly, $57/annual subscription. The "Job Opportunities" section contains ads for about five to 20 positions, mostly for senior–level jobs with non–profit organizations and universities; lots of fundraising positions.

Membership Directory of the North Carolina Center for ***Nonprofits*** (North Carolina Center for Nonprofits, Suite 506, 4601 Six Forks Rd., Raleigh, NC 27609–5210; phone: 919/571–0811) contact for price, 50 pages, published each November. You'll get a description of 592 non–profit agencies that includes name, address, phone, and contact name, but no description of the agencies.

The Carolina JobBank (Bob Adams Publications; available from Planning/Communications' catalog at the end of this book) $15.95, published each March, 360 pages. Lists hundreds of the major non–profit and private sector employers in North and South Carolina, including whom to contact

at each about job vacancies. Also included is a list of professional employment services, the addresses of the local chapter of many professional and
trade associations, and profiles of many occupations.

To locate **Job Service Offices**, contact the Employment Security Commission (P.O. Box 25903, Raleigh, NC 27611; phone: 919/733–7546).

Foundations and grants

North Carolina Giving: The Directory of the State's Foundations (Capital
Consortium, 2700 Wycliff Rd., Suite 312, Raleigh, NC 27607; phone:
919/783–9199) $162, 798 pages, 1993. Profiles over 730 foundations:
trustee, limitations, application procedures, sample grants.

A Guide to Funders in Central Appalachia and the Tennessee Valley
(Appalachia Community Fund, 517 Union Ave., Suite 206, Knoxville, TN
37902; phone: 615/523–5783) $58, over 300 pages, January 1994. Among
the 399 funders reported on are those that give grants in western North
Carolina. Includes everything you need to seek funding: contact name, types
of grants, grant application process, average grant size, plus how to write a
grant proposal, funders from outside the region that make grants in the
region, religious funding sources, and Japanese corporations with grantmaking programs.

North Dakota

You can view job announcements at any of the
state's 20 local **Job Service Offices**. Obtain the
brochure entitled *Your Step–by–Step Guide to Using
Job Service* from the **Job Service North Dakota** (1000 E. Divide Ave., P.O.
Box 1537, Bismarck, ND 58502; phone: 701/224–2825).

Ohio

The Ohio JobBank (Bob Adams Publications; available from Planning/Communications' catalog at the
end of this book) $15.95, annual, 420 pages. Lists
1,500+ of the major private sector and non–profit employers throughout
the state including whom to contact at each about job vacancies. Also
included is a list of professional employment services (always be cautious

with these services; there are some charlatans out there who have sullied this profession's reputation), the addresses of the local chapter of many professional and trade associations, and profiles of many occupations.

To obtain a list of the state's 76 **Job Service Offices**, contact the Public Information Office (Bureau of Employment Services, 145 S. Front St., P.O. Box 1618, Columbus, OH 43216; phone: 614/466–3859). Ask for the "Programs and Services Brochure."

Foundations and grants

Charitable Foundations Directory of Ohio (Office of the Attorney General, Charitable Foundations Section, 30 E. Broad St., 17th Floor, Columbus, OH 43266–0410) $7.50 (includes postage), September 1993. Reports on 2,056 charitable organizations that make grants: contact person, restrictions, purpose, number of grants awarded.

The Cincinnati Foundation Directory (MR & Company, P.O. Box 9223, Cincinnati, OH 45209; phone: 513/793–6636) $42 plus 5.5 percent sales tax for Ohio residents, 120 pages, June 1992. Describes over 220 foundations and charitable trusts: areas of interest, officers and trustees, application procedures, sample grants, financial data.

The Cleveland Foundation Directory (MR & Company, P.O. Box 9223, Cincinnati, OH 45209; phone: 513/793–6636) $50 plus 5.5 percent sales tax for Ohio residents, June 1993. Reports on about 280 Cuyahoga County foundations and charitable trusts: areas of interest, officers and trustees, application procedures, sample grants, financial data.

The Southwest Ohio Foundation Directory (MR & Company, P.O. Box 9223, Cincinnati, OH 45209; phone: 513/793–6636) $37 plus 5.5 percent sales tax for Ohio residents, 120 pages, 1991. Reports on about 235 foundations and charitable trusts in the 16 county southwest Ohio region (except for Hamilton County where Cincinnati is located): areas of interest, officers and trustees, application procedures, sample grants, financial data.

Oklahoma

To pinpoint **Job Service Offices**, contact the Employment Security Commission (2401 N. Lincoln Blvd., Oklahoma City, OK 73105; phone: 405/557–7105).

Foundations and grants

The Directory of Oklahoma Foundations (Foundation Research Project, P.O. Box 1146, Oklahoma City, OK 73101; phone: 405/235–5603) $25/prepaid, $30/billed, 131 pages, 1992. Profiles more than 200 Oklahoma foundations: contact person, application procedures, restrictions, funding emphasis, financial data.

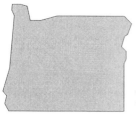

Oregon

Sound Opportunities (Nonprofit Community Network, 2708 Elliott Ave., Seattle, WA 98121; phone: 206/441–8280) biweekly, $13/four–month subscription. Features ads for about three to five positions with non–profits in Oregon plus a few internships and volunteer opportunities. Under "Jobseekers" you can place your own notice advertising your availability for work. Jobs advertised range from secretarial, maintenance work, to executive directors and everything in between.

Rocky Mountain Employment Newsletter (Intermountain Publishing, 311–B0 14th St., Glenwood Springs, CO 81601–3949; phone: 303/945–8991) 18 issues/year, $21/three–month subscription to one edition, $26/any two editions, $31/three editions, $36/four editions. Two and one–month subscriptions also available. Published in four editions: Washington–Oregon, Colorado–Wyoming, Arizona–New Mexico, and Idaho–Montana. Combined, the four editions include over 400 job openings, some with non–profits. The positions tend to orient toward the outdoors, with quite a few in natural resources, environment, and wildlife.

The *Local Office Directory* (Employment Division, Department of Human Resources, 875 Union St., NE, Salem, OR 97301; phones: 503/378–3211, 800/237–3710 within Oregon only) lists 33 local **Job Service Offices** where listings of vacancies are available.

Foundations and grants

The Guide to Oregon Foundations (United Way of the Columbia–Willamette, 718 W. Burnside, Portland, OR 97209; phone: 503/228–9131) $25, 178 pages, published in spring of odd–numbered years. Reports on general purpose foundations, special purpose foundations, and national or regional foundations with an active interest in Oregon: contact person, purpose statement, financial data, officers, and sample grants.

Pacific Northwest Grantmakers Forum Member Directory (Pacific North-west Grantmakers Forum, Suite 214, 1305 Fourth Ave, Seattle, WA 98101; phone: 206/624–9899) 106 pages, published in March of even–numbered years, the 1992 edition cost $20 plus $1.30/shipping and $1.64 sales tax for Washington state residents; check with the Forum for the price of sub-sequent editions. A good many Oregon–based foundations are among the 75 or so grantmakers described in this directory. Included in each listing are contact name's address and phone, application procedures, range of grant amounts awarded, and types of projects funded.

Pennsylvania

Opportunity NOCs (The Nonprofit Management Development Center at LaSalle University, 1900 N. Olney, Philadelphia, PA 19141; phone: 215/951–1701) monthly, $10/three–month subscription, $30/annual subscription. From 10 to 20 positions with non–profits in Pennsylvania, southern New Jersey, and Delaware are described in every issue.

The Greater Philadelphia JobBank (Bob Adams Publications; available from Planning/Communications' catalog at the end of this book) $15.95, annual, 468 pages. Lists 1,400+ of the major private sector and non–profit employers in the metropolitan area including whom to contact at each about job vacancies. Also included is a list of professional employment services (always be cautious with these services; there are some charlatans out there who have sullied this profession's reputation), the addresses of the local chapter of many professional and trade associations, and profiles of many occupations.

Obtain locations of **Job Service Offices** from the Bureau of Employment Services and Training (Department of Labor and Industry, Room 1115, Seventh and Forster Streets, Harrisburg, PA 17121; phone: 717/787–4811).

Foundations and grants

Directory of Pennsylvania Foundations (Triadvocates Press, P.O. Box 336, Springfield, PA 19064; phone: 215/544–6927) $51.95, 400 pages, 1990 edition includes 88–page 1993 update and supplement, new edition in spring 1994. Contact for information about a periodic supplement. Details over 2,300 foundations with full profiles of over 980 foundations with assets over $75,000 or issuing grants totaling more than $5,000: application guidelines, directors and trustees, major interests.

Rhode Island

Find the ten **Job Service Offices**, by contacting the Department of Employment and Training (101 Friendship St., Providence, RI 02903; phone: 401/277–3722) or see your telephone directory. Job Service staff will match job seekers with positions and refer them to potential employers.

Foundations and grants

Corporate Philanthropy in Rhode Island (D.A.T.A., 70 Audubon St., New Haven, CT 06510; phones: 800/788–5598, 203/772–1345) $5 plus $3/shipping, last published in 1989. Reports on over 250 corporate giving programs: contact person, giving priorities and interests.

South Carolina

The Carolina JobBank (Bob Adams Publications; available from Planning/Communications' catalog at the end of this book) $15.95, published each March, 360 pages. Lists hundreds of the major non–profit and private sector employers in South and North Carolina, including whom to contact at each about job vacancies. Also included is a list of professional employment services, the addresses of the local chapter of many professional and trade associations, and profiles of many occupations.

To locate **Job Service Offices**, contact the Employment Security Commission (1550 Gadsden St., Columbia, SC 29202; phone: 803/737–2400).

Foundations and grants

South Carolina Foundation Directory (South Carolina State Library, 1500 Senate St., ATTEN: Mary Bull, Columbia, SC 29211; phone: 803/734–8666) $15, 390 pages, last published in 1990, next edition expected in 1993 or 1994. Around 200 foundations are described: areas of interest, range of grants, geographic limitations, principal officer.

South Dakota

Job openings in the non–profit sector can be found by contacting a local **Job Service** office. You can obtain a list of these offices by contacting the South Dakota Department of Labor (P.O. Box 4730, Aberdeen, SD 57402–4730; phones: 800/592–1882, 605/622–2302). The offices are computerized, so you can obtain up–to–the–minute information on job openings in South Dakota and nationally.

Foundations and grants

The South Dakota Grant Directory (South Dakota State Library, 800 Governors Dr., Pierre, SD 57501; phone: 605/773–3131) free to South Dakota residents, January 1992. Over 300 grantmaking institutions are profiled: eligibility requirements, purpose statements, application procedures.

Tennessee

Job Bank (Council of Community Services, 2012 21st Ave., South, Nashville, TN 37212; phone: 615/385–2221) free, walk–in service. This organization maintains a file of job openings that non–profits send in. You can examine them at the Council's office on weekdays between 8 a.m. and 5 p.m. Do *not* request these to be sent to you. They can be seen only in–person

The Tennessee JobBank (Bob Adams Publications; available from Planning/Communications' catalog at the end of this book) $15.95, published each March, 360 pages. Lists hundreds of the major non–profit and private sector employers in South and North Carolina, including whom to contact at each about job vacancies. Also included is a list of professional employment services, the addresses of the local chapter of many professional and trade associations, and profiles of many occupations.

Directory of Community Services (Council of Community Services, 2012 21st Ave., South, Nashville, TN 37212; phone: 615/385–2221) $30/two–volume set plus $3/shipping, volume available individually for $16 each plus $1.50/shipping each. The 395–page Volume One covers over 450 agencies in Davidson County where Nashville rests. Over 520 agencies located in 22 surrounding counties are described in the 450 page Volume Two. Each agency description includes a contact person, area served, services offered, and clientele.

Salary Survey (Council of Community Services, 2012 21st Ave., South, Nashville, TN 37212; phone: 615/385–2221) $10, 13 pages, annual. Covers all levels of positions with non–profits in the 23–county area around Nashville.

To obtain a list of **Job Service Offices**, contact the Department of Employment Security (500 James Robertson Parkway, 12th Floor, Volunteer Plaza, Nashville, TN 37245–0001; phone: 615/741–2131).

Foundations and grants

A Guide to Funders in Central Appalachia and the Tennessee Valley (Appalachia Community Fund, 517 Union Ave., Suite 206, Knoxville, TN 37902; phone: 615/523–5783) $58, over 300 pages, January 1994. Among the 399 funders described are ones that award grants in Tennessee. Includes everything you need to seek funding: contact name, types of grants, grant application process, average grant size, plus how to write a grant proposal, funders from outside the region that make grants in the region, religious funding sources, and Japanese corporations with grantmaking programs.

Texas

JOBTRAC (6856 Arboreal Dr., Dallas, TX 75231; modem phone only: 214/349–0527) free. Run by volunteers, this job database offers mostly job opportunities within Texas including non–profits and teaching. Dial up the modem number (they won't publicize their voice number) and download job descriptions that interest you. You can also send your resume directly to employers by modem.

The Dallas–Fort Worth JobBank (Bob Adams Publications; available from Planning/Communications' catalog at the end of this book) $15.95, annual, 408 pages. Lists 1,000+ of the major private sector and non–profit employers in the metropolitan area including whom to contact at each about job vacancies. Also included is a list of professional employment services, the addresses of the local chapter of many professional and trade associations, and profiles of many occupations.

How to Get a Job in Dallas/Fort Worth (Surrey Books; available from Planning/Communications' catalog at the end of this book) $15.95, annual, 420 pages. This easy–to–use book tells you whom to contact for job vacancies at over 1,250 top private sector and non–profit employers in the metropolitan area. It also lists local chapters of professional and trade associations (which may publish a periodical with jobs ads or operate a local job service), local trade magazines, useful local professional publications, directories, and lists of executive search firms and of employment services.

How to Get a Job in Houston (Surrey Books; available from Planning/Communications; see the catalog at the end of this book) $15.95, annual, 410 pages. This easy–to–use book tells you whom to contact for job vacancies at over 1,200 top non–profit and private sector employers in the metropolitan area. It also lists local chapters of professional and trade associations (which may publish a periodical with job ads or operate a local job service), local trade magazines, useful local professional publications, directories, and list of executive search firms and of employment services.

The Houston JobBank (Bob Adams Publications; available from Planning/Communications' catalog at the end of this book) $15.95, annual, 408 pages. Lists 1,000+ of the major non–profit and private sector employers in the metropolitan area including whom to contact at each about job vacancies. Also included is a list of professional employment services, the addresses of the local chapter of many professional and trade associations, and profiles of many occupations.

The Texas Employment Commission operates a statewide, computer–assisted job matching system at its 100 offices. Request a list of these **Job Service Offices** from the TEC State Office (101 E. 15th St., Austin, TX 78778–0001; phone: 512/463–2222) or see the state government section of the local telephone directory.

Foundations and grants

Directory of Texas Foundations (Funding Information Center of Texas, 507 Brooklyn, San Antonio, TX 78215; phone: 512/227–4333) $119, published in spring of even–numbered years, price includes supplement published in the autumn of odd–numbered years. Describes over 900 large foundations and 620 smaller foundations: contact person, application procedures, emphasis, restrictions, grant range, trustees.

Directory of Dallas County Foundations (Dallas Public Library, Grants Information Service, 1515 Young St., Dallas, TX 75201; phone: 214/670–1487) $30 plus $3 shipping plus $2.48 sales tax, 493 pages, 1990–91 edition. Reports on over 354 private foundations: contact person, interests, officers, number of grants awarded.

Directory of Tarrant County Foundations (Funding Information Center, Texas Christian University, P.O. Box 32904, Fort Worth, TX 76129; phone: 817/921–7664) $40 plus $3/shipping plus $2.48 sales tax, 1989 edition, new edition expected in late 1992. Reports on a substantial number of foundations: types of support, fields of interest, trustees.

Utah

Informal Job Service (Utah Nonprofits Association, 1874 Connor Street, Salt Lake City, UT 84108; phone: 801/583–6579) free, call this informal service which receives job descriptions and keeps resumes on file for nonprofit sector jobs in the state of Utah.

Jobs listings are available by in–person application at the Utah **Job Service**, 720 South 200 East, Salt Lake City, UT 84111 (phone: 801/536–7000) or 5735 S. Redwood Rd., Salt Lake City, UT 84107 (phone: 801/269–4700).

To locate other **Job Service Offices**, contact the Utah Department of Employment Security (P.O. Box 11249, Salt Lake City, UT 84147; phone: 801/536–7401).

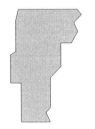

Vermont

Vermont Job Service (Vermont Department of Employment and Training, P.O. Box 308, Montpelier, VT 05601–0308; phone: 802/828–3860) free. Provides job matching services. Resumes are kept on file up to three years.

Vermont Jobs Line (Vermont Department of Employment and Training, Office of Policy and Information, P.O. Box 488, Montpelier, VT 05601; phone: 802/828–4153) free. From within Vermont, call 800/464–4473; from outside the state dial 802/828–3939. This 24–hour job hotline can be called with a touch–tone or rotary telephone. The only difference is that rotary users must clearly enunciate their choices (and pronounce the number 0 as "zero" and say each digit separately such as one two for the number 12. First you get to select one of the 12 regions within the state. Then you get to select if you want to hear the job listings received only during the last 24 hours, or all the job listings. Finally, you select which of nine general occupation categories for which you want to hear job information. At any time you can press "1" to skip to the next job listing or the asterisk to hear a job listing again (you don't get either of these options if you use a rotary phone). When you find a job that is right for you, be sure to write down its job order number given at the end of its description. Then call or visit any Employment and Training office to discuss the job and get full details on how to apply. The department does have a brochure on this service which is yours for the asking.

DET Board (Vermont Department of Employment and Training, Office of Policy and Information, P.O. Box 488, Montpelier, VT 05601; phone: 802/828–4153) free, updated daily. Anyone with a personal computer and modem can access this 24–hour a day electronic bulletin board which features job opening bulletins, which is a condensed version of the job openings available at local Job Service offices. If you find a job opening in your occupation, you should contact the local Job Service office for more information and procedures on how to contact the employer. Only the job title, wage, town, and job order number are shown. Within Vermont, call 800/924–4443 if you're using a 1,200 or 2,400 baud modem (the system cannot handle anything faster). From out of state, call 802/828–4108 or 802/828–4322. Set communication parameters at 8–N–1; duplex full. At the new user sign on, type "new" as your USER–ID. To see job openings, choose I to learn how to use the system. You can download information. The department has a short brochure that explains how to use the system. Ask for the *DET Board PC Access to Labor Market Information* brochure. If you have questions about the system, call Michael Griffen at 802/828–4153 (voice).

To locate **Job Service Offices**, contact the Department of Employment and Training (P.O. Box 488, Montpelier, VT 05601–0488; phone: 802/828–4000).

Foundations and grants

Corporate Philanthropy in New England: Vermont (D.A.T.A., 70 Audubon St., New Haven, CT 06510; phone: 203/772–1345) $5 plus $3/shipping, 1988; currently out of print but may be available at local libraries. Reports on over 125 corporate giving programs: contact person, giving priorities and interests, general philanthropic policies.

Virginia

Community Jobs/D.C. (ACCESS: Networking in the Public Interest, 50 Beacon St., Boston, MA 02108; phone: 617/720–5627) semimonthly, $29/three–month subscription, $39/six–month subscription, $69/annual subscription; but if you also subscribe to the national edition of *Community Jobs,* you can get *Community Jobs/D.C.* for an additional $5/three months, $10/six months, $20/year; see the description of *Community Jobs* in Chapter 2 under "Job ads in print."). Includes advertisements for positions with a broad range of non–profits in the Washington, D.C. metropolitan area. The vast majority of these job announcements do not appear in the national edition of *Community Jobs.*

Opportunities in Public Affairs (Brubach Publishing Company, P.O. Box 15629, Chevy Chase, MD 20825) $29/two–month subscription, $49/four months, $69/six months, $129/annual, $7.95/single issue. You'll find announcements of over 200 positions with non–profits; local, state, and federal government agencies; and private companies in government affairs, public relations, broadcasting, and publishing. In addition to job announcements, this periodical also reports on unadvertised jobs its editors have uncovered. Most job openings are in the District of Columbia area.

The Washington, D.C. Giving Guide (ACCESS: Networking in the Public Interest, 50 Beacon St., Boston, MA 02108; phone: 617/720–5627) $4/prepaid, 115 pages, 1993. Lists hundreds of non–profits in the Washington, D.C. area by subject area.

The 1993 Washington Job Source (MetCom, Inc. 1708 Surrey Lane, NW, Washington, DC 20007) $14.95 plus $3 shipping. Gives you the name, address, and phone number of the hiring contact for 2,100 non–profits, federal agencies, Congressional committees and commissions, and corporations.

Washington 93 (Columbia Books, 1212 New York Ave., NW, Suite 330, Washington, DC 20005; phone: 202/898–0662) $75, published annually each June. You'll find nearly 600 pages of addresses, phone numbers, and information on businesses and companies in the D.C. area including its Virginia suburbs. Included are chapters on national associations, labor unions, law firms, medicine and health, foundations and philanthropy, science and policy research, education, religion, cultural institutions, clubs, and community affairs.

Locate a local State Employment Service Office (Job Service) through a local telephone directory's state government section or obtain a list of the 42 local **Job Service Offices** from the Virginia Employment Commission (703 E. Main St., Richmond, VA 23219; phone: 804/786–7097).

Virginia is one of the first states to use ALEX, the Automated Labor EXchange computer service that enables job seekers to look up job vacancies in Virginia, and nationwide, themselves. ALEX terminals are located at Job Service Offices and in shopping malls, libraries, and schools.

Foundations and grants

A Guide to Funders in Central Appalachia and the Tennessee Valley (Appalachia Community Fund, 517 Union Ave., Suite 206, Knoxville, TN 37902; phone: 615/523–5783) $58, over 300 pages, January 1994. Among the 399 funders reported on are those that give grants in southeastern Virginia. Includes everything you need to seek funding: contact name, types of grants, grant application process, average grant size, plus how to write a grant proposal, funders from outside the region that make grants in the region, religious funding sources, and Japanese corporations with grantmaking programs.

Washington

Sound Opportunities (Nonprofit Community Network, 2708 Elliott Ave., Seattle, WA 98121; phone: 206/441–8280) biweekly, $13/four–month subscription. Features ads for about 20 jobs with non–profits in Washington State plus a few internships and volunteer opportunities. Under "Jobseekers" you can place your own notice advertising your availability for work. Jobs advertised range from secretarial, maintenance work, to executive directors and everything in between.

Nonprofit Community Resource Directory (Nonprofit Community Network, 2708 Elliott Ave., Seattle, WA 98121; phone: 206/441–8280) $19.95 plus $2.23/shipping (plus $1.82 sales tax for Washington residents), 128 pages, 1993. In addition to listing the names, addresses, and phone numbers for over 1,500 non–profit organizations in Washington State, this very valuable directory also tells you where to find job listings unique to Washington for each of the 20 different specialities within the non–profit sector.

Job Bulletin #2: Business, Industry, and the Public Sector (University of Washington, Center for Career Services, 301 Loew Hall, Mail stop FH–30, Seattle, WA 98195; phone: 206/254–0194) weekly, $40/three–month subscription. From 20 to 30 announcements of job vacancies appear in the typical issue. Only about 10 percent of the job announcements are for positions in the non–profit sector.

Northwest Nonprofit (Northwest Nonprofit Resources, 525 East Mission Avenue, Spokane, WA 99202–1824; phone: 509/484–6733) bimonthly, $40. One or two job ads appear under "Classifieds."

Nonprofit Computerized Label Service (Northwest Nonprofit Resources, 525 East Mission Avenue, Spokane, WA 99202–1824; phone: 509/484–6733) .10 per name. Includes names and addresses for 2,300 nonprofit organizations in the state of Washington.

Rocky Mountain Employment Newsletter (Intermountain Publishing, 311–B0 14th St., Glenwood Springs, CO 81601–3949; phone: 303/945–8991) 18 issues/year, $21/three–month subscription to one edition, $26/any two editions, $31/three editions, $36/four editions. Two and one–month subscriptions also available. Published in four editions: Washington–Oregon, Colorado–Wyoming, Arizona–New Mexico, and Idaho–Montana. Combined, the four editions include over 400 job openings, some in non–profits. The positions tend to orient toward the outdoors, with quite a few in natural resources, environment, and wildlife.

How to Get a Job in Seattle/Portland (Surrey Books; available from Planning/Communications' catalog at the end of this book) $15.95, annual, over 300 pages. This easy–to–use book tells you whom to contact for job vacancies at over 1,500 top private sector and non–profit employers in the metropolitan area. It also lists local chapters of professional and trade associations (which may publish a periodical with jobs ads or operate a local job service), local trade magazines, useful local professional publications, directories, and lists of executive search firms and of employment services.

The Seattle JobBank (Bob Adams Publications; available from Planning/Communications' catalog at the end of this book) $15.95, annual, 408 pages. Lists 1,000+ of the major non–profit and private sector employers in the metropolitan area including whom to contact at each about job vacancies. Also included is a list of professional employment services, the addresses of the local chapter of many professional and trade associations, and profiles of many occupations.

To locate **Job Service Offices**, contact the Employment and Training Division (Employment Security Department, 212 Maple Park, Olympia, WA 98504; phone: 206/438–4804).

The state also offers biennial area wage surveys that supply occupational wage and salary rates for clerical, managerial, professional, technical, and general occupations: average wage rates with high and low ranges, average hours worked, and occupational descriptions. There's a separate *Area Wage Survey* report for each of the following regions: Chelan–Douglas–Okanogan

Clallam–Jefferson, Cowlitz, Grays Harbor–Pacific, Kitsap, Lewis, Moses Lake, Pierce, Seattle PMSA (Small firms), Skagit–Island–San Juan, Spokane, Thurston–Mason, Tri–Cities, Vancouver, Walla Walla, Whatcom, and Yakima. Each report costs $1 (add $2.50 shipping and handling for your entire order; Washington state residents must add 7.9 percent sales tax). Send your check or money order to: Washington State Employment Security Department, Labor Market and Economic Analysis – Wage, P. O. Box 9046, Olympia, WA 98507–9046.

Foundations and grants

Charitable Trust Directory (Attorney General, Charitable Trust Division, P.O. Box 40106, Olympia, WA 98504–0106; phone: 206/753–0863, ext. 1) $10, 490 pages, published each January. Reports on over 1,000 charitable organizations and trusts: purpose statement, sample grants, financial data, and officers.

Pacific Northwest Grantmakers Forum Member Directory (Pacific Northwest Grantmakers Forum, Suite 214, 1305 Fourth Ave, Seattle, WA 98101; phone: 206/624–9899) 106 pages, published in March of even–numbered years, 1992 edition cost $20 plus $1.30/shipping and $1.64 sales tax for Washington state residents; check with the Forum for the price of subsequent editions. Most of the 75 or so grantmakers described in this directory are based in the Puget Sound area. Included in each listing are contact name's address and phone, application procedures, range of grant amounts awarded, and types of projects funded.

West Virginia

To locate **Job Service Offices**, contact the Bureau of Employment Programs (112 California Ave., Charleston, WV 25305–0112; phone: 304/558–2660).

Foundations and grants

West Virginia Foundation Directory (Kanawha County Public Library, Administrative Office, 123 Capitol St., Charleston, WV 25301; phone: 304/343–4646) $7.50/prepaid, 108 pages, 1992. Profiles over 100 foundations: contact person, areas of interest, restrictions, application procedures, trustees.

A Guide to Funders in Central Appalachia and the Tennessee Valley (Appalachia Community Fund, 517 Union Ave., Suite 206, Knoxville, TN 37902; phone: 615/523–5783) $58, over 300 pages, January 1994. Among the 399 funders reported on are those that give grants in West Virginia. Includes everything you need to seek funding: contact name, types of grants, grant application process, average grant size, plus how to write a grant proposal, funders from outside the region that make grants in the region, religious funding sources, and Japanese corporations with grantmaking programs.

Wisconsin

Milwaukee Associates in Urban Development Informal Job Service (750 N. 18th Street, Milwaukee, WI 53233; phone: 414/344–3933) This extremely informal job service will send job descriptions out by request if you contact them by phone, or a list of more extensive job descriptions can be viewed on their job board at the agencies headquarters.

To locate **Job Service Offices**, contact the Job Service Division (Department of Industry, Labor, and Human Relations, P.O. Box 7972, Madison, WI 53707; phone: 608/266–8212).

Foundations and grants

Foundations in Wisconsin: A Directory (Marquette University Memorial Library, 1415 W. Wisconsin Ave., Milwaukee, WI 53233; phone: 414/288–1515) $24, 237 pages, September 1993 and in even–numbered years thereafter. Profiles 791 active grantmaking foundations: officers and directors, grant range, purpose and interests, sample grants.

Wyoming

Rocky Mountain Employment Newsletter (Inter-mountain Publishing, 311–B0 14th St., Glenwood Springs, CO 81601–3949; phone: 303/945–8991) 18 issues/year, $21/three–month subscription to one edition, $26/any two editions, $31/three editions, $36/four editions. Two and one–month subscriptions also available. Published in four editions: Colorado–Wyoming,

Arizona–New Mexico, Idaho–Montana, and Washington–Oregon. Combined, the four editions include over 400 job openings, some in non–profits. The positions tend to orient toward the outdoors, with quite a few in natural resources, environment, and wildlife.

To get the addresses of the 16 local **Job Service Centers** in Wyoming, contact the Job Service of Wyoming (Department of Employment, P.O. Box 2760, Casper, WY 82602; phone: 307/235–3200).

Foundations and grants

Wyoming Foundations Directory (Laramie County Community College, 1400 E. College Dr., Cheyenne, WY 82007; phone: 307/778–1205) contact for price, spring 1992. Details over 70 foundations including the name of the contact person, purpose statement.

The Montana and Wyoming Foundation Directory (Eastern Montana College Library, 1500 N. 30th, Billings, MT 59101; phone: 406/657–1686) $10, 102 pages, last issued in summer 1993. Reports on 20 foundations in Wyoming: contact person, application procedures, areas of interest, and geographic preferences.

Chapter 32

Cover letters and resumes

Once you've found the job vacancies, you still have to write an effective cover letter and resume to get the job — unless you're applying for a job that requires submission of only a specified form. There are a lot of fine resume and cover letter books on the market that will help you prepare good cover letters and resumes — and some not so fine books. I've scoured more of them than I care to remember and have refined their best advice for you in this chapter. I've tried to be as concise as possible so you don't have to spend any more time than is necessary to devise an effective resume and cover letter.

The next step in the job search process requires you to persuade the prospective employer that you are worth interviewing. That's where your cover letter and resume make the difference. Once you get the interview, it's up to you to make a good enough impression to be offered the job at the salary you want.

This chapter suggests ways to write an effective application letter to accompany your resume, in response to a job ad and as a "blind" application. Then it explains how to prepare an attractive and effective resume. For the student right of out school, these guidelines remove some of the mystery from applying for jobs. For the seasoned professional, they offer a sound refresher course and debunk many of the myths built up over the years, particularly concerning the content of a resume.

Finally, Chapter 33 reviews ways to effectively prepare for your job interview and recommends productive interview behaviors that can benefit even the most seasoned worker.

Cover or target letters

Cover letters and resumes go hand–in–hand. A target, or cover letter explains why you are particularly well–suited to the specific job for which you are applying. The resume outlines your professional experience, education, and other relevant accomplishments in some detail and can be used for most any job for which you apply.

The purpose of the cover letter and resume is to market you to a potential employer well enough to get her to invite you to a personal interview. Because the person who does the hiring usually scours scores of applications (sometimes hundreds in today's job market), your cover letter should, in a persuasive, professional, polite, and personable manner, point out your specific qualifications for the job so effectively that the employer will carefully examine the resume your cover letter accompanies. As Dr. Krannich and William Banis put it in *High Impact Resumes and Letters*, "your letter should be the sizzle accompanying the sell." While the resume can, and should, be mass produced, the cover letter for each job application should be individually typed and targeted to the specific job.

Cover letter guidelines

Use your own personal stationery or blank paper and the appropriate business letter format for your cover letter. It is very bad form to use the letterhead of your current employer when applying for a job. Use high quality white or light–colored bond paper.

If at all possible, the letter itself should be addressed to a specific person. If the advertisement or job announcement failed to name the person to whom you apply, it's usually worth a phone call to learn his name. Just ask the receptionist or secretary in the department that is doing the hiring. Sometimes you'll run into a brick wall where nobody will tell you to whom to write. One option is to consult the directories described in this book to identify the proper person. Then call the agency or school to confirm that the individual still works there (personnel do change after directories are published). If you cannot identify a name to which to write, simply address your letter to the "Director of Human Resources" or to the "Director of X," the division or department in which you wish to work.

You'll also want to use these directories if you are writing a "blind" letter seeking employment when there is no job advertised — as illustrated in the first sample cover letter at the end of this chapter.

Cover letter content

An effective cover letter is written with a professional tone and style and should include the following items:

☐ **Clearly identify the job** you seek in the first paragraph or sentence.

☐ **Indicate why you are applying** for this particular position. Try to link your interests to the employer's needs. If you have a compulsion to state your career objective, your cover letter is the place to do it. Tailor your career objective to the job you are seeking. If your career objective doesn't match the job well, your whole application may wind up in the circular file and the reader may never bother to even read your resume and see how great you'd be for the job.

☐ **Describe your qualifications.** Explain why you are particularly well–suited for this specific position. Carefully review the job description or job announcement or ad to determine what skills are sought and how you meet them. In your cover letter, show how you meet these requirements. Refer to items in your enclosed resume and emphasize your qualifications vis–a–vis the employer's needs. In a sense, you should re–write the employer's ad around the qualifications described in it. This approach is low–keyed, but assertive while not appearing to be boastful, hyped–up, or aggressive.

☐ **Refer the reader to the enclosed resume** for details of your experience and education.

☐ **Request the next step** in the hiring process: an interview, an answer to this letter, or a request for references (be assertive, but friendly). Make the employer an open–ended offer she can't refuse, as is done in the first sample cover letter at the end of this chapter. This approach softens the request for an interview without putting the employer on the spot to say "yes" or "no" right away. The follow–up phone call lets you know whether or not you have any chance to get interviewed. If you don't have a chance, you can move on to more promising job opportunities without waiting any longer. Conversely, the employer may find you sufficiently interesting to invite you to an in–person job interview. Either way, you get results quickly. Alternatively, you can end the letter with the conventional, "Thanks for your time and consideration. I hope to hear from you in the near future." Just be prepared to wait since many employers contact only job candidates they wish to interview and never even acknowledge receiving the application of someone they don't intend to interview.

☐ **Provide any specific information** the employer sought in his job announcement or ad. If a job ad requests references, you should give their names, addresses, and phone numbers near the end of your cover letter or on a separate sheet. As the discussion on resumes urges, do

not list references in your resume. Always make sure that the people you give as references will speak favorably about you and are willing to serve as references. If an employer requests your salary history, include that on a separate sheet, not in the cover letter. Do *not* put salaries in your resume.

📂 **Thank the reader** for her time and consideration.

If you are writing a so–called "blind" cover letter to learn if a job opening exists, you will want to adjust your letter accordingly. This sort of approach letter is designed for you to gain access to an individual who will either provide you with contacts, leads, and information on job opportunities within her agency or elsewhere. Be sure to learn the correct name of the person to whom you write. The various directories described throughout the *Non–Profits' Job Finder* or a phone call to her company will get you her name.

Cover letter style

Your cover letter tells the employer a lot about your competency. No matter what kind of a job you seek, typographical errors suggest that you would be a careless employee. A poorly written cover letter suggests that you do not communicate effectively.

Cover letters should be direct, powerful, and error free. Make like a good newspaper copy editor: eliminate unnecessary words, and carefully check grammar, spelling, and punctuation. Avoid using the passive voice ("should have been," "it was done by me"). It's suggestions like this one that make us regret paying so little attention in high school English class. Don't try to be cute or too aggressive like the preceding sentence. Avoid pomposity and long sentences. And don't use no most excellent slang of no sort, no way, dude.

Keep the letter short and to the point. There's no reason to overwhelm the reader with a lengthy cover letter that repeats a lot of your resume.

Keep your letter positive. Highlight your past accomplishments and skills as well as your future value to the employer.

References

As mentioned earlier, the ad for the job for which you are applying may have requested references. You should identify your references near the end of your letter or on another sheet of paper. *Don't list references in your resume since you may want to use different references for different jobs.* In addition, it is prudent to let your references know to which positions you have submitted an application. If you know a potential employer is likely to contact your references, you would be sagacious to send your references a copy of your cover letter and the ad for the job so they can customize their responses to better fit the job.

For each reference, be sure to give the person's correct name and title, and complete address and phone number including area code, so the reference can be contacted easily. If a reference's first name is gender ambiguous (Chris, Leslie, Shelley, Michael Jackson), avoid embarrassment and use "Mr." or "Ms." before the reference's name so your potential employer gets the sex right when he contacts your reference. A fundamental principle of applying for a job is to make it as easy as possible for the potential employer to follow–up your application because some employers simply toss out an application if they can't reach references or obtain other relevant information about the job candidate. It's a buyer's market, and as the applicant, you are the seller.

Be certain to have permission to use these names as references. Use only references you are certain will comment favorably on your performance and ability to work with others. Be prepared to offer additional references if asked.

The resume

Since the individual doing the hiring has to examine so many resumes, you are best off if you keep yours relatively short and sweet. Remember: your resume is both a sales pitch and a summary of your qualifications. Like it or not, those 60–second spots for political candidates nearly always have more impact than a five–minute or half–hour commercial. The same reasoning applies to resumes.

The recent college graduate isn't likely to have any problems keeping his resume down to one–page while the experienced professional may have a tough time limiting her resume to just four pages. The keys to making your resume stand out from the crowd — in addition to its substance — are to organize it well and produce an attractive, professional–looking document.

Resume content

By following several general guidelines you can make the content of your resume more effective.

❑ *Include only pertinent information*. Do not include material unless it gives potential employers a reason to hire you.

Include only information from which you can confidently expect a favorable reaction. When in doubt, leave information out; don't gamble on adverse reactions. A resume simply is not the place to put anything negative about yourself. Remember, you are marketing yourself to the prospective employer as the best person for the job. Would the folks at Dow Chemical, so anxious to build a clean image today, advertise that they manufactured the napalm used to burn and kill civilians in Vietnam or would cigarette advertising voluntarily include warnings on the cause–and–effect relationship of smoking and cancer and other diseases?

❑ *Be scrupulously honest*. For example, in 1976, one Illinois municipality offered its village manager job to a man who appeared to have built a successful career in city government in California. Unfortunately for him, the local newspaper learned of his phony credentials when interviewing one of his past employers and exposed the rascal. It seems he failed to earn the degree from Purdue University that he claimed to possess and was ten years older than the 55 years he listed on his resume. He withdrew his name from consideration for the job before the city fathers and mothers could withdraw it for him. During the past few years, many high–level government *and non–profit sector* employees around the country have lost their jobs, and their careers, for misrepresenting themselves on their resumes or job applications.

Most resume fraud, however, does not become public knowledge. If a discrepancy is found during a job interview, the job simply is not offered. Fraud discovered after someone has been hired, usually results in the employer quietly asking the employee to resign with the not–so–subtle threat of dismissal hanging over his head. An executive at a credential verification service estimates that 30 percent of all resumes contain some fraudulent educational information. And with an increasing number of employers verifying this information, honesty and accuracy are essential for any resume or job application. Think about it, how could you ever trust somebody on the job if he lied to get the job?

There are a number of items of information that belong in your resume. An effective resume includes the following information presented in a clear, concise, and well–written style:

📁 ***Applicant identification***. Your name should go at the top of the first page. If your resume is typewritten, underline your name. If produced on a word processor, place your name in a typeface and style that makes it stand out. See the sample resumes at the end of this chapter. Be sure to include your home address and home telephone number (including area code). If you don't want anybody at work to know you are looking for a job, do not put your work phone on your resume. This is where you can indicate any preference for where you want to be contacted simply by writing: "Contact at [phone number]." If you think it will help you land the job, furnish your birth date. Most job seekers, especially those over 40, are best off if they do not reveal their age in their resume. You may want to produce an "age proof" resume that downplays your age and draws the reader's attention to your abilities and accomplishments. Two excellent books go into great detail on how to prepare an "age proof" resume: *The Over 40 Job Guide* by Kathryn and Ross Petra ($12.00, 352 pages, 1993), and *Resumes for the Over–50 Job Hunter* by Samuel Ray ($12.95, 216 pages, 1993) (for your convenience, both are available from Planning/Communications' catalog at the end of this book).

📁 ***Education***. Identify your college degree and any advanced degrees earned. Give the names of the schools that awarded your degrees and the years in which they were received. Include the city and state in which the school is located if that is not apparent from its name. Recent graduates may wish to list major scholarships or honors received. Also note relevant post–graduate education. Recent graduates may want to also list major extracurricular activities and organizational offices they held.

The longer you've worked, educational information becomes less important to potential employers while practical experience becomes more significant. *For the recent graduate*, the education section should precede the section on professional experience. The more seasoned professional will want to place the experience section before the education section. Job candidates who lack a college degree should indicate the highest level of education they have had, whether it was a high school degree, or some college or junior college education without receiving a degree.

If you attended college, but did not graduate, give the name of the school and how many years you attended (University of Chicago, 1991–1993).

If you never attended college, don't leave out the education section. Omitting it will simply call attention to your lack of formal higher education. One option is to include the education heading and under it, print "Self–educated." Be sure to list any work–related courses or training you've had. Add a section to your resume entitled "Other Interests" or "Hobbies" where you can list items that show your intellectual activity or other interests that may help you stand out from the crowd.

📁 ***Professional experience***. Jobs in your professional field should be described under a heading such as "Professional Experience" or "Work Experience." Jobs should be listed in reverse chronological order with the most recent first. For each position, furnish the following information:

Job title. Place your job title first. Use some emphasis to make it stand out: bold face, italics, borders, or boxing it if your resume is typeset or prepared on computer, underlined if prepared on a typewriter.

📁 ***Employer's name, address, and phone number***. If there is even one former employer you do not want a potential employer to call, leave out the phone numbers of all past employers. Do *not* give the name of your supervisor here; just give the name of the company, non-profit, or government agency.

Period of employment. If you've frequently changed jobs, like every two or three years, you don't want to advertise it. Employers like to hire people they think will stay with the agency for a long time. It costs them time and money to train a new employee. So, if you've changed jobs frequently, place the dates of employment within the heading for each job as illustrated by the first sample resume at the end of this chapter. On the other hand, if you've

Maximizing resumes of recent graduates

For the student or recent graduate with no professional experience, it is appropriate to list nonprofessional jobs and part–time, summer, or volunteer work if you label the section something like "Work Experience." In addition, persons with little or no professional experience can list major school projects that resulted in a written product and projects they may have conducted with a citizen group or a planning commission. See the first sample resume at the end of this chapter for an example of a resume for an entry–level job candidate just graduating from school.

If you have no publications to list, you could label the publications section "Papers" and list selected papers you've written that you feel are pertinent and will generate a positive reaction from a potential employer.

Obviously, if you have no organization memberships, honors, or additional professional activities, leave these sections out of your resume. But again, I strongly recommend that you obtain a student membership in your field's professional organization. Such membership helps illustrate your dedication to your profession.

generally held your jobs for four or more years, place the dates of employment in the left–hand margin as shown in the second sample resume at the end of this chapter.

Responsibilities, duties, and accomplishments. This may be the most important text in your resume. It is your opportunity to tell potential employers what you did in your former positions. Using short phrases rather than full–blown sentences presents this information concisely without appearing to be conceit or braggadocio. Unless jobs outside the profession in which you are seeking work reflect on your ability to perform your professional tasks, this list of jobs should concentrate on the professional positions you have held.

📁 *Organization memberships and honors.* Identify the professional organizations to which you belong and offices you have held in them, professional certifications or licenses you have earned, and professional honors you have been awarded. Do not use abbreviations nor acronyms. A potential employer feels pretty dumb when he doesn't recognize the acronym or abbreviation. One of the bonuses of providing this information is that if the person reading your resume belongs to these organizations, this will establish a common bond that will often enhance your chances of being hired. If you don't belong to the leading professional associations in your field, you may very well lose points. So, join your professional organizations. Many offer lower rates for student members and a few, like the American Planning Association, offer very low rates for unemployed members.

Do not include membership in political organizations — that's not any employer's damned business, especially a government employer! You can include germane civic and community organization memberships, particularly if you are, or have been, an officer or chaired an important committee.

📁 *Publications.* Clearly identify major relevant publications such as books, plans, reports, budgets, and magazine or newspaper articles so the reader can find them if she wishes. Experienced workers should not include papers or projects from college or graduate school unless they were published. List publications in chronological order with the most recent last or in reverse chronological order with the most recent first.

📁 *Additional professional activities.* List other professional activities such as participation in professional conference programs, guest lectures, commission memberships, courses taught, etc.

📁 *References.* As explained earlier, never identify references in your resume. At the end of your resume, insert a line like ''References available upon request.'' If the job announcement requests references, include their names, addresses, and phone numbers in your cover letter.

Correcting fallacies about resumes

Several common misconceptions about resumes continue to survive despite all the advice job counselors have given. Some items simply do not belong in a resume.

✗ *Salary*. The purpose of your resume is to get you an interview. Don't undermine it! If your resume reveals your past earnings, it could scare a prospective employer into thinking you are too high–priced even if you are willing to work for less or the same as in your current position. Even worse, listing salaries might unwittingly lead the potential employer to reduce the salary she was prepared to offer. Salary should come up only at the end of the job interview after you've had a chance to demonstrate your value to an employer as well as learn about the worth of the position. You cannot realistically discuss nor negotiate salary if you prematurely mention it in your resume. However, if the ad for a job requests your salary history, submit it on a separate sheet, but not in your resume. Negotiating salary is a skilled art, advice on which can fill a book of its own. For sound advice on negotiating salary, see Ronald and Caryl Krannichs' *Dynamite Salary Negotiations: Know What You're Worth and Get It!* ($13.95, 1994, 164 pages; available from Planning/Communications' catalog at the end of this book).

✗ *Career Objective*. If you have the insatiable urge to state your career objective in writing, describe it in your cover letter. This approach permits an applicant to express his career objectives in terms applicable to a specific job. *Do not place career objectives in your resume.*

✗ *Military Experience.* Your military rank and dates of service should be left out of your resume unless they have a direct bearing on the job you're seeking. If your military achievements and skills make you more employable or you achieved a high rank that looks impressive, include this information. If not, leave it out.

✗ *Hobbies.* Many employers do not care about an applicant's hobbies or outside interests. Frankly, a list of hobbies and outside interests only clutters your resume with irrelevant information. There is also the danger that your hobbies may scare off a potential employer. For example, the head of a non–profit in California says he is reluctant to hire anyone who lists skiing or other cold–weather sports on a resume because he thinks such people would vacation a lot on weekends and be unavailable for necessary weekend work. Other employers are reluctant to hire persons with a lot of outside interests because they think it will be hard to get them to do extra work at home or work late hours. Conversely, some employers like their employees to have outside interests.

There's an old story still circulating of the job candidate who won his position over equally–qualified applicants because the director wanted a fourth for bridge at lunch — admittedly not a sound hiring criterion. But nobody in good conscience can state that every agency director follows sound hiring procedures. So, list hobbies and outside interests only at your own risk. If your qualifications are any good, you'll make it to an interview where the interviewer can ask about these activities if they are really important to her.

If you do not have a college degree, you might want to include a list of hobbies in your resume to establish some "intellectual" credentials.

Resume appearance and design

Although most employers are interested in the content of the resume rather than its appearance, design expectations have risen thanks to the accessibility of word processing and laser printers. Today well–designed, typeset–quality resumes are the standard. It used to cost a small fortune to produce a typeset resume. Today, typeset–quality can be produced by anyone with a word processing program and laser printer. Do not use a dot–matrix printer. The results look amateurish even in letter quality mode. Resist the urge to use them.

Nearly everybody can have access to high–quality resume design at a reasonable cost. Many resume preparation services will convert a one– or two–page typewritten resume into a classy–looking document for fee ranging from $30 to $200. Any resume preparation service that charges $100 or more for a two–page resume should include a major editing or rewrite and redesign of your resume for that price. Resume preparation services appear in the yellow pages under "Resume Service."

There are some really good computer programs designed specifically for easily producing beautiful resumes that grab a reader's attention (of course, once the appearance gets their attention, the content has to keep it). One of these programs is *WinWay Resume for Windows* ($69.95, 1993; available from the catalog at the end of this book).

If you don't have a laser printer or good deskjet or bubblejet printer, there is still an alternative that is time consuming, but costs little. If you can prepare your resume on a personal computer, but don't have a laser printer, take a floppy disk with your resume file on it to one of the many photocopying shops that rents time on desktop computers and laser printers. If you can't find a copy shop that uses the same word processing program you have, find out if its word processing program can import your resume file. You'll probably have to do some reformatting using the shop's word processing program. Be sure to save a copy of the finished resume on your floppy disk so you can bring it back for easy, quick revisions.

Use the copy shop's laser printer to print one copy of your finished resume on high–quality white paper. Then photocopy additional copies on the shop's best photocopying machine. It's a lot less expensive this way since these shops tend to charge around a dollar for each page printed on the laser printer while photocopies usually cost less than 10¢ per page.

To assure an attractive, readable resume, type or print it neatly on 8.5–inch by 11–inch paper that is at least 20–pound weight. Unless you've got some very good reason to use bright colored paper, avoid it. Your best bet for a professional–looking resume is a conservative paper color like white, off–white, ivory, light tan, or light gray. Use a dark ink or toner such as black, navy, or dark brown. The exact format or design is up to you. Whatever you choose, keep it clean and professional looking. Two possible designs are suggested by the sample resumes that follow.

Sample cover letters and resumes

The first sample resume and cover letter are for a recent graduate seeking an entry–level position with a non–profit community development organization. The cover letter is an example of a "blind" cover letter. A resume designed this nicely immediately illustrates the applicant's excellent graphic skills. For your enjoyment, there are over 20 references to the Kinks.

The second sample resume and cover letter show an experienced worker applying for a higher–level position in response to a job listing on a job hotline. This resume is designed to show how to present your experience when you've risen through the ranks with an employer so it does not look, at first glance, like you simply changed jobs every 18 months. There are dozens of references to my favorite movies in this resume and cover letter.

Both resumes are variations of the traditional chronological resume. I chose not to include samples of functional resumes or other trendy formats for the simple reason that most *employers do not like them!* Despite all the hype about functional and other "modern" resumes, most employers still prefer to receive a chronological resume because it is the most straightforward presentation of a job candidate's credentials.

"Blind" cover letter for entry—level position

1720 Denmark Street
Sleazy Town, Illinois 60635
March 15, 1993

Lola Victoria, Director of Graphic Support
Shangri—La Community Assistance Project
1312—4 Waterloo Sunset Boulevard
Scrapheap City, Illinois 61701

Dear Ms. Victoria:

As you well know, it's nearly impossible to build affordable and attractive quality housing in the inner city
in this age of government cutbacks. But amid this decline
in assistance to the neighborhoods, the Shangri—La Community Assistance Project has shown that the impossible can
still be accomplished, if you give the people what they
want.

I'm very interested in learning more about your work,
especially your 'Rush Hour Blues" project, as well as the
possibilities of joining your design team. As the enclosed
resume indicates, prior to receiving my bachelor's degree
in architecture last year I served as an architect's and engineer's assistant.

Perhaps your schedule would permit us to meet briefly
to discuss our mutual interests. I will call your office
next week to see if such a meeting can be arranged.

Thank you for your time and consideration. I look forward to meeting you.

Sincerely,

Ray Davies

Ray Davies

Enclosure

Raymond D. Davies
1720 Denmark Street
Sleazy Town, Illinois 60635
708/453–0009

Education

Berkeley Mews Institute of Technology
Bachelor of Architecture, July 1993

- Completed the Architectural Curriculum as well as investigated the realms of digital photography and black and white photographs with their uses in the architectural field.

Misty Water Magnet High School, 1989

- Two years of mechanical drawing and two years of architectural drawing.

Experience

A Well Respected Copy Center

- Customer Service Representative and shift supervisor in charge of all computer–related services: resume design and preparation, desktop publishing of copy center brochures, advertising, signs, and posters.
- Responsible for seeing jobs through from crude originals to finished presentation quality product.

Village Green Preservation Society

- Architectural Assistant responsible for designing picture book "Do You Remember Walter" for educating elementary school children on the need for historic preservation.

Better Things Architects

- Engineering Assistant responsible for updating and finishing architectural and engineering drawings for the "Don't Ever Change" low budget residential development.

References

Portfolio and slide presentation available upon request

Response to ad for advanced–level position

1949 Dread Pirate Roberts Drive
Ottumwa, Iowa 52501
December 6, 1993

Inigo Montoya, Vice President
The Shoeless Joes' Foundation
4523 Fire Swamp Drive
Chisholm, MN 55719

Dear Mr. Montoya:

Your announcement on the <u>Foundation Journal's</u> Job Hotline for a Director of Foundation Giving immediately
grabbed my attention as a potentially challenging and very
professionally rewarding opportunity. As my enclosed resume
indicates, I have been working for nearly 20 years in financial planning, the last 12 years with the Field of Dreams
Foundation where I have risen from the position of Assistant Director of Fund Raising Programs to Director of Strategic and Financial Planning.

I joined the Field of Dreams Foundation after three
years as Senior Financial Advisor for the Herbert Potter Financial Consulting Service where I initiated the service's
nationally–known 'Do–Gooder Investment Program.''

I would like to learn more about this position as well
as have an opportunity to meet with you to discuss our mutual interests. I will call you next week about any questions we may both have and to arrange an interview if, at
that time, we both feel it is appropriate.

Thank you for you time and consideration. I look forward to meeting you.

Sincerely,

Raymond Kinsella

Raymond Kinsella

Enclosure

Raymond Kinsella

1949 Dread Pirate Roberts Drive
Ottumwa, Iowa 52501
Phone: 515/882–1701

Professional Experience

1982+   Field of Dreams Foundation (7215 Florin Rd., Guilder, IA 52511)

Director of Strategic and Financial Planning. 1988+
Supervise the foundation's six–person Strategic and Financial Planning Section. In addition to basic management and administration, responsible for preparation of the foundation's annual budget, development, and strategic plans.

Chief Financial Planner. 1985—1987
Headed the division within the Strategic and Financial Planning Section responsible for devising new funding programs. Programs created included the Moonlight Graham One At Bat Second Chance Program, the Fire Swamp Recovery Fund, the Clarence Goodbody Win Your Wings Fund, and the Gizmo Gremlins Hulkster Film Festival Fund.

Assistant Director of Fund Raising Programs. 1982—1985
Assisted Director in managing fund raising programs and designing new fund raising drives.

1979–
1982   **Senior Financial Advisor,** Herbert Potter Financial Consulting Service (320 Sycamore, Potterville, NY 11946; 607/543–0100)
Provided investment advice to savings and loan institutions, Initiated special program at BCCI to finance international small businesses. Created the much–copied "Do–Gooder Investment Program."

1975–
1978   **Assistant Planner,** Department of Economic Development, 432 S. Wainwright Dr., Bedford Falls, NY 10506; 607/678–3400)
Conducted planning studies on real estate values, development potential, and tax increment financing proposals.

Education

Masters of Urban Planning, University of Illinois–Urbana, June 1975
  Teaching Assistant, Sept. 1973–June 1975
B.S. (finance), UCLA, June 1973
  Dean's List, 1970–1973
  Chairperson, R.O.U.S. Cheese Festival, 1972

Organization Memberships and Honors

American Association of Foundation Executives, 1980+
National Society of Financial Planners, 1976+
  New York Chapter Vice–President, 1978–1980
Metropolitan Development Commission, 1981–1989
Regional Finalist, White House Fellowship, 1980

Publications

"If You Build It, He Will Come," in *Foundation Times,* December 9, 1991, pp. 9–
  22.
"The Making of a Funding Angel: Every Time a Bell Rings," in *Give Till It Hurts
  Quarterly,* June 3, 1989, pp. 13–20.
Easing His Pain: The Jerry Salinger Story, published by Planning/Communications
  Press, 1986, 240 pages.
"Miracle Max and the Crystal Bill," in the *Sunday New York Times,* Feb. 29,
  1983, pp. 574–592.
"Zuzu's Petals: Financial Wisdom Means Environmental Protection," in *Planning*
  magazine, May 8, 1981, pp. 5–8.

Additional Professional Activities

Speaker at American Association of Foundation Executives National Conference:
  "It's a Wonderful Life for the Princess Bride in Her Field of Dreams," March
  1990
  "Fezzik and Vizzini: Count Ruggin's Kidnap of Financial Theory," April 1987
Guest lecture series, University of Iowa, spring semester 1982: "Can This Be
  Heaven If It's Really Iowa?"

References available upon request

Chapter **33**

Performing your best at your job interview

In the increasingly competitive job market, a job ad or job hotline listing often draws well over 100 responses from qualified individuals. An invitation to appear for a personal interview indicates that your cover letter and resume interested the potential employer enough to make you a serious candidate. Now it's up to you to do your best at the job interview to clinch the job. Many well–educated, intelligent, well–qualified candidates lose jobs because they are uncomfortable in interview situations or fail to prepare adequately. Others just have a natural aptitude for personal interviews. Any well–qualified job candidate can improve his performance in job interviews by following the guidelines suggested here and in books on job interviewing such as the Krannichs' *Interview for Success* and *Dynamite Answers to Interview Questions* (both are available from Planning/Communications' catalog that begins on page 311).

Few positions with non–profit entities require a written examination. Instead there is an oral quasi–examination, more accurately called an interview. Some employers put you before a panel of several people who evaluate you. Others simply have the personnel director, her assistant, or a division head interview you. When asked to appear for an interview, try to learn who will conduct the interview and who else will be present so you can be adequately prepared.

Preparing for the interview

The obvious function of the personal interview is to give your potential employer an opportunity to thoroughly evaluate you, and you a chance to sell yourself. It also hands you the opportunity to learn much more about the employer and the agency or institution for which he works. You want to be able to carry on a fairly intelligent conversation with your interviewer, even if he can't. By knowing what is expected of you and by undertaking a few simple preparations, you can make a more favorable impression and minimize any nervousness you may feel.

Interviewers will size you up in terms of the following qualities:

Initial impression	Fitness for the job
Past job performance	Maturity
Analytic ability	Judgment and prudence
Appearance and manner	Leadership
Motivation	Potential to grow in the job
Ability to communicate	Overall personality
Initiative	Mental alertness
Self–confidence	Compatibility with other staff

Some employers maintain a standard rating form and use a point system to rate candidates. Prior to your interview, try to obtain a copy of the rating form from the Personnel Department so you can tell exactly on what qualities you will be evaluated. Most won't give one to you, but who knows, maybe one will. If they say you can't have one, don't argue or try to talk them into giving you one.

This checklist of fundamental steps you should take before you meet your interviewer will enhance your performance at the interview:

❑ *Be certain of the exact time and place of the interview.* If you are unsure of how to get there, just ask. Write this information down and don't lose it. If you are really nervous about finding the interview location, check it out on a local street map or take a test drive there.

❑ *Arrive at the interview on time or a little early.* There is no excuse for tardiness for a job interview. Innumerable jobs have been lost because the candidate was late for the interview. If it becomes obvious you are going to be more than five minutes late, call and let the interviewer's secretary know. Try to arrive about 15 minutes early.

❑ *Know how to pronounce the interviewer's name correctly.* If in doubt, call in advance and ask her secretary how to pronounce it.

❏ *Learn all you can about your potential employer and the position for which you are applying*. When applying for work with any non–profit entity, you'll score points with the interviewer if you are reasonably familiar with what it does. You should have enough of an idea of what the entity does so you can explain how you can contribute to its success. And if you can't learn all you would like to know about it, be prepared to ask pertinent questions at the interview. The questions you ask at the interview are often more important than the answers you give to the interviewer's questions.

Another group interview today?

At least try to learn enough so your potential employer won't feel you are too much of an outsider to learn the vagaries of the agency for which you would be working. Use the directories described in the *Non–Profits' Job Finder* to learn more about the potential employer. By all means try to learn all you can about the person or persons who will interview you and make the hiring decision so you can present the side of you which will appeal the most to their sensibilities. It is possible that other people you know in your field may be able to tell you something about your interviewer and the company for which he works.

❏ *Make a list of points you want to be sure to make in the interview* at appropriate moments. You may have forgotten to make these points or facts about yourself at your last interview. Placing them firmly in mind before this interview should assure that you don't forget them again. Even though you should never pull out such a list at the interview, the mere act of writing the list will help you remember the points.

Many interviewers will query you about your career goals. Whether or not you were once a Boy Scout, be prepared! Think this one out carefully because nearly every interviewer will sock you with some question about your career goals even though, as recommended in the preceding chapter, you should not put your career goals in your resume.

❏ *Plan to bring several items to the interview*. Believe it or not, some interviewers lose a candidate's resume and cover letter just before the interview. So be sure to bring a clean copy of each with you. If requested, bring letters of reference and work samples. Students may substitute high–quality term papers or projects. Bring these materials in a folder or brief case and offer them only if asked or if they graphically illustrate a point. The interviewer's desk is probably cluttered enough as is.

Questions interviewers ask

Be prepared to answer the questions that inevitably surface in any job interview. According to the authors of *Interview for Success,* most of the following questions about your education, work experience, career goals, and yourself tend to surface in virtually every job interview. Obviously the first set of questions that deal with education are more likely to be asked of recent graduates than seasoned professionals who have work experience that will interest an interviewer more than the job candidate's education.

- Tell me about your educational background.
- Why did you choose to attend that particular college?
- What was your major, and why?
- Did you do the best you could in school? If not, why not?
- What subject did you enjoy most? ...the least? Why?
- If you started all over, what would you change about your schooling?

Recent graduates are likely to also be asked:

- What was your grade point average? (The more work experience you have, the less likely this inquiry will be made.)
- Why were your grades so high?... so low?
- What leadership positions did you hold?
- How did you finance your education?
- What were your major accomplishments in each of your former jobs?
- Why did you leave your last position? (If asked why you left any of your former jobs, give reasons that do not suggest you are a job shopper or jumper. Acceptable reasons include a return to school, better pay, new challenges, more responsibility, and a desire for a different type of work.)
- What job activities do you enjoy the most? ...the least?
- What did you like about your boss? ...dislike?
- Which of your jobs did you enjoy the most? Why? ... the least? Why?
- Have you ever been fired? Why?
- Why do you want to work for us?

- Why do you think you are qualified for this position?
- Why are you looking to change jobs?
- Why do you want to make a career change?
- Why should we want to hire you?
- How can you help us?
- What would you ideally like to do?
- What is the lowest pay you would take? (Always deflect this question. See the discussion on salaries later in this chapter.)
- How much do you think you are worth in this job?
- What do you want to be doing five years from now? (Working here with a promotion or two, obviously.)
- How much do you want to be making five years from now?
- What are your short–range and long–term career goals?
- If you could choose any job and agency, where would you work?
- What other types of jobs are you considering? ... other agencies?
- When would you be able to start?
- How do you feel about relocating, travel, and spending weekends or evenings in the office?
- What attracted you to our department?
- Tell me about yourself.
- What are your major strengths?
- What are your major weaknesses? (Never say you don't have any. Turn a negative into a positive with a response like, "I tend to get too wrapped up in my work and don't pay enough attention to my family. My wife keeps suggesting that I should join Workaholics Anonymous ")
- What causes you to lose your temper?

SYLVIA   **by Nicole Hollander**

- What do you do in your spare time? What are your hobbies?
- What types of books and magazines do you read?
- What role does your family play in your career?
- How well do you work under pressure? … in meeting deadlines?
- Tell me about your management philosophy?
- How much initiative do you take?
- What types of people do you prefer working for and with?
- How _____ (creative, tactful, analytical, etc.) are you?
- If you could change your life, what would you do differently?
- Who are your references? (Have a printed list with names, addresses, and phone numbers ready to submit.)

Stupid interviewer tricks: Illegal questions

Unfortunately, despite great strides over the past decade, illegal questions continue to arise in job interviews, even in the non–profit sector. Sexism, in particular, is alive and well in the hearts and souls of many job interviewers. While equal employment opportunity laws make it illegal to ask certain questions during an interview, some interviewers ask them anyway. If you are prepared, you can fend them off effectively and still score points with the interviewer. If the questions don't get asked, you've got no problem.

Illegal or inappropriate questions include:

- What's your marital status?
- How old are you?
- Do you go to church regularly?
- What is your religion?
- Do you have many debts?
- Do you own or rent your home?
- What social and political organizations do you belong to? Unless you are applying to work for a political organization of some sort, this question is totally inappropriate. Be wary if the interviewer steers the conversation to politics. Do not be evasive, but temper your remarks to camouflage radical or extremist views. Keep in mind that in some communities a traditionally "liberal" viewpoint is considered "radical." Your political views are really nobody's business but your own. But don't say that in an interview unless you have found an inoffensive way to express that view. Try to say no more than is necessary to answer the interviewer's broad line of questioning about politics.

- What does your spouse think about your career?
- Are you living with anyone?
- Are you practicing birth control?
- Were you ever arrested?
- How much insurance do you carry?
- How much do you weigh?
- How tall are you?

If an interviewer spouts one of these illegal questions, don't go nuclear, dude, and shout "That question is illegal and I ain't gonna answer it!" You may be right, but this sort of reaction does not display any tact on your part, which may be what the interviewer is testing, albeit tactlessly. The authors of *Interview for Success* and *Dynamite Answers to Interview Questions* suggest that humor is an effective response. For example, if asked whether you are on the pill, you could respond, "Sure, I take three pills every day, vitamins A, B, and C, and thanks to them I haven't missed a day of work in three years."

Asked if you are divorced, you might respond, "I'd be happy to answer that question if you could perhaps first explain what bearing being divorced, or not being divorced, could have on someone's ability to perform this job?"

As you might have guessed by now, women are the main targets of these unjustifiable questions. But if you're prepared, you can neutralize them. For example, some interviewers will ask women with small children, "What if the kids get sick?" A sound response to this question goes along the lines of, "I have arranged for contingency plans. I have a sitter on standby, or my husband can take a vacation day." This sort of answer indicates to your potential employer that you are a professional (not that you should have to prove your professionalism because you're a woman) and that you've anticipated the problem.

Married women with a family are often asked, "How can you travel?" An interviewer could be trying to find out if the employer will have to pay for the woman's other responsibilities. An employer may be wondering if she is going to put her family before her job. A good answer would be, "Of course I can travel when it's important to my job. I'd be happy to do it. All I have to do is make the proper arrangements."

If an interviewer learns that your spouse works for a company that likes to move its employees around every three or four years, she may ask, "What are your plans if your spouse receives orders to relocate?" That's actually a reasonable question to ask of *either* partner in a two-income household, but for some mysterious reason it is rarely asked of the husband. A good answer is to say, "My husband and I have discussed this issue and we've decided that my work is important for my professional growth and we will work out a plan when and if that time comes." Once a woman has been working for an employer for a while and has proven her worth, she'll have a better bargaining position if spousal relocation threatens her job.

Try to decide how you will handle illegal or inappropriate questions before you go to an interview. With a little preparation, you can turn a negative into a positive when such questions are posed. Your answers to such questions could turn out to be your strongest and most effective of the whole interview.

Questions you should ask

Prepare questions before you go to the interview so you won't be speechless when the interviewer asks you if you have any questions. This gives you a good opportunity to show how much you know about the employer by asking intelligent questions about the employer. You may want to ask about the nature of the job and agency, opportunities to exercise initiative and innovation, chances for advancement, and status of the agency. Save questions about fringe benefits (health insurance, leave time, conference attendance) and salary for the end of the interview. As explained later in this chapter, you are best off if the interviewer raises these issues.

The job counselors suggest that you be prepared to ask the following questions if the interviewer has not already answered them:

- What duties and responsibilities does this position involve?

- Where does this position fit into the organization?

- Is this a new position?

- What would be the ideal person for this position? Skills required? Background? Personality? Working style?

- With whom would I work in this job?

- Can you tell me something about these people? Their strengths, weaknesses, performance expectations?

- What am I expected to accomplish during the first year?

- How will I be evaluated?

I was **sure** I had your application filed here somewhere..

- On what performance criteria are promotions and raises based? How does this system operate?

- Is this a smoke–free office? (Ask this question only if it makes a difference to you. If you ask it, the interviewer will probably want to know if you are a smoker or if you don't want any smoking near you.)

- What is the normal salary range for such a position (assuming it was not stated in the advertisement for the job and the interviewer has not mentioned the salary range).

- Based on your experience, what types of problems would someone new in this position be likely to encounter?

- How long have you been with this agency? What are your plans for the future? (These two questions are appropriate if the interviewer would be your supervisor or superior.)

- What is particularly unique about working for this institution/division/department?

- What does this organization's future look like?

Personal appearance

Face facts: clothes, grooming, and cleanliness certainly do not reflect on how decent or qualified a person is for a job, or how well someone will perform on the job. Just look at Albert Einstein, or, at the other extreme, look at the immaculately–groomed gentlemen who brought us Watergate, Iran–Contra, and the fairly recent savings and loan scandals. But since the interviewer does not know you personally, your appearance can greatly influence his first impression of you — and first impressions count a lot at job interviews. You will make a much better first impression if you are well–dressed and well–groomed.

Don't take chances with appearance even if it means showing up better dressed than your interviewer. Research shows that women elicit a more favorable reaction from interviewers of either sex when they wear a dress or suit, the classic pump, nylons, and a bra. Jeans, shorts, culottes, mini–skirts, sandals, dirty or unkempt hair, an exposed middle, and flamboyant clothing evoke unfavorable responses. Carry a purse or attache case, but not both. It's hard not to look clumsy trying to handle both. If you opt for the attache case, keep a slim purse with your essentials inside the brief case.

Men should wear a suit and tie. Men make a less favorable impression with a sport coat, and a downright unfavorable one when wearing a sweater or boots. Shorts, T–shirts, jeans, or sandals turn off any interviewer. Some researchers insist that a maroon tie inspires confidence. Others have found that the shorter, more neatly trimmed the hair and beard, if any, the better the impression.

Whether or not your native culture places as much of a premium on cleanliness as the American culture does, be sure to bathe and use deodorant. On the job you'll be expected to be clean and relatively odor–free. Smelling like a locker room at your job interview *will* cost you the job no matter how ideal you are for it.

Whatever your everyday mode of dress and grooming may be, you've got to play the game when job hunting. Sometimes you will be better groomed and clothed than your interviewer, but remember that it is *your* appearance that counts. After you've landed the job, you can resume your normal work appearance if it varies from that suggested here and does not violate office standards.

For more information on how to dress for an interview, see any of the dozens of books on interviewing. They'll essentially tell you what you've just read — but they'll take 25 pages to do it.

Conduct at the interview

Common sense and courtesy, above all else, should govern your conduct at a job interview. For example, be punctual and, if possible, arrive a few minutes early in case there are forms to complete. It only hurts your chances to keep an interviewer waiting.

Similarly, common sense dictates that you do your best to make a good first impression since, fair or not, first impressions are quite strong and seldom change later in the interview. A friendly, warm smile helps establish a good first impression that carries throughout the entire interview. A natural smile in the right places throughout an interview can mean the difference between a favorable and unfavorable response.

Greet your interviewer(s) with a solid handshake — something a bit softer than the Hulkster might use — no matter what your sex is. Most interviewers do not like a "wet fish" handshake.

Throughout the interview try to maintain good poise and posture; sit straight and avoid leaning on your elbow or talking with your hands over your mouth. Look alert and interested throughout the interview. Demonstrate that you can be a wide awake, intelligent listener as well as a talker. If nervous, hide it. Keep your hands still in your lap; do not tap your pencil or twist your purse strap. Don't fiddle with objects on the interviewer's desk, or with your fingernails. Chewing gum, or smoking without being invited to do so, usually makes a bad impression since both are generally regarded as signs of nervousness.

Naturally, you will want to establish and maintain good eye contact. Nearly every interviewer is conscious of eye contact; it is the surest way to convince him you know what you are talking about.

Above all else, be yourself and be honest. Since most interviews follow a simple question and answer format, your ability to respond quickly and intelligently is vital. Confused and contradictory answers can cost you the job. The best preventative against contradictory answers, logically enough, is the truth. An honest answer that seems a little unflattering to you is far better than a white lie that may tangle you up in a later question. If you don't know the answer to a specific question, the best thing you can say is, "I don't know." The odds are good that the interviewer knows the "right" answer to the question and a bad guess can only put you in a poor light.

Following several additional interviewing pointers will enhance your chances of winning the job:

📁 ***Follow the interviewer's lead.*** Most interviewers like to think they are in control. Some like to do most of the talking and judge you by your reactions. Because others believe it is your job to sell yourself, they hardly speak at all. When selling yourself, be modest about your accomplishments while getting your points across. Nobody likes, or hires, a braggart. If you seem too self–involved, the interviewer will sense, perhaps rightly so, that you will always place your interests ahead of those of the company–and nobody wants to hire somebody like that! Don't exaggerate your skills or accomplishments since most interviewers pick up on truth stretching very quickly and it hurts your chances for the job. Try to offer concrete examples of your better points.

📁 ***Do not take notes during the interview.*** A job candidate taking notes annoys and distracts some interviewers. If you must write something down, make a remark like, "That's very interesting. Do you mind if I jot it down?" Your best bet is to write notes of anything you need to remember after the interview.

📂 ***Job interviewers like candidates who are enthusiastic and respon-
sive.*** Let the interviewer know you are genuinely interested in the job.
If you are passive or withdrawn during the interview, the assumption
can easily be made that you will behave that way on the job. Some
employers want passive employees, though. So you will have to use
your judgment to determine if your interviewer wants a passive or active
employee.

📂 ***Even if you need the job desperately, do not let the interviewer know
you do.*** Candidates who call attention to their dire straits are less likely
to be hired. Hiring decisions are not based on your need, but on your
ability, experience, and attitude.

📂 ***Keep your answers as complete and concise as possible*** since many
interviewers can give only 30 minutes to an interview. Devote more
time to answering important questions that require in–depth responses
than to less significant questions. Some hiring executives recommend
never spending more than one minute to answer a question. If the
interviewer wants you to elaborate, she'll ask you to.

📂 ***Never denigrate a former employer.*** If you had difficulties, suggest
that some of the blame must have rested with you.

📂 Since the last few minutes of an interview can sometimes change things,
do not be discouraged if you have the impression that the interview
has been going poorly and you have already been rejected in the
interviewer's mind. Some interviewers who are interested in hiring you
will try to discourage you just to test your reactions. Remaining confi-
dent, professional, and determined will help make a good impression.

📂 ***Salary is a subject best broached toward the end of an interview,
preferably by the interviewer.*** Some experts believe an applicant
should ask for as much money as possible to establish a bargaining
position, and that employers offer as little as possible for the same
reason. However, ads for most jobs identify a salary range.

Other job announcements simply say, "Salary open." The interviewer may choose not to tell you the amount she has to offer and may
ask how much you want. Indicate that you are more interested in a job
where you can prove yourself than in a specific salary. If interested, the
interviewer will usually suggest a figure. Try to find out in advance the
standard or average salary for the type of position for which you are
applying. Use the salary surveys described in chapters two through 31
of the *Non–Profits' Job Finder* to learn what you should be offered. You
should also know the salary level beneath which your needs will not
permit you to go. For a whole book of detailed advice, see *Dynamite
Salary Negotiations: Know What You're Worth and Get It!* ($13.95,
1994, 164 pages; available from Planning/Communications' catalog
that begins on page 311).

📂 When given the opportunity, be prepared to offer a closing statement. This will be your last chance to mention any beneficial points you hadn't had an opportunity to raise during the interview and to summarize the positive contribution you can make to the department.

📂 A job offer is rarely made at the interview. The interviewer may want to discuss your application with other staff and may have other candidates to interview. Occasionally a job is offered on the spot. If absolutely certain you want it, you can accept it. However, it is best to ask for 48 hours to decide. But do not give the impression you are playing off one potential employer against another. You can easily lose both job offers that way.

📂 Since most interviews last a half hour or less, an inconspicuous glance at your watch will suggest when your time is almost up. Be alert for signs from the interviewer that the session is almost over, such as when he looks at his watch. Do not keep talking when the session appears to be ending. Summarize your thoughts and stop. Be sure to thank the interviewer for her time and consideration. Tell her to be sure to get in touch with you if she should have any further questions.

📂 Should you send a thank you note right after the interview? Many career counselors say that research shows that a thank you note enhances your chances. But some interviewers regard them as a bother. You certainly should note, for yourself, any further contact your interviewer may have suggested. Follow her instructions exactly, and don't muddy the waters by immediately sending unsolicited correspondence. If the interviewer indicated you will hear from her by a certain date and you don't, write a brief note to remind her about a week after you were supposed to hear from her. Express appreciation for the time and consideration she gave you, and briefly note your continuing interest in the position. You have little to lose at this point by refreshing her memory, and you might get a favorable response.

After the interview

If you don't get a flat rejection or the polite "know" that comes in the type of letter that says, "We will keep your resume in our files and let you *know* if anything ...," keep in touch if there is anything in the letter that suggests you should. Unless you make a nuisance of yourself, you will be able to stay in the foreground if another vacancy opens.

It's a close call as to whether you should listen to the many job counselors who encourage writing a follow–up letter right after the interview. You will have to use your impressions of the interviewer to determine whether a follow–up letter will help or hurt you.

SYLVIA   **by Nicole Hollander**

Following these suggestions should, at least in theory, reduce the hiring decision to one based on qualifications. Not all employers make their hiring decisions the same way. So during your interview be sensitive to hints of what criteria the interviewer will use to make his hiring decision and temper your remarks to comply with them. In general, though, following the suggestions made in this chapter will place you in good stead with a potential employer.

When accepting a job offer, you should send the employer an acceptance letter in which you clarify your assumptions about the job (salary, training, fringe benefits, responsibilities) and indicate your expected date of employment. Once an employer has decided to hire you, you can usually get the starting date changed to one more acceptable to you as long as you are reasonable. Make certain that all conditions of employment are clear and that you have a job offer in writing before you give notice to your current employer that you are leaving. Try to give one month notice if possible, but certainly no less than two weeks.

When rejecting a job offer, you should send a letter as soon as possible that declines the offer and expresses your appreciation for the employer's interest and confidence in you.

When you get rejected, but would still like to work for that employer at some future time, it doesn't hurt to send a pleasant letter thanking the interviewer for her time and expressing your disappointment at not being selected. Emphasize your interest in her department and ask to be kept in mind for future consideration. Suggest that you believe that you would work well together and that you will continue to follow the progress of her agency. Such a letter shows your continuing interest, your recognition that you were not the only qualified applicant, and your genuine desire to work for that agency. Such a thoughtfully–written, brief two– or three–paragraph letter can leave a very favorable impression and enhance your chances should you ever apply there again or encounter the interviewer in another work–related situation.

Even if you didn't possess these job–quest tools before, you are now prepped to prepare a convincing cover letter and a thorough, yet readable resume with which to interest an employer. Finally, you know how to prepare for that strange phenomenon called the personal interview so you can convey the best impression possible.

The *Non–Profits' Job Finder* helps you find the type of job you want in the location you desire, and gives you a leg up on other job seekers who are unaware of the job sources described herein. Armed with the information in this book, you can identify non–profit sector job openings that most job seekers will never know existed because they limit their job search to positions discovered by word of mouth, personal contacts, and the local classifieds.

To find sources of job vacancies in local, state, or the federal government, see the **Government Job Finder**. To locate sources of vacancies in the private sector, see the **Professional's Private Sector Job Finder**. Both are available in bookstores and through the catalog at the end of this book. These books provide the same service for job seekers in government and the private sector that the *Non–Profits' Job Finder* delivers for folks seeking positions in the non–profit sector. Some of the job sources contained the *Non–Profits' Job Finder* also appear in one or both of the other job finder books because some job sources include jobs in more than one employment sector. However, each job finder book contains *many more* job sources for each occupation that do not appear in the other job finder books.

In addition, a computerized version of these three books for MS–DOS computers is now available. Called **The Ultimate Job Finder**, this software program enables you to search and retrieve descriptions of all job sources for specific specialties in the private sector, non–profit sector, and/or government sector–all at once! It combines the power of all three books into one computer program. See the catalog at the end of this book for details.

Successful job hunting takes time and requires effort. But by using your common sense and the job–finding techniques explained in the *Non–Profits' Job Finder*, it's quicker and easier — and your chances of finding satisfactory employment will soar even in the confusing and difficult economic times that face us all in the last decade of the twentieth century.

Reader Feedback Form

We'd like to make the next edition of this book even more helpful. You, our readers, are a source of valuable information and suggestions. So, please use this form to:

✍ Tell us if a job source you've tried to reach has moved or changed its phone number. If you can't reach it, chances are pretty good that we can track it down and send you the updated information.

✍ Tell us about any changed addresses or phone numbers you've found;

✍ Tell us how we can make the next edition of the *Non–Profits' Job Finder* more helpful; and

✍ Let us know of any useful job sources that somehow escaped our attention or started operating after this book was written.

If you run out of space, just attach another sheet. Please send your comments to me at Planning/Communications, 7215 Oak Avenue, River Forest, IL 60305–1935. **Feel free to photocopy this page. Send any corrections or changes to me as soon as possible so I can include them in the free** *Update Sheet* **described on page 300.**

Thanks for your help and support.

Daniel Lauber

Daniel Lauber

_____
_____
_____
_____
_____
_____

Purely optional: Clearly print your name, address, and evening phone number in case we need to reach you for more information. **If you're asking us to find a job source you can't track down, please include a self–addressed stamped envelope and your home phone number.**

About the author

Author Daniel Lauber, AICP, worked for local and state government in Illinois as an award–winning city planner from 1972 through 1980. Since then he has served local and state governments as a planning consultant and, since 1985, as a land–use attorney.

He is the author of the **Government Job Finder, Professional's Private Sector Job Finder, Professional's Job Finder, Non–Profits' Job Finder, The Compleat Guide to Finding Jobs in Government, The Compleat Guide to Jobs in Planning and Public Administration,** and **The Compleat Guide to Jobs in Planning.**

Mr. Lauber has explained how to unlock the secrets of the hidden job market on CNBC–TV's "Steals and Deals" program and on over 80 radio stations throughout the country. He is also a frequent speaker at job fairs and job clubs.

At age 35 he was elected the youngest president of the 26,000–member American Planning Association while attending the Northwestern University School of Law full–time. He is currently President of the American Institute of Certified Planners.

He received his Masters of Urban and Regional Planning in 1972 from the University of Illinois–Urbana, and B.A. in sociology from the University of Chicago in 1970. He received his J.D. from Northwestern University School of Law in 1985.

He has written dozens of articles on planning and law issues in professional publications and the popular press. He created the "Condo Watch" column for the *Chicago Sun–Times* in 1979. When not immersing himself in the preparation of this book, he spends most of his time as an attorney on zoning cases and on behalf of people with disabilities who wish to live in group homes. He also does computer consulting for a number of non–profits and edits and designs numerous monographs and newsletters.

Unfortunately, he can't follow his own advice. His resume runs a lot longer than the four page maximum recommended in Chapter 6. No wonder he's a consultant.

Free Update Sheet

As the *Non–Profits' Job Finder* explains in Chapter 1, job sources are much like people and other businesses: they move, they change their phone number, they go out of business, and new ones spring up. It took a full year to identify and verify all the job sources described in this book. By the time you read this, a small percentage of them will have moved or gone out of business. A few new ones will have begun.

We're constantly monitoring these changes. We rely on our readers to use the **Reader Feedback Form** on page 298 to let us know of changes in job sources they discover. We confirm any changes they report and add them to our ongoing **Update Sheet.**

Books bought directly from Planning/Communications after June 1, 1994 will include the latest *Update Sheet,* assuming one is warranted. If you bought your book in a bookstore, you can still obtain a free *Update Sheet* by following these simple instructions:

Anytime **after June 1, 1994,** you can obtain your free *Update Sheet* by cutting out the coupon at the top of the next page and sending it with a self–addressed, stamped (one ounce postage) number ten business envelope (that's the one that is 9–1/2 inches wide) to:

PLANNING/ COMMUNICATIONS

7215 Oak Avenue

River Forest, IL 60305–1935

This offer ends when the next edition

of the *Non–Profits' Job Finder* is published.

Coupon for free update sheet is on the next page

Updated information on the job sources in the 1994–1995 edition of the

Non-Profits' Job Finder

To get your **free *Update Sheet*,** cut out the "bowling ball" coupon above and send it along with a stamped (one ounce postage), self–addressed, number ten business envelope to:

PLANNING/ *COMMUNICATIONS*
Non–Profits' Job Finder Update Sheet
7215 Oak Ave
River Forest, IL 60305

**No photocopies! You *must* send the original
coupon with your stamped, self–addressed envelope.
If you don't follow these instructions, you'll get no response.**

☞ Do not mail before June 1, 1994. ✍

The first *Update Sheet* won't even be prepared until then. This offer expires when the next edition of the *Non–Profits' Job Finder* is published.

Photocopies not accepted   *Only this original coupon will be accepted*

Index

As explained in Chapter 1 (that's the chapter that told you how to get the most out of this book — which, naturally, nobody wants to read), this Index supplements the Table of Contents to help you find job sources for specialties that are not located in the chapter where you would intuitively expect them to be. When you locate a job source by using this Index, be sure to also look at the other entries in the same section of the chapter. There will often be additional job sources for that specialty there. For example, if you find a periodical for a particular specialty, be sure to also look at the entries under "Job services," "Directories," and "Salary surveys."

A

Catalog of job-quest books and software

PLANNING/COMMUNICATIONS

**7215 Oak Avenue
River Forest, Illinois 60305**

Phone orders: 800/829-5220

This is the catalog at the end of the book. For your convenience, Planning/Communications carries this selection of the most effective career books and software to help you get a new job. Several of them are noted in the text of the *Non-Profits' Job Finder*. Some are available in bookstores. But since most are hard to find in bookstores, we've made them available to you by phone and mail order.

Ordering information appears on the last three pages of this catalog.

America's Job Finders for the 1990s

You simply can't get a new job *unless you know where they are adver-tised.* Daniel Lauber's three job finder books and computer software get you to over 5,000 of the best places where job vacancies are advertised for all three sectors of the economy.

Non--Profits' Job Finder, 3rd edition

$16.95, paperback: ISBN 0--9622019--8--7, 1994, 336 pages
$32.95, hard cover: ISBN: 1--884587--02--X

This is the book you're reading now. It gets you to all the best places where job openings, internships, and grant opportunities in the non--profit sector are announced. For reviews, see the back cover and very first page before the title page.

Government Job Finder, 2nd edition

$16.95, paperback; ISBN 0--9622019--7-9, 1994, 352 pages
$32.95, hard cover: ISBN: 1--884587--01--1

"**Dynamite job hunting tool.**...the **most complete** compen-dium of resources for government jobs I've ever seen."
— *Joyce Lain Kennedy, the dean of America's career authors*

By the author of the *Non--Profits' Job Finder,* this book presents details on over 1,750 sources of job vacancies in local, state, and federal government, in the U.S. and abroad. New for 1994 are 20 percent more job sources and a free *Update Sheet.*

"So **authoritative** we call it the Bible. **Recommended** as the first step to finding government jobs." — *Police Career Digest*

"**Everything you wanted to know** about locating government vacancies (and possibly a few things you never even thought about)...**unlocks** seemingly limitless (and some-times obscure) data about finding positions in local, state, and federal government agencies. Easy--to--use." — *Journal of Career Planning and Placement*

"It steers you to...where you can actually find job openings. It will **help you find a job.**" — *Job Training and Placement Bulletin*

"**Outstanding**" — *Career Opportunities News*

"**Recommended**...affordable...**outstanding.**" — *Library Journal*

Order form begins on page 322
To order: 800/829-5220 weekdays, 9 a.m. to 6 p.m. CST

Professional's Private Sector Job Finder

$18.95, paperback: ISBN 0–9622019–6–0, 1994, 536 pages
$36.95, hard cover: ISBN: 1–884587–00–3

"A real powerhouse for job leads."

—*Joyce Lain Kennedy, America's premier careers writer*

Daniel Lauber, author of the *Non–Profits' Job Finder*, reports on over 2,400 sources of job vacancies in all aspects of the private sector in the all–new *Professional's Private Sector Job Finder*. Included are a chapter on international jobs in the private sector, full details on dozens of new online and computerized job services, and a free *Update Sheet*.

"**Excellent** reference book for job–hunters and career consultants....Unlike the scam artists who promise to provide job seekers lists of job openings in Alaska, **the author delivers** useful information on **where jobs are** advertised outside of the daily papers." — *Bloomsbury Review*

"**Exceptional**... In over 500 pages, the *Professional's Job Finder* describes more than 2,100 sources of job leads in the private sector.... This resource book is **one of the most complete sources** of information that I have seen." — *Search Bulletin: Career Opportunities for Executives and Professionals*

"This book is a little **different.** Leaving most of the motivational babble to other writers, [Lauber] steps beyond the local classifieds to mine specialized resources that can **give job seekers just the edge they need.... exceptional...**" — *Booklist*

"Handy, affordable reference for professionals seeking employment in the private sector. An **outstanding** compendium of resources....Additional sources include directories of businesses, corporations and agencies, and salary surveys....**clear, comprehensive....unique** and **valuable...**" — *Library Journal*

The Ultimate Job Finder

$49.95, comes on 3.5–inch floppies, 5.25–inch floppies available on request, requires Microsoft Windows 3.1 and 3 megabytes free space on hard disk drive. Write for availability of MS–DOS, Macintosh, and CD–ROM versions available later in 1994.

Harness the power of your personal computer to find sources of job vacancies in all sectors of the economy. *The Ultimate Job Finder* combines all 5,000+ job sources in Daniel Lauber's three job finder books described above into one search and retrieval software program. Just type in your occupation, and hit [ENTER]. You instantly get details on your screen for every job source for that occupation — from all three job finder books. Scroll through them and print out the ones you want to pursue.

"*The Ultimate Job Finder* **sparkles**...reasonably priced...**pleasant to use**...**remarkable.** Most other electronic employment databases cost thousands of dollars." — *Joyce Lain Kennedy,* author of the *Electronic Job Search Revolution*

Feel free to photocopy this catalog
To order: 800/829–5220 weekdays, 9 a.m. to 6 p.m. CST

Jobs With Non-Profits

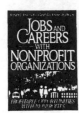

Jobs and Careers with Nonprofit Organizations
$15.95, 1994, 232 pages

Two years in the making, this book is the perfect companion to the *Non–Profits' Job Finder* described on page 312. It identifies major non–profit organizations that offer attractive job alternatives, job search strategies, and contact information on hundreds of domestic and international non–profit organizations. By Ronald and Caryl Krannich.

Good Works: A Guide to Careers in Social Change
$18.00, 428 pages, 1991, 1994 edition available May 1, 1994

Get details on over 800 non–profit employers: address, phone, director's name, purpose, budget, staff positions, number of staff openings each year, number of part–time employees, internships, where vacancies are advertised, and how to apply. Forward by Ralph Nader.

Great Careers: The Fourth of July Guide to Careers, Internships, and Volunteer Opportunities in the Non–Profit Sector
$34.95, 1990, 605 pages

Great Careers is the book that helps you decide which non–profit career to pursue. It's **filled with details** on types of jobs and many job sources for social services, legal aid, the arts, women's issues, consumer advocacy, environment, social change, research, philanthropy, foundations, disabilities, hunger and homelessness, animal rights, labor unions, children and youth, international non–profit organizations, and many other non–profit fields.

Jobs in Washington, DC: 1001 Great Opportunities for College Graduates
$11.95, 1992, 217 pages

"Must reading for anybody seeking a job in Washington, D.C." See page 225 of the *Non–Profits' Job Finder* for full details on this valuable and popular book.

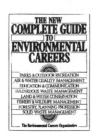

The New Complete Guide to Environmental Careers
$15.95, 1993, 362 pages

Get full details on environmental career opportunities with government, non–profits, and private companies in planning, parks and recreation, environmental protection, natural resource management, forestry, communications, air and water quality management, hazardous waste management, solid waste management, education, and communication. Also covers schooling required, internships, and career strategies. By the Environmental Careers Organization.

Order form begins on page 322
To order: 800/829-5220 weekdays, 9 a.m. to 6 p.m. CST

Job Opps 94: Job Opportunities in the Environment
$16.95, 1993, 224 pages

Learn about government agencies, non–profits, and private sector businesses likely to hire environmental personnel this year. See page 93 for a description of this very popular book. From Peterson's Guides.

Government Careers

The Complete Guide to Public Employment
$19.95, 1994, 528 pages

Called the "**seminal book** on public employment," this book helps you decide what career to pursue in government or with non–profits by providing in–depth information about career opportunities in all branches of the public employment sector.

The Complete Guide to Public Employment also helps people who wish to leave government learn how to shift their government skills into the related worlds of non–profits, trade and professional associations, contracting and consulting, foundations and research organizations, political support groups, and international institutions. By Caryl and Ronald Krannich.

The Book of U.S. Government Jobs
$15.95, 1994, 224 pages

Called a "**treasure trove of information**" this book gives a thorough overview of the federal hiring process, civil service exams, veterans and military dependents hiring, overseas employment, the postal service, opportunities for people with disabilities, and federal occupation lists. Author Dennis Damp identifies the types of jobs available and how to get them. Includes sample civil service exam questions and answers.

"**Extremely helpful and informative.** I particularly like this author's gumption in **dispelling the mystery** of the generic federal employment application. The author lavishly supplies agency contact information."—*Small Press*.

International Careers

Guide to Careers in World Affairs, 3rd Edition
$14.95, 1993, 422 pages

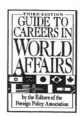

Brand new edition by the editors of the Foreign Policy Association, this book tells you all you need to know about getting hired in many different aspects of world affairs. See page 138 of the *Non–Profits' Job Finder* for full details.

Feel free to photocopy this catalog
To order: 800/829-5220 weekdays, 9 a.m. to 6 p.m. CST

The Almanac of International Jobs & Careers
$19.95, 1994, 348 pages

An all-new edition of the Krannichs' popular compilation of names, addresses, and phone numbers for over 1,000 key employers in the international arena. For the full scoop on this book, see page 138. It's the perfect companion to *The Complete Guide to International Jobs & Careers* described immediately below. By Caryl and Ronald Krannich.

Complete Guide to International Jobs & Careers
$13.95, ISBN 0-942710-69-X, 1992, 306 pages

This book presents the **best approaches for entering the international job market** and describes, in detail, each of the different sectors of the international job market so you can decide which is best for you. See page 137 for full information about it.

International Internships and Volunteer Programs
$18.95, 1992, 233 pages

See page 138 for full details on this guide to internships and volunteer opportunities outside the U.S. By Will Cantrell and Francine Modderno.

Work, Study, Travel Abroad
$13.95, 1994, 502 pages, available beginning April 1994

By the Council on International Educational Exchange, this book gives you to full details on exchange programs, government grants, and scholarships to work or study abroad. See page 146 of the *Non-Profits' Job Finder* for full details.

How to Get a Job in Europe   ### How to Get a Job in the Pacific Rim
$17.95, 1992, 520 pages   *$17.95, 1992, 424 pages*

For Europe or the Pacific Rim, get details on over 1,000 potential employers plus local professional associations, periodicals, and directories; executive search firms, and employment services. A new edition of each title will be published sometime in 1994. We'll send you the latest edition.

Finding the Right Job for You

Change Your Job, Change Your Life:
High Impact Strategies for Finding Great Jobs in the 90s
$14.95, 1994, 363 pages

Loaded with **practical "how to" advice,** this highly acclaimed book covers everything from understanding today's job market and identifying the best jobs for the 1990s to assessing skills and mastering every step in the job search and hiring processes. It also includes unique chapters on relocating to another community, starting a business, and identifying useful job search resources. It's the **perfect guide** for anyone making a job or career change.

Order form begins on page 322
To order: 800/829-5220 weekdays, 9 a.m. to 6 p.m. CST

What Color is Your Parachute?

$14.95, 1994, 464 pages

The latest annual edition of Richard Bolles' perennial best–seller, this book really does help you find your calling in life with the most effective career and job–hunting methods.

Career Design Software

$99.95, specify 3.5–inch or 5.25–inch floppy disks, requires hard drive, MS–DOS single–user version; write for multi–user version price

Based on the career development system that is the foundation of *What Color is Your Parachute?*, this software lets you proceed at your own pace to uncover your interests and hidden skills, set goals, determine your career direction, negotiate, prepare for interviews, and much more. Includes automated resume preparation software.

Zen and the Art of Making a Living
A Practical Guide to Creative Career Design

$16.00, 1993, 597 pages

The most innovative career guide since *What Color is Your Parachute?*, Laurence Boldt's book is not just about getting a job. The first part helps you discover what you really want to do and identify what work will be deeply satisfying. The second part furnishes practical action steps to finding or creating that work (including the very insightful advice to get the *Non–Profits' Job Finder*). Over 120 worksheets help you find your way to a more rewarding job and career.

Graduating to the 9 to 5 World

$11.95, ISBN 0–942710–50–9, 1991, 195 pages

Here's one of the essential career books for everyone in Generation X (okay, so it's a lousy label, but the media insists we use it). This book will give you a real "Welcome to the Working Week" (with apologies to Elvis Costello). It's **every student's passport to the realities of the working week**. Prevent "9 to 5 shock" by learning what it's like to work in a structured world where office politics, productivity, and performance take center stage. Learn how to use your first 90 days on the job to greatly enhance your career.

Internships 1994

$29.95, ISBN 1–56079–149–7, 1993, 424 pages

See page 30 of the *Non–Profits' Job Finder* for a full description of this annual book from Peterson's Guides.

Summer Jobs 1994

$15.95, 1993, 320 pages

Get the full scoop on this guide to mostly outdoor summer jobs on page 25 of the *Non–Profits' Job Finder*. From Peterson's Guides.

Finding a Job in Specific Cities

Job Hotlines USA: The National Telephone Directory of Employer Joblines
$24.95, new edition each May, 128 pages

   Career Communication's annual book lists job hotline phone numbers for over 1,000 universities, colleges, private sector employers, and government units, both alphabetically and by city and state. See page 13 of the *Non–Profits' Job Finder* for details.

How to Get a Job Series

   These easy–to–use books tell you whom to contact for job vacancies at over 1,500 top non–profit and private sector employers, organized by industry in each city and its surrounding metropolitan area. For details, see the descriptions of each under the appropriate state in Chapter 31 of the *Non–Profits' Job Finder*. We'll always send you the latest edition. **Price: $15.95 each**

How to Get a Job in Atlanta
How to Get a Job in Boston
How to Get a Job in Chicago
How to Get a Job in Dallas/Ft. Worth
How to Get a Job in Houston
How to Get a Job in New York

How to Get a Job in the San Francisco Bay Area
How to Get a Job in Seattle/Portland
How to Get a Job in Southern California
How to Get a Job in Washington, D.C.

The Bob Adams JobBank Series

   See the description of each title under the appropriate state in Chapter 31 of the *Non–Profits' Job Finder*. As always, we will send you the latest edition of each title. **Price: $15.95 each**.

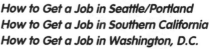

Atlanta JobBank
Boston JobBank
Carolina JobBank
Chicago JobBank
Dallas–Ft. Worth JobBank
Denver JobBank
Detroit JobBank
Florida JobBank
Houston JobBank
Los Angeles JobBank
Minneapolis JobBank

Metro New York JobBank
Ohio JobBank
Phoenix JobBank
Philadelphia JobBank
St. Louis JobBank
San Francisco Bay Area JobBank
Seattle JobBank
Tennessee JobBank
Metro Washington DC JobBank

Order form begins on page 322
To order: 800/829-5220 weekdays, 9 a.m. to 6 p.m. CST

Winning Resumes and Cover Letters

High Impact Resumes and Letters:
How to Communicate Your Qualifications to Employers
$12.95, 1992, 254 pages

Twice excerpted in the *National Business Employment Weekly*, this highly praised best–seller has set a new standard for resume and letter writing guides. This easy–to–follow guide walks you through the steps necessary to write resumes and cover letters with impact, ones that stand out from the crowd. It helps you "think out" your resume rather than simply imitate some model.

"If we had money for only one book on resumes, this would be our choice."
—*Career Opportunities News*

The Resume Catalog: 200 Damn Good Examples
$15.95, 1988, 316 pages

Yana Parker's classic set of resume examples includes tips on strengthening resume content. Other resume books come and go, but this remains one of the very best.

Dynamite Resumes: 101 Great Examples
$9.95, 1992, 137 pages

From the authors of *High Impact Resumes and Cover Letters* comes a unique guide for transforming ordinary resumes into outstanding ones that grab the attention of potential employers. Numerous examples illustrate the key principles for revising a resume. Included are two unique chapters that critically review resume guides and computer software used specifically for resume writing. By Ronald and Caryl Krannich.

WinWay Resumes for Windows
$69.95, 1993, requires Windows, includes both size floppy disks

All these resume books in this catalog give good advice, but you need WinWay Resumes for Windows to easily create the resume with the "look that gets hired." Choose from among 35 resume styles. Use any of the many fonts on your computer. Update your resume with ease. Includes a spell checker and action verb glossary.

Resumes for Re–Entry: A Handbook for Women
$10.95, 1993, 180 pages

Here's the definitive guide for women entering or re–entering the work force. Filled with examples and tips for navigating today's highly competitive job market, this book shows you how to use powerful language and present your interests, skills, and qualifications to grab the attention of potential employers.

Resumes for the Over 50 Job Hunter

$12.95, 1993, 208 pages

Samuel Ray shows you how to turn your age and experience into an asset in the eyes of potential employers. Includes 95 sample resumes, tips for successful networking, how to follow up, and how to negotiate the best deal.

Electronic Resume Revolution

$12.95, 1994, 256 pages

If you've read the *Non–Profits' Job Finder* carefully, you know there's an electronic revolution in hiring with hundreds of job–matching services and computerized resume and job databases becoming the new way to get a job. Premier careers writer Joyce Lain Kennedy teams up with Thomas Morrow to show you how to create a winning resume for this electronic resume revolution. Learn how to prepare your resume for electronic scanners and for computerized resume databases and job–matching services. The authors present over 30 sample resumes to get you past the computer and in front of the person who does the hiring. Also learn how to prepare a video resume.

Job Search Letters that Get Results

$12.95, ISBN 0–942710–70–3, 1992, 232 pages

The companion volume to *Dynamite Cover Letters,* this book includes 201 examples of the six most important types of letters every job seeker needs to write: cover, approach, thank you, rejection, withdrawal, and acceptance letters. By Caryl and Ronald Krannich.

200 Letters for Job Hunters

$17.95, 1993, 344 pages

Nobody does it better than author William Frank with his collection of over 250 types of job letters to cover every situation in the job search: answering want ads, cold calls, hidden jobs, part–time employment, follow–up letters, and much more.

Dynamite Cover Letters and Other Great Job Search Letters

$9.95, 1992, 135 pages

"A **really good book.** Filled with **common sense**…tells all the important things without forcing the reader to consume 350 pages….blends savvy with easy–to–read text with examples of all kinds of job search letters." — *Career Opportunities News*

Order form begins on page 322
To order: 800/829–5220 weekdays, 9 a.m. to 6 p.m. CST

Interviews, Salary, and Networking

Interview for Success:
A Practical Guide to Increasing Job Interviews, Offers, and Salaries
$11.95, 1992, 218 pages

One of the most comprehensive and practical interview preparation books available today, *Interview for Success* is packed with solid advice on getting interviews and then using them to your advantage to win the job at the salary you want. The authors, Caryl and Ronald Krannich, present everything you need to know to do your best at your job interview, including how to handle stress. Included is a checklist of 54 interviewing maxims.

Dynamite Answers to Interview Questions
$9.95, 1992, 163 pages

"No more sweaty palms" —that's what the authors of this lively book promise. The perfect companion volume to *Interview for Success* (described immediately above), this book outlines the best answers to key job interview questions. Included are sample answers to hundreds of questions crafty interviewers are likely to spring. Learn how to turn negative responses into positive answers that can mean the difference between getting hired and being rejected.

Dynamite Salary Negotiations
$13.95, 1994, 164 pages

Praised by the *National Business Employment Weekly*, this book dispels myths and explains how to determine your true value, negotiate salary and employment terms, and finalize your job offer. It shows how to respond to ads that request a salary history or salary requirements and much more. By Ronald and Caryl Krannich.

The New Network Your Way to Job and Career Success
$12.95,1993, 188 pages

Pinpointing a practice often presented as merely a vague concept, this book shows you how to make the connections that get you to the jobs that aren't widely advertised. Learn to identify, link, and transform networks to gather information and obtain advice and references that lead to job interviews and offers. By Caryl and Ronald Krannich.

How to Order

Complete the order form that begins on this page, or call us toll–free at 800/829–5220 to order (call 708/366–5200 if you need more information before ordering), Mondays through Fridays, 9 a.m. to 6 p.m. Central Standard Time.

Be sure to include postage according to the formula given at the end of the order form and enclose your payment (check, money order, VISA, or MasterCard —individuals and private companies must prepay).

We will always send you the current edition of a book. Call or write for special quantity discounts or resale prices. *Please note that prices are subject to change without notice.*

PLANNING/COMMUNICATIONS

7215 Oak Avenue
River Forest, Illinois 60305–1935

To order: 800/829–5220
For information: 708/366–5200
Weekdays: 9 a.m. to 6 p.m. Central Standard Time

All orders from individuals or businesses must be prepaid by check, money order, VISA or MasterCard. Purchase orders are accepted only from libraries, universities, bookstores, or government offices.

Order Form

Title	Price	x #	= Total
America's Job Finders for the 1990s			
Non–Profits' Job Finder (paperback)	$16.95	x ____	= $_____
Non–Profits' Job Finder (hard cover)	$32.95	x ____	= $_____
Government Job Finder (paperback)	$16.95	x ____	= $_____
Government Job Finder (hard cover)	$32.95	x ____	= $_____
Professional's Private Sector Job Finder (paperback)	$18.95	x ____	= $_____
Professional's Private Sector Job Finder (hard cover)	$36.95	x ____	= $_____
The Ultimate Job Finder (computer software)	$49.95	x ____	= $_____
Careers with Non–Profits			
Jobs and Careers with Nonprofit Organizations	$15.95	x ____	= $_____
Good Works: A Guide to Careers in Social Change	$18.00	x ____	= $_____
Great Careers: The Fourth of July Guide...	$34.95	x ____	= $_____
Jobs in Washington, DC...	$11.95	x ____	= $_____
The New Complete Guide to Environmental Careers	$15.95	x ____	= $_____
Job Opps 94: Job Opportunities in the Environment	$16.95	x ____	= $_____

Government Careers

The Complete Guide to Public Employment	$19.95	x ____	= $_____
The Book of U.S. Government Jobs	$15.95	x ____	= $_____

International Careers

Guide to Careers in World Affairs	$14.95	x ____	= $_____
The Almanac of International Jobs & Careers	$19.95	x ____	= $_____
The Complete Guide to International Jobs & Careers	$13.95	x ____	= $_____
International Internships and Volunteer Programs	$18.95	x ____	= $_____
Work, Study, Travel Abroad	$13.95	x ____	= $_____
How to Get a Job in Europe	$17.95	x ____	= $_____
How to Get a Job in the Pacific Rim	$17.95	x ____	= $_____

Finding the Right Job for You

Change Your Job, Change Your Life	$14.95	x ____	= $_____
What Color is Your Parachute?	$14.95	x ____	= $_____
Career Design Software	$99.95	x ____	= $_____
Zen and the Art of Making a Living	$16.00	x ____	= $_____
Graduating to the 9 to 5 World	$11.95	x ____	= $_____
Internships 1994	$29.95	x ____	= $_____
Summer Jobs 1994	$15.95	x ____	= $_____

Finding a Job in Specific Cities [fill in name of city or state from list on page 318]

Job Hotlines USA	$24.95	x ____	= $_____
How to Get a Job in _____ [from list on page 318]	$15.95	x ____	= $_____
How to Get a Job in _____ [from list on page 318]	$15.95	x ____	= $_____
How to Get a Job in _____ [from list on page 318]	$15.95	x ____	= $_____
_____ JobBank [from list on page 318]	$15.95	x ____	= $_____
_____ JobBank [from list on page 318]	$15.95	x ____	= $_____
_____ JobBank [from list on page 318]	$15.95	x ____	= $_____

Winning Resumes and Cover Letters

High Impact Resumes and Letters	$12.95	x ____	= $_____
The Resume Catalog: 200 Damn Good Examples	$15.95	x ____	= $_____
Dynamite Resumes: 101 Great Examples	$ 9.95	x ____	= $_____
WinWay Resumes for Windows	$69.95	x ____	= $_____
Resumes for Re–Entry: A Handbook for Women	$10.95	x ____	= $_____
Resumes for the Over 50 Job Hunter	$12.95	x ____	= $_____
Electronic Resume Revolution	$12.95	x ____	= $_____
Job Search Letters that Get Results	$12.95	x ____	= $_____
200 Letters for Job Hunters	$17.95	x ____	= $_____
Dynamite Cover Letters & Other Great Job Search Letters	$ 9.95	x ____	= $_____

Interviews, Salary, and Networking

Interview for Success	$11.95	x ____	= $_____
Dynamite Answers to Interview Questions	$ 9.95	x ____	= $_____
Dynamite Salary Negotiations	$13.95	x ____	= $_____
The New Network Your Way to Job and Career Success	$12.95	x ____	= $_____

Subtotal: $_____

☛ **Illinois residents only:** Add 7.75% sales tax   + $_____

Feel free to photocopy this catalog
To order: 800/829-5220 weekdays, 9 a.m. to 6 p.m. CST

☛ **Shipping:** ($3.75 for ~~first item,~~ ~~$1 for~~ + ___$ 3.75___
each additional i~~tem, see next line~~)

☛ **Additional items:** _____ x $1/each = $_____

☛ ***Overseas orders:** Add an <u>additional</u> $12 per book
for air mail (if actual postage is less, we will
refund the difference to you) + $_____

* = *Orders sent to U.S. possessions and military addresses
do not require this additional overseas postage.
They are shipped via Priority Mail.*

☛ **Total enclosed:** $_____

❑ Check here to receive Planning/Communications'
free catalog of 175 job–quest books and software.

Ship to:

Please print clearly or ty~~pe~~

Name _____

Address _____

_____

For UPS delivery, give full stree~~t~~

City–State–Zip _____

❑ **Enclosed is my ch**~~eck~~
$_____ **mad**~~e to~~
Planning/Communications

❑ **Please charge $_____ to my**
VISA or MasterCard

Card number:

_____

Expiration date: _____

Signature (if charging this order):

_____

Please sign your name exactly as it appears on
your VISA or MasterCard.

Home phone number: _____/_____

~~Pa~~**yment terms**

~~A~~ll checks must
~~be i~~n U.S. dollars
~~dra~~wn on an U.S.
~~ban~~k.

Orders from
individuals or private
businesses **must be
prepaid.**

Purchase orders
are accepted only
from libraries,
colleges, universities,
bookstores, and
government offices.

SEE PAGE 322 FOR ORDERING INSTRUCTIONS